NOTHING GOOD IS ALLOWED TO STAND

Work with patients with severe neuroses very often has to cope with the phenomenon that every progress in the analytic or therapeutic work is followed paradoxically by a clinical deterioration. There are a number of dynamic factors that converge to bring about this negative therapeutic reaction, including many-layered guilt and shame, aspects of envy and jealousy, attachment to negative affects, turning trauma from passive to active, conflicts within the superego, and the defensive use of omnipotence of responsibility.

In *Nothing Good Is Allowed to Stand*, Wurmser, Jarass, and their colleagues consider these and other factors insightfully, such as the extent to which traumatization lives on in self-directed aggressions of the superego in the claim of omnipotence; the significant role of deep conflicts between opposite values and loyalties in bringing about the prohibition of anything "good" and thus of the negative therapeutic reaction in particular and masochism in general; and the extent to which envy, jealousy, and resentment can be encountered in the "inner object," the "inner judge" (i.e., the superego), and how they are directed against the self.

Léon Wurmser, M.D. is a Training and Supervising Analyst at the New York Freudian Society. His publications include *The Power of the Inner Judge* (Jason Aronson, 2000), *Jealousy and Envy* (with Heidrun Jarass; Analytic Press, 2007), and *Torment Me, but Don't Abandon Me!* (Jason Aronson, 2007). He maintains a private practice in Towson, MD.

Heidrun Jarass, M.D. is a Training and Supervising Analyst at the Institute for Psychoanalysis of the German Psychoanalytic Society, Nürnberg. A psychoanalyst in private practice, she has been active in psychoanalytic research, focusing on the psychodynamic processes in supervision, and has presented her work with severely ill patients at international meetings. She co-edited (with Léon Wurmser) *Jealousy and Envy* (Analytic Press, 2007).

PSYCHOANALYTIC INQUIRY BOOK SERIES

JOSEPH D. LICHTENBERG

Series Editor

Like its counterpart, *Psychoanalytic Inquiry: A Topical Journal for Mental Health Professionals*, the Psychoanalytic Inquiry Book Series presents a diversity of subjects within a diversity of approaches to those subjects. Under the editorship of Joseph Lichtenberg, in collaboration with Melvin Bornstein and the editorial board of *Psychoanalytic Inquiry*, the volumes in this series strike a balance between research, theory, and clinical application We are honored to have published the works of various innovators in psychoanalysis, such as Frank Lachmann, James Fosshage, Robert Stolorow, Donna Orange, Louis Sander, Léon Wurmser, James Grotstein, Joseph Jones, Doris Brothers, Fredric Busch, and Joseph Lichtenberg, among others.

The series includes books and monographs on mainline psychoanalytic topics, such as sexuality, narcissism, trauma, homosexuality, jealousy, envy, and varied aspects of analytic process and technique. In our efforts to broaden the field of analytic interest, the series has incorporated and embraced innovative discoveries in infant research, self psychology, intersubjectivity, motivational systems, affects as process, responses to cancer, borderline states, contextualism, postmodernism, attachment research and theory, medication, and mentalization. As further investigations in psychoanalysis come to fruition, we seek to present them in readable, easily comprehensible writing.

After 25 years, the core vision of this series remains the investigation, analysis and discussion of developments on the cutting edge of the psychoanalytic field, inspired by a boundless spirit of inquiry.

PSYCHOANALYTIC INQUIRY BOOK SERIES

JOSEPH D. LICHTENBERG
Series Editor

Vol. 39
Nothing Good Is Allowed to Stand:
An Integrative View of the
Negative Therapeutic Reaction
Léon Wurmser & Heidrun Jarass (eds.)

Vol. 38
Self Experiences in Group, Revisited: Affective Attachments, Intersubjective Regulations, and Human Understanding
Irene Harwood, Walter Stone, & Malcolm Pines (eds.)

Vol. 37
The Abyss of Madness
George E. Atwood

Vol. 36
Manual of Panic Focused Psychodynamic Psychotherapy – eXtended Range
Fredric N. Busch, Barbara L. Milrod, Meriamne B. Singer, & Andrew C. Aronson

Vol. 35
World, Affectivity, Trauma:
Heidegger and Post-Cartesian Psychoanalysis
Robert D. Stolorow

Vol. 34
Change in Psychoanalysis:
An Analyst's Reflections on the Therapeutic Relationship
Chris Jaenicke

Vol. 33
Psychoanalysis and Motivational Systems:
A New Look
Joseph D. Lichtenberg, Frank M. Lachmann, & James L. Fosshage

Vol. 32
Persons in Context:
The Challenge of Individuality in Theory and Practice
Roger Frie & William J. Coburn (eds.)

Vol. 31
Toward an Emancipatory Psychoanalysis:
Brandchaft's Intersubjective Vision
Bernard Brandchaft, Shelley Doctors, & Dorienne Sorter

Vol. 30
From Psychoanalytic Narrative to Empirical Single Case Research:
Implications for Psychoanalytic Practice
Horst Kächele, Joseph Schachter, Helmut Thomä & the Ulm Psychoanalytic Process Research Study Group

Vol. 29
Mentalization:
Theoretical Considerations, Research Findings, and Clinical Implications
Fredric N. Busch (ed.)

Vol. 28
Transforming Narcissism:
Reflections on Empathy, Humor, and Expectations
Frank M. Lachmann

Vol. 27
Toward a Psychology of Uncertainty:
Trauma-Centered Psychoanalysis
Doris Brothers

PSYCHOANALYTIC INQUIRY BOOK SERIES

JOSEPH D. LICHTENBERG
Series Editor

Vol. 26
Living Systems, Evolving Consciousness, and the Emerging Person: A Selection of Papers from the Life Work of Louis Sander
Gherardo Amadei & Ilaria Bianchi (eds.)

Vol. 25
Sensuality and Sexuality across the Divide of Shame
Joseph D. Lichtenberg

Vol. 24
Jealousy and Envy: New Views about Two Powerful Feelings
Léon Wurmser & Heidrun Jarass (eds.)

Vol. 23
Trauma and Human Existence: Autobiographical, Psychoanalytic, and Philosophical Reflections
Robert D. Stolorow

Vol. 22
Psychotherapy and Medication: The Challenge of Integration
Fredric N. Busch & Larry S. Sandberg

Vol. 21
Attachment and Sexuality
Diana Diamond, Sidney J. Blatt, & Joseph D. Lichtenberg (eds.)

Vol. 20
Craft and Spirit: A Guide to Exploratory Psychotherapies
Joseph D. Lichtenberg

Vol. 19
A Spirit of Inquiry: Communication in Psychoanalysis
Joseph D. Lichtenberg, Frank M. Lachmann, & James L. Fosshage

Vol. 18
Kohut, Loewald, and the Postmoderns: A Comparative Study of Self and Relationship
Judith Guss Teicholz

Vol. 17
Working Intersubjectively: Contextualism in Psychoanalytic Practice
Donna M. Orange, George E. Atwood, & Robert D. Stolorow

Vol. 16
The Clinical Exchange: Techniques Derived from Self and Motivational Systems
Joseph D. Lichtenberg, Frank M. Lachmann, & James L. Fosshage

Vol. 14
Affects as Process: An Inquiry into the Centrality *of Affect in Psychological Life*
Joseph M. Jones

Vol. 13
Self and Motivational Systems: Toward a Theory of Psychoanalytic Technique
Joseph D. Lichtenberg, Frank M. Lachmann, & James L. Fosshage

PSYCHOANALYTIC INQUIRY BOOK SERIES

JOSEPH D. LICHTENBERG
Series Editor

Vol. 12
Contexts of Being: The Intersubjective Foundations of Psychological Life
Robert D. Stolorow & George E. Atwood

Vol. 10
Psychoanalysis and Motivation
Joseph D. Lichtenberg

Vol. 8
Psychoanalytic Treatment: An Intersubjective Approach
Robert D. Stolorow, Bernard Brandchaft, & George E. Atwood

Vol. 2
Psychoanalysis and Infant Research
Joseph D. Lichtenberg

Out of Print titles in the PI Series

Vol. 15
Understanding Therapeutic Action: Psychodynamic Concepts of Cure
Lawrence E. Lifson (ed.)

Vol. 11
Cancer Stories: Creativity and Self-Repair
Esther Dreifuss-Kattan

Vol. 9
Female Homosexuality: Choice without Volition
Elaine V. Siegel

Vol. 7
The Borderline Patient: Emerging Concepts in Diagnosis, Psychodynamics, and Treatment, Vol. 2
James S. Grotstein, Marion F. Solomon, & Joan A. Lang (eds.)

Vol. 6
The Borderline Patient: Emerging Concepts in Diagnosis, Psychodynamics, and Treatment, Vol. 1
James S. Grotstein, Marion F. Solomon, & Joan A. Lang (eds.)

Vol. 5
Toward a Comprehensive Model for Schizophrenic Disorders: Psychoanalytic Essays in Memory of Ping-Nie Pao
David B. Feinsilver

Vol. 4
Structures of Subjectivity: Explorations in Psychoanalytic Phenomenology
George E. Atwood & Robert D. Stolorow

Vol. 3
Empathy, Volumes I & II
Joseph D. Lichtenberg, Melvin Bornstein, & Donald Silver (eds.)

Vol. 1
Reflections on Self Psychology
Joseph D. Lichtenberg & Samuel Kaplan (eds.)

NOTHING GOOD IS ALLOWED TO STAND

An Integrative View of the Negative Therapeutic Reaction

Edited by

Léon Wurmser
Heidrun Jarass

Routledge
Taylor & Francis Group
NEW YORK AND LONDON

First published 2013
by Routledge
605 Third Avenue, New York, NY 10017
4 Park Square, Milton Park, Abingdon, Oxon OX14 4RN

Routledge is an imprint of the Taylor & Francis Group, an Informa business

Library of Congress Cataloging in Publication Data
Nothing good is allowed to stand : an integrative view of the negative therapeutic reaction / edited by Leon Wurmser, Heidrun Jarass.
p. cm. — (Psychoanalytic inquiry ; 39)
Includes bibliographical references and index.
ISBN 978-0-415-53198-6 (hbk. : alk. paper) — ISBN 978-0-415-53199-3 (pbk. : alk. paper) — ISBN 978-0-203-11003-4 1. Psychotherapy—Complications. 2. Psychotherapist and patient. I. Wurmser, Leon. II. Jarass, Heidrun.
RC480.5.N66 2012
616.89'14—dc23
2012007454

ISBN: 978-0-415-53198-6 (hbk)
ISBN: 978-0-415-53199-3 (pbk)
ISBN: 978-0-203-11003-4 (ebk)

Typeset in Garamond
by EvS Communication Networx, Inc.

CONTENTS

CONTRIBUTORS

Melvin Bornstein, MD is a supervising and training analyst at the Michigan Psychoanalytic Institute, and Associate Clinical Professor, Department of Psychiatry, at Wayne State University and the University of Michigan. He is also the Editor of *Psychoanalytic Inquiry*.

Jörg Frommer, MD is a training analyst and head of the Department of Psychosomatic Medicine and Psychotherapy, Otto-von-Güricke-University, Magdeburg. His research interests include psychoanalytic theory, psychosomatic and counseling, qualitative methods, psycho-oncology, and trauma.

Mathias Hirsch, MD is a psychiatrist and psychoanalyst practicing in Düsseldorf, Germany. He has published extensively in the areas of sexual abuse and the family, psychoanalytic psychology of the body, guilt and guilt feelings, and psychoanalytic therapy of traumatized patients.

Heidrun Jarass, MD is a training and supervising analyst at the Institute for Psychoanalysis of the German Psychoanalytic Society, Nürnberg. A psychoanalyst in private practice, she has been active in psychoanalytic research, focusing on the psychodynamic processes in supervision, and has presented her work with severely ill patients at international meetings. She coedited (with Léon Wurmser) *Jealousy and Envy* (Analytic Press, 2007).

Joseph Lichtenberg, MD is Director Emeritus of the Institute of Contemporary Psychotherapy and Psychoanalysis, and past President of the International Council for Psychoanalytic Self Psychology. Editor-in-Chief of *Psychoanalytic Inquiry*, he has authored and edited numerous books and articles, including *Psychoanalysis and Motivational Systems: A New Look (Routledge, 2010).*

Shelley Orgel, MD is a training and supervising analyst at the Institute for Psychoanalytic Education, formerly called the Institute at the NYU School of Medicine, where he has also been the Director. Former Chair of the Board on Professional Standards (BOPS) of the American Psychoanalytic Association, he is an associate editor of the *Psychoanalytic Quarterly* and has published papers on clinical issues, psychoanalytic education, applied analysis, and numerous book reviews.

Anna Ornstein, MD is Professor Emerita of Child Psychiatry at the University of Cincinnati, Lecturer in Psychiatry at Harvard Medical School, and a supervising analyst at the Boston Psychoanalytic Institute and Massachusetts Institute of Psychoanalysis.

Cordelia Schmidt-Hellerau, PhD is Professor of Clinical Psychology at the University of Zurich, and a training and supervising analyst at the Swiss Psychoanalytic Society and at the Boston Psychoanalytic Society and Institute. Her research area is psychoanalytic theory/Freudian metapsychology, in particular drive theory. She has published books and articles in several languages and works in private practice in Chestnut Hill, Boston, MA.

Gerd Schmithüsen, MD is a training and supervising analyst at the Psychoanalytic Institute of Cologne-Düsseldorf, where he was Director from 2004 to 2008. Since 2008 he has been the Director of Training and a member of the Sponsoring Committee for the Croatian Psychoanalytic Study Group. He maintains a private practice.

Léon Wurmser, MD is a training and supervising analyst at the New York Freudian Society. His publications include *The Power of the Inner Judge* (Jason Aronson, 2000), *Jealousy and Envy* (with Heidrun Jarass, Analytic Press, 2007), and *Torment Me, but Don't Abandon Me!* (Jason Aronson, 2007). He maintains a private practice in Towson, MD.

FOREWORD

Joseph Lichtenberg

Courageous people examine their disappointments and failures. They do so to learn what they could do better and what the limits of reasonable expectations are for themselves and others. Freud was just such a courageous person. Freud's writings on negative therapeutic reactions (NTR) are a hallmark beginning for psychoanalytic explorations of therapeutic failure. To my mind, Freud had less to say about what might be done better than he had to say about the limitations of the method—the patient's impenetrable archaic superego or adhesive libido or death instinct. Much has been written since then on NTR and much has changed in both analytic theory and technique. A principal change that affects the explorations in this volume is the broadly accepted dyadic perspective, whether conceived in terms of I-thou, transference-countertransference, a self-selfobject matrix, projective identification, intersubjectivity, or the relational perspective. Beyond the analytic dyad are the influence of culture, social mores, morality, spirituality, and transgenerational transmission, and beyond these are the situations people find themselves in both as children and adults—persecution, war, totalitarian regimes, abuse, cults, and other forms of victimization—the snares of stress and acute trauma.

Nothing Good Is Allowed to Stand bears the imprint of Léon Wurmser as editor, author, and erudite thinker. From its origins, psychoanalysis has tilted between its scientific and humanistic traditions (Lichtenberg, 1985). Under Wurmser's leadership, this contemporary exploration of NTR draws on the empirical tradition for its careful observation of clinical detail and the assessment of evidence for the inferences each author forms. But the book's unique contribution emerges from the richness of the humanistic tradition being brought to bear on understanding the role of conscience and of positive, but especially negative, emotions in all human endeavors. Through the clarity of the many clinical illustrations, generalized, often off-putting, terms like *archaic superego* move into a particular person's struggle with how he or she wrestles with moral precepts and ideals, with guilt and shame. Archaic means early, stuck back in an infant's primitive, concretized view of good and bad. Archaic can mean stuck in a time warp of a stultified resistance to openness to change and positive influences.

Archaic can mean stuck in connections to others that restrict freedom to develop the rhythms of one's own strivings. Archaic means not only the individual's history, but the history of humankind's wrestling with placing values outside the individual into gods or God. Exploring the archaic means asking what kind of gods or God we construct. Do our ideals tilt each individual's imagination toward flexibility or rigidity, or is the tilt toward justice and compassion or jealousy and retribution?

Nothing Good Is Allowed to Stand is a multiauthored book, multi- and distinguished. Single-authored books have traditionally been preferred by publishers and maybe by readers. The reasoning is that single authorship assures more cohesion and continuity of presentation. And that is true. But this argument omits the factor of differing potentials for cohesion that a particular subject offers. When the definition of the subject is far from clear and the territory covered by the topic is diverse, as is true of NTR, then the shifting but integrated perspectives of multiple authors are needed. As stated by Gilbert and Sullivan's mythic Mikado: the punishment fits the crime. The success of a multiauthored book lies in the caveat—shifting but integrated perspectives. Wurmser and Jarass, working closely with their authors, have achieved a delicate balance for the reader by using kaleidoscopic shifts in explanations derived from clinical stories while consistently reminding the reader of the same core factors contributing to NTR: overwhelming shame and guilt, irreconcilable loyalties, absoluteness of expectation and demand, blocked progression of time, and jealousy, envy, and resentment. By having multiple authors give their emphasis, each factor is illuminated in a different frame of a particular lived experience. And by having multiple authors bring their differing personal, cultural, historic, and theoretical perspectives, each reader is challenged to think and rethink his or her own clinical and, maybe more importantly, personal experiences. To use Wurmser's evocative metaphor, multiplicity allows the dynamic facets of NTR to unfold "as if painted onto a Chinese fan."

Focusing on the clinical narratives, the reader will encounter dyads in which problems centered on the narcissistic wounds of unfolding bodily and mental changes, the fear of penetration by the analyst's offerings, early trauma leading to a fear of annihilation, an analyst's absorption with a feeling of time standing still, and internal objects opposing progress and the development of autonomy. The reader will find guilt over separation, the analyst turning into an omnipotent threatening mother opposing separation and independence, violent storms of rage and suicidal depression, and a compulsion to disappoint and fail associated with an implacable, cruel, dehumanizing superego. The reader will find trauma from the totalitarian assumptions of lack of reciprocity in human relations, a belief that improvement in analysis gratifies the analyst at the expense of the patient, early abandonment, and the need to avoid feeling alive and taking ownership of one's trauma and risking being mortally humiliated. Diverse factors indeed!

The profound contributions of the editors and authors of *Nothing Good Is Allowed to Stand* go a long way to resolve the conundrum of NTR and the parodies the concept has at times been reduced to:

Analyst: I have offered you an accurate interpretation of your associations. You should be improving.
Patient: Accurate? What about …?
Analyst: Okay. Now I understand. Your desire is for …
Patient: Now I feel terrible. You are right—I have awful urges and now I am both guilty and horribly ashamed. I am evil and worthless and nothing you can say or do will convince me otherwise.

Answers to this conundrum are offered by different authors. Some question the assumption inherent in "accurate interpretation." These authors offer alternative or novel formulations and especially express the willingness to look deeply into the analyst's own reactivity and sensitivity. Some authors describe the slow careful work with the patient's archaic superego to free conscience from its dictatorial polarized rigidity. Other authors give importance to the analyst's mode of delivery—the sensitivity to implicit shaming, the awareness of the patient's (and the analyst's) narcissistic vulnerability, and the patient's loss of humanity from the suffering of trauma. Wurmser offers his valuable contribution: "NTR is a very frequent *phenomenon*, but not an *explanation*…. Sometimes even the best understanding in really very severe neuroses does not change the reaction—an almost immovable determination to destroy the best one is, one gets, one wants, one has." Earlier I suggested that an understanding of NTR has been enhanced by a shift of focus from a primarily intrapsychic perspective to a balanced intrapsychic/intersubjective perspective. Since Freud's initial discussion of NTR, the presumed centrality of guilt associated with oedipal conflicts has shifted to a balanced assessment of the importance of guilt *and* shame, and the significance of attachment security in early infancy. These shifts provide threads for the reader to trace in both the clinical cases and theories. Here I will characterize the salience of a contemporary appreciation of shame. The seminal exploration of shame is largely indebted to Léon Wurmser and the group of other American psychoanalysts who have participated in a long running study group at the American Psychoanalytic Association meetings. For an understanding of NTR, shame must be regarded not only as a useful brief regulating affect experience, but also as a more lasting affective *state* with pathological implications. Indeed the same can be said of guilt. As a brief regulatory affect, guilt offers moral and ethical guidance. As an affect *state*, from the "this or that I do, did, or want to do is bad and wrong," guilt moves to "I am bad and evil. I am unworthy of seeing, hearing, or believing anything I or anyone says is good about me." A guilty affect state leads the individual to *reject* anything good thought or said about him or her. In contrast, a shame affect state often results in the individual being *unable* to see or hear any good. A shame state is a turn-off whether it takes place by slowing down, withdrawing, turning inward, or dissociating. Good is shrugged off as if it didn't exist until the shame state abates or is worked through. The working through often occurs at an implicit level of mutual recognition rather than in response to a specific interpretation. An individual's disposition for and vulnerability to shame states means that NTRs even when reversed have an unfortunate likelihood of recurrence—as indicated in some of the case reports and in the clinical story I will relate.

By chance when Léon asked me to write this foreword I was preparing a presentation for an American Psychoanalytic Association meeting panel on sibling relationships. I decided to present my first supervised case now begun over 50 years ago. Based on my reading of *Nothing Good Is Allowed to Stand*, I began to understand aspects of my experience with Mrs. H I had not recognized before. I assume many readers of this book will have similar experiences as they engage in their clinical explorations. I will describe my analysis with Mrs. H emphasizing the phenomenology of NTR that happily we were able to largely resolve.

Mrs. H came for analysis because of a cancer phobia that gradually morphed into a fear of becoming pregnant. In the consultative interview, she manifested immediately the heightened tension and difficulty in talking freely that became painfully characteristic throughout. Each comment was stated in a burst of words and only in response to a question. Her only comment that had a ring of spontaneity and intensity was toward the end of the interview when I asked her if there was any person important to her that she had not spoken of. She replied: "No. I have a twin. She is 10 minutes younger. I never let her forget it. I bossed her all the time. I was always the smart one—she the pretty one." During the next 4½ years she elaborated this theme: She did better in school, forced her sister to give her a favorite doll, she was energetic and her sister was lazy, she was better at sewing, cooking, managing money, and had married first.

These years of analysis were marked by persistent silences lasting on one occasion for seven consecutive hours. She isolated daily events and events during sessions. She would feel ashamed, depressed, and hopeless about her defensiveness. Mrs. H treated each issue of the arrangements—hours, fees—as a struggle for domination. Whatever the decision she would rail against it in pained victimized silence, but what her feelings meant was never to be discussed. The prototypic interaction was that nothing was to be discussed or negotiated as though between equals. On entering or leaving the office, she avoided looking directly at me. On several occasions outside of the office, Mrs. H looked straight at me, but persistently denied she had seen me. The major source of her selective blindness was her fear/conviction that I thought her worthless, couldn't stand another minute of her lack of associative productivity, and that she was not the pretty one. She was certain nothing good was to be seen on my face. This picture of a tense, inhibited, laconic, ashamed woman contrasted with her personality outside the analysis, where she could be garrulous, gossipy, aggressive, energetic, and flirtatious.

Looking back, I regard her silences and generalized communicative impairment as a form of NTR. I did not and could not at the time know the source but once triggered the manifestations set up a downward spiral of shame leading to avoidance and more shame. In the shame state nothing good existed for her. And on my side was my inexperience, uncertainty, and feelings of helplessness—all shame inducers. On the plus side was my general self-confidence and the patience learned from my years of working with psychotic and borderline patients.

A major turning point in our understanding of her proneness for NTR came unexpectedly in the fifth year. As part of her many gains in her outside life, she had discontinued contraception, become pregnant, and without difficulty had given birth to a daughter, Liz. When Liz was 16 months old, Mrs. H began to talk anxiously about Liz's play with another child of the same age. As she talked about the aggressive elements in their play, to my surprise I recognized that she strongly identified with the underdog. Her poignant feeling for the child's losing possession of a toy or being pushed around was in stark contrast to the manner in which she usually talked about rivalry. This provided a strong indication that Mrs. H had blocked awareness of all memory of a period when her twin sister and not she had been the dominating one. Catching up and overtaking proved to be a prototype for her entire early development. Mrs. H, the older by 10 minutes, but by 2 pounds the smaller of the premature twins, had been slower in maturation than her larger sister. As soon as she could, when she was 3 or 4, she used her energetic nature to struggle and scramble ahead in every area. Her narratives of how she bested her twin were often accompanied by a burst of uncontrolled laughter at her sister's discomfort. Interpretations of the meaning of the laughter, especially its fragmentary appearances in the transference, led Mrs. H to a full recognition of her sadistic enjoyment of turning the tables on someone and opened our path to recognizing a source of guilt. The opposite, being the underdog of a pair, was felt by Mrs. H as a complete humiliation. Mrs. H found it hard to recognize and accept how her vulnerability to take the alternate extreme positions of humiliated underdog or the one who overcomes and enjoys it sadistically influenced her development and her current difficulty in allowing anything good to stand. She lived in fear that she might revert to being the one (the twin) who can't talk as she did in undertaking the analysis. And her mood was affected. The mother's response to the more cheery, less finicky, larger twin was more giving while her reaction to the patient's contrasting tendencies, so like the mother's own, was a mixture of shared depression and disapproval.

A puzzling symptom was her opening her mouth and feeling she could not close it. The symptom seemed to both of us a manifestation of anxiety but otherwise escaped explanation. In a session about 2 months before termination after a second successful pregnancy and birth, she described Liz asking to give the 3-month-old baby the bottle. She related how Liz was unable to hold the bottle steady on the baby's lips and the nipple went in too far. For the first time in a year, Mrs. H experienced the symptom of the open mouth she couldn't close. She then related that she had been told by her older sister that often their mother would feed the more rapidly responsive twin and turn over the more finicky baby to her. The open mouth symptom was a somatic marker of both the pragmatic ineptness of the child feeder and the preferential abandonment by the mother. It went along with her transference belief that I didn't want to be bothered with her and would have preferred another. Especially in the early stages of the analysis, this implicit attribution was at times actualized in an underlying enactment that characterized many of our silences and dominance struggles. In these moments, unlike the preferred easy twin, she was the baby who couldn't or wouldn't and I was the caregiver who was puzzled, inept, and would have liked an easier initial analysand. But following her childhood model (and mine), neither of us would accept a defeated pessimistic stance but would and did struggle to persevere.

Looking back, I recognize in Mrs. H's development the major factors that Wurmser cites for understanding NTR: overwhelming guilt and shame (shame states being predominant); irreconcilable loyalties between experiencing her twin as a person to love and a rival to best (rivalry and the guilt of sadistic victory predominating); absoluteness of the expectation she would have to be better in every way; a time lock in the humiliating state of being the one who couldn't talk; and "the unholy trinity of jealousy, envy, and resentment." I am certain many readers will similarly find greater recognition of these factors as they puzzle over the phenomenon of NTR in their clinical endeavors.

Reference

Lichtenberg, J. D. (1985). Humanism and the science of psychoanalysis. *Psychoanalytic Inquiry*, *5*, 393–369.

INTRODUCTION

Léon Wurmser and Heidrun Jarass

> Største seir er nederlag,
> Til seir i fall!
>
> (Ibsen, "Brand," 1866/1991)[1]

We begin with a few quotes from some recent supervisory sessions: The first instance is that of a medical student who in a systematic way destroys every success and in whose analysis progress immediately and predictably has to be paid for with a shattering deterioration. The analyst reports: "Only in severest pain, with tragic mutilation, and in terror of deaths she feels that her parents love her. It is an automatized masochistic pattern: 'Hurt me, and I see in the tears in your eyes how much you love me.' I cannot afford anything good. Everything good needs to be annihilated." In short, there is a kind of primordial equation: *Everything good = over-excitement = traumatic flooding with affects = sexualized aggression and aggressively charged love and sexuality.*

In the second instance, an analyst speaks of the self-righteousness and vindictiveness of his otherwise remarkably successful woman patient, as expressed by her masochistic triumph, with the content: "It is too good to be true," but also, "It is the parents who are at fault when they have not bought me any gloves and my hands freeze."

In a third case of supervision: "He claims that his mother is a very envious woman, and so is his wife; therefore the work inhibition: 'I cannot be successful; I could be envied.' The same occurs in treatment."

And in a fourth instance, a colleague reports about her patient who has been in analysis for a number of years: "She twists everything. I say something that I think is empathic. She immediately turns it into something critical and torments me with it. No joy, no pleasure is allowed to stand. Without letting me know, she has been rather successful, but immediately feels she does not deserve it and hides it from me." The patient's consistent use of "judging instead of exploring" (Paul Gray, personal communication) has easily tempted the therapist to rush in as defender of the poor self against the perceived threat from the implacable inner judge. The inner judge embodies the voice of "the evil mother."

Already in these vignettes we recognize a problem of treatment that occurs very frequently and is very hard to endure. It is a problem that keeps cropping up in our literature, but, it seems to us, has found rather less attention than it deserves. It is not seen in all its complexity and multilayered dynamics, but rather reduced to some single factor. There are not a few analysts who doubt that the concept can be justified.

After having worked for many years with a number of particularly difficult patients where every sign of progress and every insight almost inevitably had been followed by a more or less massive retrogression, often over a period of a decade of analytic work and longer, the two of us felt interested, not to say compelled, to study intensively the widely divergent ideas about what Freud (1923) had called the "negative therapeutic reaction" and the views emerging in the roughly 90 years since then. In our book on jealousy and envy (Wurmser & Jarass, 2007), we have already reflected upon some of these experiences, but a more focused study of the phenomena and what underlies them became desirable. This was the more so as the rather voluminous literature about them profiled valuable partial aspects, but hardly provided a synthesis of most that appeared to be clinically relevant.

The phenomena are clear, but their conceptualization varies widely. To remain close to them we chose a less theoretically prejudicial and committal title: "Nothing Good Is Allowed to Stand."

Freud's Understanding of the Dynamics Behind the Phenomenon

Psychoanalytic theory understands as negative therapeutic reaction (NTR) a powerful deterioration of the analytic patient's clinical condition that follows upon an important insight, other signs of progress during treatment, or having received support and praise. It is therefore a phenomenological term, though one for which in the literature a considerable number of psychodynamic reasons were and are adduced. It is probable that its observations may have strongly impelled Freud to introduce the structural model of id, ego, and superego.

The phenomenon is described by Freud for the first time in 1918 when he writes that his patient (the "Wolf Man") "showed the habit of producing transitory 'negative reactions'; every time something had been conclusively cleared up, he attempted to contradict the effect for a short while by an aggravation of the symptom which had been cleared up" (p. 69). At this point he explains it, in analogy with children, as an assertion of autonomy and defiance against a prohibition, followed by submission, as if they were "stopping [the symptom, respectively the censored behavior] of their own accord."

Five years later, he gives this phenomenon a much deepened interpretation. In *The Ego and the Id* (1923), he stresses the paradoxical, surprising, and disappointing nature of this phenomenon: "Every partial solution that ought to result, and in other people does result, in an improvement or a temporary suspension of symptoms produces in them for the time being an exacerbation of their illness; they get worse during the treatment instead of getting better" (p. 49). It is a specific form of resistance, rooted in the fear of getting better, but analyzing it (as hitherto) as an expression of defiance against the analyst, or as a fixation on the gain from being ill, or as due to "narcissistic inaccessibility," is of little avail. Based on his new conceptualization of the superego, the central new factor with which Freud now explains the negative therapeutic reaction is an unconscious feeling of guilt that requires punishment by suffering. Yet, this guilt feeling is mute (*stumm*): "He does not feel guilty, he feels ill" (p. 50), and the resistance against this insight is very strong. Such an unconscious sense of guilt may not only be due to the patient's own drive wishes but also to "*borrowed guilt*" (p. 50), the guilt feelings or actual guilt within the family (Eickhoff, 1989, 2004; Hirsch, 1997, chapter 4, this volume; Jarass, chapter 5, this volume; Levy, 1982; Plenker, 2000). An alternative way of phrasing the same issue of intensive unconscious guilt is by presenting it as criticism and punishment by a cruel inner judge (i.e., by a "sadistic superego," and the submission of the self to this inner tyrant; see Wurmser, chapter 1, and Jarass, chapter 5, this volume). Freud (1923) sees this cruelty of the superego as an expression of the death instinct turned against the self (p. 53).

One year later, in "The Economic Problem of Masochism" (1924), he replaces the concept of "the unconscious feeling of guilt" with those of "the *need for punishment*" (p. 166) and "*moral masochism*" (p. 169), so intense because of the repression of oedipal wishes of a sexual and murderous nature. The meaning of the NTR would then be, more generally: "I cannot allow myself any success because the success I really want to achieve or have achieved is the conquest of one parent and the elimination of the rival." In that sense, the dynamic meaning of the NTR would be the same as what he had described in 1916 as "those who are wrecked by success," but now specifically related to the transference. As formulated later on by Sandler (1980; Sandler, Dare, & Holder, 1973): "In people who show this reaction, improvement can be thought of as representing the gratification of an internally forbidden wish and is consequently experienced as a threat" (1980, p. 14).

Finally, in "Analysis Terminable and Interminable" (1937), Freud assumes constitutional factors to account for the intensity of the aggression and thus of the *death instinct vested in the superego.*

Newer Theoretical Approaches

For Karen Horney (1936), the reaction is stimulated by a good interpretation that leads to different, partly coexisting responses:

1. Against the background of intense *competitiveness*, there occurs a compulsive disparagement of, and hostility against, a "good interpretation," any possible progress that would be seen as a triumph for the analyst: the affect of *resentment*.
2. On the basis of grandiose ideas and wishes for perfection and admiration, set up against a profound fear of being exposed in any weakness or failing (*narcissism as defense against shame anxiety*), the patient feels humiliated by any interpretation that implies some failing (which most do): the affect is primarily that of *shame*; the patient has to retaliate by belittling and thus trying to humiliate the analyst (turning passive into active).
3. Possible success is equated with crushing rivals and evokes the danger of being similarly crushed in retaliation as they would crush their rivals: Thus there is both a fear of success and a fear of failure (a *shame-guilt-dilemma*); "NTR is a special form of the fear of success" (p. 36); the predominant affect appears to be *envy*._
4. Interpretation is experienced as an unjust accusation, thus evoking *unconscious guilt* and the need to prove the analyst wrong and damaging.
5. On the basis of a strong need for affection due to massively frightening circumstances in childhood, interpretation is felt as a falling short of love and experienced as rejection; there is a constant *oscillation between rivalry and a need for affection*. A good interpretation implies an "acute frustration of the patient's excessive need for affection" (p. 40). This exaggerated need for affection is traced back by Horney to the double anxiety of the patient's own hostility and that of the retaliation from without. Reassurance could come only from unconditional love. Thus the basic affect in this form appears to be jealousy. She summarizes her findings by explaining NTR as derived from the two currents of intense hostility against the analyst and the fear of success. She concurs with Freud that it is "*a feature of every severe neurosis*," adding the words "in our culture" (p. 41), and advocates a strong technical emphasis on what today would be called the here-and-now of the transference, over reconstructions of childhood conflicts.

In Horney's analysis there is a strong hint of the importance of shame conflicts in the causation of NTR—a factor that has become much more prominent in modern works (see below).

Subsequently, the focus shifted for Melanie Klein and her school to the paramount motivation for NTR being *envy* and of the defenses against it (Klein, 1957, p. 185), or, in addition, narcissistic defenses against an unconscious *depressive state* or position (Rivière, 1936; Rosenfeld, 1975). Rivière's connection of NTR with the depressive position leads her also to place great emphasis on the role of unconscious love and caring about the objects: the patient's sense that he or she does not deserve help so long as justice has not been done to the love objects (Plenker, 2000, p. 636).

Klein "points out that to deny oneself success is a defense against the guilt for having attacked the good object due to envy and that it also depends on the patient's incapacity to accept a useful interpretation with gratitude" (Maldonado, 1989, p. 332). According to Rosenfeld (1975), it is the "*omnipotent inner structure*, loaded with envy" that attacks the dependent part of the self: "The attack against the dependent self serves to reinforce the narcissistic structure's delusional possession of the breast that denies all need and all envy" (Maldonado, 1989, p. 232).

Olinick (1964) picks up on the attitude of *anal defiance* and hence negativism, mentioned by Freud in his comments about the Wolf Man, and focuses on the dread of regression to what Anna Freud had called the "*primary identification* with the love object": "This is feared as a loss of intactness, or annihilation of the self, and is defended against by negativism ... this dreaded helplessness and emotional surrender is inherent in the *ambivalent identification with a depressed, pre-oedipal maternal* [emphasis added] love object" (p. 545). He summarizes:

> I may now denote this reaction as a depressive, sadomasochistic rage, which is projected and induced in the other person, in a desperate effort at defense against the expectation of inner loss and helpless regression. Negativism is the linkage between the various parts of the picture, the common denominator among the various elements. (p. 546)

He pointedly juxtaposes: "Sadomasochism 'projects' depression, and negativism 'rejects' depression" (p. 546). The main therapeutic task appears to be "the analysis of the *'primary identification' with the depressed, pre-oedipal mother*" (p. 547). In Olnick's Panel report of 1970, he defines NTR as "an acute, recurrent, negativistic emotional crisis in a sadomasochistic person who is prone to depression; it represents a category of superego resistance.... Negativism as part of the negative therapeutic reaction defends against a *loss of self* inherent in the ambivalent relationship with a depressed, pre-oedipal maternal love object" (pp. 666–667).

Limentani (1981) states:

> Most Kleinian analysts have tended to rely on the interpretation of the patient's envy as a mainstay in counteracting the patient's destructive attack on the analyst and his work, whilst the majority of analysts, particularly from North America, have tended to rely on Freud's concept of unconscious guilt and masochism. (p. 381)

He ascribes its genesis to a defense against unbearable pain rooted in trauma, particularly severe early separation: "The pain involved is excruciating and is remembered sufficiently clearly to be avoided at all costs, but the memory of the event to which it relates is often neither accessible nor available (as in most cases of early separation from mother, disturbed weaning, etc.)" (p. 388). The NTR is "a particularly stubborn defense against the re-experiencing of pain and psychic suffering associated with early trauma" (p. 389), a defense directed against any sign of independence. Concretely, it means: "Every step towards insight was equal to being allowed to grow up and this he could not accept" (p. 386).

Yet, it is also very meaningful to turn this argumentation around: It is precisely severe, chronic, and early traumatization that would lead to a *clinging to pain*, to an *attachment to negative affects* altogether, what Arthur Valenstein (1973) described as the core of the NTR:

> Primitive affect states occurring during periods of marked regression are likely to be as far as it is possible to go therapeutically toward the recovery of the events or circumstances of the early preverbal period. And such primitive affect states appear to be consequent to the propensity of such individuals to relive in later life and in the intense transference recrudescence what they cannot cognitively remember, namely, the aura of early experience including the *sense* of self and self-object. This is especially so if, as is usually the case, they are strongly fixated to early trauma associated with pain; then they readily regress to primitive affect states characteristic of such trauma. (p. 375)

In a specific reference to the NTR he adds:

> Such patients appear to react refractorily to correct interpretation with regression to primitive negativistic states. They become immersed in painful affects to which they appear to cling. I believe that such affects are emphatically held to because they represent the early self and self-object. Giving up such affects, coincident with mostly correct, but insufficiently deep interpretations would be equivalent to relinquishing a part of the self and/or self-object at the level which those affects represent. (p. 376)

Such a compulsive clinging to pain and sadness assumes the character of a relationship that substitutes for the mother and can become a powerful motive for the NTR, as if to say: "I do not allow being robbed of the suffering. It is the only intimate Other (*Du*) I know." In contrast to Freud and Sandler he therefore holds the opinion that this "nuclear determinant of the 'negative therapeutic reaction' is located developmentally much earlier than definitive superego formation" (p. 390).

This *central role of separation anxiety* in its genesis is also stressed by Maldonado (1989); separation leads to "feelings of possessive jealousy and envy towards the object" (p. 335), now of course mainly the analyst, and a need for vengeance. It is what Freud observed already in 1918: the role of defiance against the analyst.

Grunert (1979) has talked about *defiance as a defense* against the wishes of the patient to surrender to, *and to fuse with*, the other (p. 16). She sees the thwarted and "offended" wishes to give oneself (*Hingabewünsche*) and a protective search for autonomy as a major motivational factor in what appears as defiance in the NTR—"a wish to protect oneself against narcissistic injury" (p. 16). She sees in it "an expression of a disturbance in the process of detachment and individuation" (p. 1). She strongly warns against *premature interpretation of aggression*; it shakes the confidence in self and analyst which is so necessary for the working through of the process of detachment and individuation in the transference (p. 26). Similarly Milton H. Horowitz (in Olinick, 1970) is of the opinion "that repeated emphasis on the patient's aggression tended to increase the expression of the aggression" (p. 661) and becomes a self-fulfilling prophecy. More broadly speaking, Renik (1991) also finds that

> despite the emphasis usually placed on the role of aggression, I have the impression that conceptualizing a negative therapeutic reaction primarily in terms of the vicissitudes of aggression rarely points the way toward opportunities for productive analytic work.... (p. 101)
>
> [W]hat appear to be manifestations of destructive aggression in negative therapeutic reactions are often better conceptualized in light of the way they serve libidinal and defensive purposes, particularly preservation of the image of a loveable and loving object. (p. 103)

In the case presented by Renik (1991):

> His negative therapeutic reaction was only one in a long series of my patient's efforts to reassure himself against his disavowed dread perceptions of his mother, transferred on this occasion to his analyst ... he *created the image he feared most*, but in a form he

> could unconsciously contradict and invalidate … he was counting on me to maintain a reality of benevolent dependability that contradicted his complaints," that is his claim that the analyst is as cold and rejecting as his mother. (pp. 94, 97)

In contrast, the role of the *masochistic triumph* (and with that the centrality of aggression) is highlighted by Kernberg (1975); he speaks of

> the need to defeat oneself as a necessary price to pay in order to defeat an unconsciously hated and envied helping figure.… Self-destruction here serves the purpose of "triumphing" over the envied object. The more serious cases of "negative therapeutic reaction" are linked with such "triumph" over others, in this case, the therapist and his life-affirmative tendencies. (p. 126)

In contrast to the cases studied by Freud where the major cause lies in unconscious guilt feelings, there are patients with more serious psychopathology who present narcissistic personality structures and "whose unconscious need to defeat the therapist is related to *oral envy and revengeful destruction* of potential external sources of love and gratification" (p. 126).

Many authors maintain the hypothesis of the predominance of autodestruction, death instinct, or Thanatos as the origin of the NTR, presumably as part of the inborn apparatus, whereas some contemporary writers would rather attribute this prevalence of self-directed destruction to early traumatic experiences (Renik, 1991, p. 100).

There has also been some inclination to understand the term and hence presumably the phenomenon itself as a sign of a faulty attitude and technique on the analyst's side (Plenker, 2000; Rivière, 1936), to interpretations tackling conflicts from the drive side instead of from the defenses (Fenichel, 1945), lack of empathy (Mayr, 2001; Ornstein, 2007, who contests the usefulness of the term altogether, see chapter 8, this volume), and especially due to too strong an interest in healing instead of the dispassionate search for understanding, the priority of cure instead of the priority of truth (Schubart, 1989), especially of insight into sexuality. In the words of Pontalis (1980):

> I would suggest that the NTR is never so manifest as in the subjects where the "therapeutic" aspect of the endeavor—care, treatment and cure—is significant, with the corollary of a massive repression of sexuality. At base, perhaps such subjects are asking us to *cure them of sexuality*, an ineducable, incurable sexuality which is for them, as in the perversions, charged with hatred, envy and violence. Rather than measure up to the madness of Eros, they choose the lost cause of a battle with Thanatos. (p. 28)

Schubart (1989) sees even the concept with its judgmental connotation ("negative") as an expression of Freud's own ambivalence between the interest in insight and the therapeutic purpose (p. 1073). The dominance of wishes to heal instead of exploring the meanings or even of attempts to educate the patient are an expression of countertransference (i.e., that the analyst shares with the patient the conviction that greed, envy, and wishes for destruction are in reality destroying the analysis and his or her own self-esteem as analyst). As a reaction formation the analyst uses the therapeutic zeal or resorts, like Freud, to "the triumph of the military metaphor" (p. 1085).

A number of authors have commented about the overextension of the term, in Sandler's (1980) comments on Rivière's views: that she first more or less equates it with "not getting well," and then shows that "not getting well" is an unavoidable indirect result of a great variety of resistances, not only those which stem from an unconscious sense of guilt. Negative therapeutic reaction is far more specific and cannot simply be treated as synonymous with resistance to recovery and a negativistic attitude. Pontalis (1980) finds that "today, the notion seems to have faded away, in its specific sense. Having been recognized everywhere, it cannot now be located anywhere" (p. 24).

Similar criticism is expressed by Maldonado (1989), Klug (2000), and Maguire (1990). The latter distinguishes three distinct categories of negative reaction that enter into analysis and analytic therapy:

1. Resistance, an integral element of the therapeutic process that, even in its most severe forms, may remain amenable over time to interpretative intervention.
2. The negative therapeutic reaction, a paradoxical phenomenon not infrequently associated with the apprehended development of the transference neurosis, which arises out of the treatment process and yet rapidly becomes extraneous to, and subversive of, this process.
3. Therapeutic stalemate, a species of negative reaction that must be distinguished from both resistance and the negative therapeutic reaction in the specific sense, a specificity formulated by Maldonado (1989) as the "contrasting improvement-worsening relation" and "the *paradoxical* nature of the response [by the patient] and the resulting surprise impact on the countertransference" (p. 327).

Maguire (1990) is even more specific:

> I subscribe to the original Freudian descriptive constraints that would restrict the status of the negative therapeutic reaction to a specific and implicitly time-limited response to interpretation; conversely, I assign a negative attitudinal reaction to the analytic

> procedure to some condition of stalemate, especially if such a reaction constitutes a sustained disruption of the analytic process that affects outcome and transcends a simple untoward reception of an interpretation or series of interpretations dealing with a particular conflictual issue. (p. 65)

The interactional or relational aspect of this reaction has been stressed. For example, Pontalis (1980) states, referring more generally to resistance:

> To say "He is in resistance" or "I am in resistance" is identical. It is the means of evacuating in the direction of one subject what is the effect of a process to which both the analyst and *his* patient, the patient and *his* analyst are subject—not to say subjected. (p. 23)

Bergmann-Mausfeld (2006) sees NTR grounded in a

> pathological accommodation … as an adequate reaction to pathogenic intersubjective experiences during the critical period of primary dependency.... Due to early pathogenic interactions and the intensification of earliest unfulfilled needs, later experiences of a good-enough-mothering and of desired "adequate" reactions are experienced as non-fitting, inadequate and jeopardizing the patient's identity in a fundamental way. (p. 251)

In the encounter with the "living" analyst, the patient touches upon something that she experiences as an overwhelming "*too-much*" and thus on deeply frightening, always frustrated needs, in particular "the need for emotionally alive interaction where she could have experienced herself in her aliveness globally held and responded to" (p. 265).

Shelley Orgel (2007, chapter 2, this volume) adds a very valuable perspective, adumbrated in slightly different contexts before by Arlow (1984), Schmithüsen (2004, chapter 3, this volume) and Chodorow (2003): the wish to deny and to block the movement of time, and with that of change, of progress, of aging, and of course, of the movement toward that ultimate separation, death. Orgel (this volume) writes:

> What has been labeled a negative therapeutic reaction, then, expresses a resistance (defense) against accepting the imperative cost of the wished-for aims of analysis itself. Living acquires meaning as we face the necessity of separation, including, in adults, the realities of aging and death. One purpose of negative therapeutic reactions, in some patients I have worked with, is to stop time, to keep the illusion of eternal youth, to refuse to grow up.

It signifies in intensified form "an inevitable, universal resistance to change" and attempts to hold on whereas, inevitably, interpretation means loss and separateness.

A second aspect highlighted by Orgel (this volume) is the equation of insight (or interpretation) with penetration: "For them interpretation is an invasive action, one that is often eroticized in fantasy." The outcome is a compromise formation between defense of boundaries and wish to merge: "Insofar as analysands feel interpretations are instruments of the analyst's ... phallic power, taking them in, absorbing them, becomes dangerously exciting, infuriating, terrifying and guilt ridden..."

Shame and the Negative Therapeutic Reaction

As mentioned above, increasing attention has been paid over the years to the importance of shame in the NRT, beginning with the role of "borrowed shame," besides that of borrowed guilt (Eickhoff, 1989, 2004) and the frequent references to "narcissistic injury" (Horney, 1936; Kohut, 1971; Renik, 1991; Rosenfeld, 1975; Rothstein, 1984). In patients with a childhood history of massive and repeated traumatization, the feeling of shame is prominent. Kohut (1971) refers to "situations in which the child's legitimate claims for the approving attention of the grownups had not been responded to, but in which the child had been belittled and ridiculed at the very moment when he most proudly had wanted to display himself" (p. 232). He speaks of traumatic states "which occur typically in the middle and even in the later stages of the analysis of narcissistic personalities, paradoxically often in response to correct and empathically given interpretations which should (and in the long run do) facilitate analytic progress" (p. 232). To ascribe this negative therapeutic reaction to guilt is usually not correct: "Their predominant tendency is to be *overwhelmed by shame*, in other words, they react to the breakthrough of the archaic aspects of the grandiose self, especially to its unneutralized exhibitionism" (p. 232).

According to our own experience (Wurmser, 2000, 2007, chapter 1, this volume; Jarass, chapter 5, this volume), traumatogenic shame very commonly pertains to the intensity of feelings in general, the great anxiety to express them, and the anxiety of inner and outer loss of control: feelings of neediness, of longing, of tenderness, of being moved, of being hurt. One aspect of transference may indeed consist in trying by the negative therapeutic reaction to evoke in the analyst a countertransference reaction of distancing and angry rebuff. Looking for the acceptance by such a figure and merger with him or her would remove the shame of feeling and wishing too strongly, but it means an almost incorrigible masochistic bondage, and a renewed and deepened sense of disgrace.

Much of this hypertrophy of the superego consists in the dominating fantasy of the *omnipotence of responsibility* set up as protection against traumatic helplessness, and, connected with this, the splitting of the superego functions (see Wurmser, chapter 1, this volume).

Affective flooding in traumatic states turns into overexcitement, and such overstimulation has to lead to very painful disappointment and the overwhelming sense of shame for "having been made the fool again." Everything that is good and supposedly helpful is equated with traumatic affective flooding, resulting in a deep equation of intense affect with sexualized aggression and aggressively experienced sexuality, closeness, and love. This traumatic, passively experienced process is again and again turned around into something actively reenacted: Every joy, every gratification, every expectation, everything good has to be broken off and changed into something negative and bad. Dangerous, mortifying, shame-laden excitement appears to be more important than guilt: "It is too dangerous to sense pleasure and joy; it will be abruptly taken away or it will become unbearably intense and totally unfulfillable." Thus the inner judge, the archaic superego, has to prevent all pleasure. The negative therapeutic reaction has a crucially important source in this preemptive thwarting of joy and pride in success (Jarass & Wurmser, 2007).

The negative therapeutic reaction quite typically enacts in the transference and countertransference what I called the "symbiotic circle" and a fatal form of the "shame-guilt dilemma":

> Every separateness is experienced, both subjectively and usually also accurately as family reality, as if it were something murderous. Abandoning the other means injuring, if not killing her or him. Accordingly, being abandoned is equated with unbearable pain or death. This means that with every step of independence one feels burdened with great guilt; every self-willedness, every success has to be punished as great temerity. Autonomy just like disobedience and defiance are declared mortal sins. This is what we can call "*separation guilt*." If one retreats from this daring step and submits to the binding other, one loses one's own self, one's dignity, one's identity. However, sacrificing one's own self in order to preserve a human relationship is looked at with withering self-contempt; the victim-self, the passive dependent self, is looked at with searing shame. Sooner or later, this *dependency shame* has to lead to open or hidden rage and to defiance, to renewed breaking away, and thus the circle is closed. (Wurmser, 2007, p. 39)

This dilemma between dependency shame and separation guilt is only a special case of the very frequent, deep conflict between opposite duties, ideals, and values. A good example is Claudius in *Hamlet* (III, iii, lines 40–43): "My stronger guilt defeats my strong intent,/And like a *man to double business bound*,/I stand in pause where I shall first begin,/And both neglect."[2]

It appears that the views developed over the many years of analytic experience and presented here largely complement each other (Danielian & Lister, 1988) and deal with different levels or various root motivations of this phenomenon. It is important, however, not to overextend the concept. Pontalis (1980) puts the analyst's task when faced with a NTR well:

> [I]f we wish to retain some chance of crossing with our patient the dry, *sterile* desert (which is how his internal space appears to him who seeks to protect it), it seems to me that we have to recognize fully the *legitimacy* of his negative reaction, that is to say accept being starved and blinded. (p. 30)

If we want to summarize what we have found to be most helpful in the recognition of the dynamics, we might say that work with patients with severe neuroses very often has to cope with the phenomenon that every progress in the analytic or therapeutic work is paradoxically followed by a clinical deterioration. There are a number of dynamic factors that converge in bringing about this clinical phenomenon. Foremost among them are: many layered guilt and shame, the role of envy and jealousy, attachment to negative affects, turning trauma from passive to active, conflicts within the superego, and the defensive use of omnipotence of responsibility.

The main points are:

1. The extent to which traumatization lives on in self-directed aggressions of the superego and in the claim of omnipotence of responsibility.
2. The great role of deep conflicts between opposite values and loyalties in bringing about the prohibition of anything "good" and thus of the "negative therapeutic reaction" in particular, the broad area of masochism in general.
3. The extent to which envy, jealousy, and resentment can be encountered in the "inner object," the "inner judge," (i.e., the superego), and how they are directed against the self.

An Overview of this Book

The main point of chapter 1 (a case description) lies in the splitting of the superego, above all in the form of the patients' being torn between irreconcilable loyalties or between overwhelming shame and equally overwhelming guilt, and with that the narrowness of their path between these two abysses of (largely opposite) types of self-condemnation. When demands that are taken as absolute get into conflict with each other or with outer reality no solution is possible. This absoluteness of expectation and demand, directed against the self and others, is, therefore, a guarantee for massive self-condemnation and constant disappointment in the other. An especially striking element is the patient's attempt to block the progression of time, "as if time stood still." Behind it we find the unholy trinity of jealousy, envy, and resentment. All the other facets of the dynamics of the case presented are, as it were, unfolded, as if painted onto a Chinese fan.

Shelley Orgel's two main points in chapter 2 have already been summarized above. He goes from the "axiom that all change involves loss" and emphasizes the one dynamic and particularly salient factor that has emerged in the case presentation in chapter 1, the attempt by many of these patients to block the progression of time: "For some, the unfolding bodily and mental changes time brings seem too narcissistically wounding to bear." In addition, there is in some the deeply feared and warded off equation of all insight and therapeutic interventions with penetrations, mostly of a phallic nature. It reminds LW of a patient who dreamed that LW was using an ophthalmoscope and she had to fight him off, literally "in-sight"—symbolizing an intense shame conflict. Both dynamics stand in contradiction to the view held by Freud (and others, like Sandler) that guilt is the main motivation for the NTR. Very importantly, he ends his paper saying that "the NTR did not announce a limitation or an end to our work, but was an inevitable and valuable part of an ongoing psychoanalytic process."

In chapter 3, Gerd Schmithüsen adds to the study of this phenomenon, which is seen in "patients who have been extremely traumatized when they were very young" when "the analyst cannot avoid experiencing feeling as if time were standing still." It is strictly an issue of the countertransference and is not consciously experienced by the patients themselves. He brings detailed excerpts out of the dialogue in sessions from the psychotherapy of a deeply troubled patient. He ascribes this phenomenon to "a radical defense": "Through this phenomenon defenses are actively, albeit unconsciously, brought into play, which prevents any further development of the catastrophic fear; the fear that developed when the child was separated from the maternal object at a time before the ego had been consolidated." He speaks of an "underlying, nonsymbolized, and as such incomprehensible fear of annihilation or fear of psychic death," that is being repeated now in the transference relationship: "The everlasting present serves as a defense against the awareness of loss, separation and death." He concludes:

> Patients try to avoid being reconfronted with their transference fear of being annihilated and the resulting intense hopelessness by actively but unconsciously projecting a standstill in time into the analyst; that is, the feeling "as if time stands still".... In this way, they induce a state of deadness in the analyst, who is over

> long periods of time present physically but psychically inaccessible for the analysand as well as for the analyst himself. In my opinion, this is a central aspect of the NTR although an appropriate appreciation of this aspect is lacking in analytic literature on NTR.... [The analyst] should be able to allow himself to be used as a container and to work on his countertransference, using his understanding of the transference–countertransference relation. It is this aspect that is constructive and one that potentially makes the therapeutic process move again, and that has been completely disregarded in literature on the NTR and causes serious misunderstandings between analyst and patient and can lead to retraumatization and the abrupt termination of the analysis.

Both chapters 3 and 5 pay particular attention to countertransference feelings and images in the understanding of the NTR, as beacons shining in the darkness of severe stalemate and despair. In a somewhat less pronounced way, this is also true for the case vignette in chapter 6.

In chapter 4, Mathias Hirsch understands it so: "By negative transference and projective identification, the therapeutic object turns into a hostile object because it demands too much the giving up of the destructive internalized object" (see also 2001, p. 50). For him the crucial factor is thus the separation from the destructive introject: "Progress in therapy may also [besides the oedipal conflicts] be understood as separation from the dependency on internal objects opposing progress and the development of autonomy. Such departure from parental objects also causes guilt, namely *separation guilt*." Hirsch depicts also the splits within the superego, the conflicts between opposite parts of conscience and ideals, in particular those parts of the superego that demand autonomy versus the one that expects submission and dependency. It is the conflict and dialectic between separation guilt and dependency shame that is outlined above and in chapter 1 (see also Wurmser, 1981/1994, 2000, 2007).

The phenomena designated under the heading of NTR are intimately interwoven with today's topical issue of trauma; Hirsch notes "the great difficulty traumatized persons have separating from the very objects once responsible for the trauma." This eminently marks the transference relationship: "The analyst turns into the omnipotent, threatening, devouring mother object preventing free will and independent identity." Hence, "in my view, the NTR is not so much an expression of a step toward autonomy but, on the contrary, a failed separation."

In chapter 5, Heidrun Jarass deals with her own and her patient's often extremely trying experiences during 12 years of a still ongoing treatment, with a patient who had often been seen and treated as floridly psychotic, but whose diagnosis continues in doubt. What is certain, however, is that almost regularly dramatic improvements and periods of increasing competency and deep insights were suddenly interrupted by violent storms of rage and suicidal depression—the negative therapeutic reaction. Certainly, there is much evidence for a bipolar disorder, both in him and in his family, but such a diagnosis would hardly do justice to the complexity of the case. In the background, salient facts are that the grandfather was a general in the Nazi army and the father had been schooled from age 11 on in a Napola (National Political Academy), a place of education and indoctrination for the children of the Nazi elite, with all the cruelty, prejudice, and dehumanization this entailed. Some of the dynamics may be visualized in this sequence:

1. Severe, cumulative, many layered relational traumatization.
2. Massively archaic nature of the superego as a consequence of the traumata, in the form of implacability, cruelty, and absoluteness of judgment and as dehumanization and "digestion." Parallel to this there are severe superego sanctions directed against strongly repressed affects, especially of murderous jealousy toward his brother, who was clearly favored by his father, but who undertook a very serious suicide attempt that left him partly paralyzed.
3. Turning of these superego aggressions against the outside in all his intimate relationships, particularly in the one with the analyst/therapist and with wife and children, something that was often "explained" by outsiders in supervision and intervision as manipulation and sadism.
4. These superego aggressions also reflect a very strong fixation on early anal fantasies that keep circling around digestion and evacuation: since early childhood, fascination with loud machines and cyclical processes in excavators, images of violent expulsion and dismemberment, smearing and generally destroying of any kind. We also have to think in this connection of the direct family tradition of the Nazi world and Auschwitz as *anus mundi* ("the anus of the world").
5. The denied and repressed family guilt in regard to possibly stolen Jewish property, resonating and being confirmed in the pervasive feelings of personal shame and guilt, in the commandments of silence in family and transference, and in the compulsion to disappoint and to fail (like the case in chapter 1).
6. Reality thus keeps being denied, but it is repeated in the compulsion to destroy, and is so confirmed.

Of particular importance for the therapist is her weaving together of this vicious circle in the patient with her own suffering under the Nazi past.

Another aspect of countertransference, insight into which proved especially helpful, is that in the understanding of the dynamics, the metaphor of "digestion" shows throughout its Janus face: as a current, frequently used image for mentalization on the one hand, and on the other as a reflection of archaic fantasies of a mostly anal nature, of dismemberment and chopping to pieces.

Just as in some of the other chapters, the approach to the problem of the NTR appears in a double form: as a classical psychoanalytic exploration of inner conflict, on an I-It level, and that of the "real relationship," more of an I-You character.

Chapter 6 offers quite a different take on the understanding of certain forms of NTR. The broad psychohistorical context within which the phenomena surrounding the NTR are examined is, as in the previous chapter, also of great relevance, a study by Jörg Frommer in the former German Democratic Republic that was (re-)united with Western Germany in 1990. This time it is less the totalitarian, racist, and genocidal dictatorship of the Nazis than the immediately ensuing rule by the Communist regime, with its thorough penetration of all layers of society and family with the help of a system of informers, bugging, denunciation, terror, and execution. As part of the "legacy" of both totalitarian dominions and their "transgenerationally charged destructive forces," especially in the form of "borrowed guilt" and "borrowed shame," the author examines a particular defense which he calls "omnipresence." As he defines it, "omnipresence refers to the compulsive attempt to eliminate all boundaries of development within a social area and render them inoperative. This includes lifting all physical borders." He wonders whether this defense may be specific to post-totalitarian personalities or may rather be a ubiquitous phenomenon of postmodern societal development.

However, he writes,

> the experience of being treated in a dehumanizing manner from early childhood on, cannot remain without consequences for self- and world experience. We know from psychoanalytic trauma research that psychic survival from this sort of trauma brings forth, at the very least, a partial identification with the perpetrator, which in the form of "totalitarian" inner objects ... brutalize the conscious and, even more, unconscious psychic life of the traumatized person. Accompanying factors are massive problems in the areas of guilt and shame as well as consistent destructive and autodestructive behavior. In a recent and strongly autobiographical essay about life in totalitarian societies, the Magdeburg psychoanalyst Ludwig Drees wrote: "the prevailing affect within these societal formations is fear, a monstrous fear of being eliminated from the community, of dropping out; the awakening of ancient fears of annihilation".... This fear leads to collective processes of psychic regression accompanied by massive denial of reality and the readiness to assume seemingly paranoid ideologies.

Accordingly, Frommer resorts to Martin Buber's philosophy, with its distinction between the world of "I-You" (*Ich-Du*, in English often infelicitously rendered *I-Thou*) and "I-It" (*Ich-Es*), by focusing on "the loss of 'Thou' in the significant other as a result of political repression." "The loss of security due to the collapse of basic assumptions of reciprocity in human relationships" has to result in a "traumatogenic mentalization deficiency." Consequently, in the phenomena of the defense of omnipresence, "the struggle against real (external) repression has … become an unbearable inner conflict, in which the projection of totalitarian superego parts into the outside world makes a nearly indispensable contribution towards the preservation of psychic equilibrium. This is especially the case when actual repression has ceased."

What about the NTR in these cases?

> The loss of "Thou" in the other person manifests itself as "empty" countertransference. As a consequence of the feeling of having no "other," no partner, patients produce "an experience in the counter-transference of helplessness, pointlessness and emptiness" … (Rose, 2001, p. 1). Robbed of his most important aide to orientation, the analyst experiences a fundamental feeling of being lost. This increases the chances of his being seduced by masked proposals to enter into destructive acting out.… The more activity on the external stage, the less obvious the emptiness of the internal world.… A highly dynamic succession of events suggesting mobility, fulfillment and success over a longer period of time is misidentified as progress.… These phases alternate with catastrophes, during which everything built at that point collapses like a house of cards in an existentially threatening manner. This is accompanied by helplessness and the shattering of a feeling of "we" between analyst and analysand.… Apparent progress can signalize deeper blockades, apparent regress be a sign of successful analysis.

Cordelia Schmidt-Hellerau proposes, in chapter 7, a radical reconceptualization of psychoanalytic drive theory. Instead of going out from the often dogmatically held view of a dual drive theory of libido and aggression, she postulates a duality of sexual and preservative drives, adding that "both drives have the capacity to become aggressive in order to reach their goals, and [I] define aggression as the intensification of either one, the sexual or the preservative drive." She calls the drive for self- and object preservation "Lethe" ("Forgetting" in Greek, the name of the river of forgetting in the netherworld), and talks about "lethic energies." She views anxiety as "the expression of the self-preservative drives in response to a realistic or imagined danger for the subject's (or the object's) well-being and survival—hence the release of quantitatively increased lethic energies reaching into the area of disease—or even death." She suggests that "the anxiety to fall ill as well as intermediate illnesses are an unavoidable and necessary transitional phase on the reconstructive way from a traumatized, deadened self-state to a safely established representation of a well-preserved self and object." NTR is, according to her, not a resistance against getting better, but a sign of getting better and should be interpreted as such, that these worries and affections are symptoms "that turn over a page" and that they should be interpreted progressively as a newly achieved capacity to elicit the analyst's object preservative as well as the patient's own self-preservative concerns. "Instead of interpreting them as a resistance against getting better, as a regressive move, and as an expression of aggression turned inwards, we interpret to our patients that these symptoms can be understood in the context of their progression and be worked through like any other neurotic symptoms." The unconscious guilt seen by Freud as the main motive she understands as a denial of helplessness: I have done it; I am not passive and helpless.

Although we have reservations about Dr. Schmidt-Hellerau's theories (especially the use of Lethe for the drive for preservation and the absence of dealing with modern motivational theories, especially Joseph Lichtenberg's), we thought the inclusion of a quite different approach would be valuable. Personally I (LW) have never found the use of aggression as basic drive satisfactory and in practical terms saw Freud's earlier theory of a self-preservative drive as more satisfactory while at the same time assuming a much greater complexity than just a duality of basic drives.

Anna Ornstein, in chapter 8, puts her point very succinctly:

> Once we consider psychoanalysis as a process that involves both participants, we can no longer speak about "proper technique" and "correct interpretations," and without these conditions being met, the concept of negative therapeutic reaction loses its usefulness. Not that I did not have failures in my practice but in the analyses that failed, I was a full participant. Presenting such a case could not have demonstrated that there are patients "who respond to the analyst's best efforts and felt signs of progress by getting worse." With the clinical example, I hoped to indicate that the nature of the patient's psychopathology may indeed be responsible for situations where the analyst's own resources are severely tested; cases where narcissistic rage plays a prominent role are most likely to result in a negative outcome or difficult and lengthy termination.

We find her view to be very valuable as a counterpoint to much smugness by analysts or therapists, but, as we will now deal with in the following final section, we do not think that this can be the whole story. Disruptions and stalemates are broader and somewhat different clinical categories than NTR, and narcissistic rage is certainly an important one of the many motives that may lead to the NTR.

The book's final chapter, by Melvin Bornstein, fittingly links up with what we are going to say at the end of this prologue and quotes what one of us (Wurmser, 2007) wrote some years ago about "the fundamental dialectic between a technical and theoretical view of psychoanalysis and a philosophy of the basic human relationship." After an impressive parcours of his own developing thinking over several decades about the problems of sadomasochism, and especially of the NTR, he reaches a basically philosophical conclusion that "there is a glaring gap in our clinical psychoanalytic model: the whole person is not considered." He asks instead for "a conceptualization that would contain the intimate humanity of the analyst and the patient in the clinical situation … so to some degree they are partners, two human beings in a dialogic relationship." And significantly he adds: "We analysts cannot be therapeutically effective while hiding to avoid humiliation and shame."

Bornstein sees a source of the NTR in the need to avoid feeling alive and taking ownership of one's trauma because of the fear of exposing too much affect, knowledge, and vitality, and of being mortally humiliated in this. "Traumas are central to the clinical difficulties in creating narratives." Instead of feeling overwhelmed and totally helpless and utterly vulnerable, it is easier "to deny our personhood, agency, and reflexivity, and to withdraw into sadomasochistic fantasies where … one experiences control in a simple, one-dimensional fashion without any agency or reflexivity" (reflexivity meaning "introspection with the goal of discovering the activities of the mind"). If the analyst is to feel alive in a dialogue with a most severely traumatized patient, states Bornstein, it is required that one live with the helplessness and the finality of the trauma. "I found sadomasochism always appeared in the service of helping to defend against an experience of being alive with the motivation to find a way to make a narrative of trauma." Rather than seeing the NTR as "negative," he views it as an "expression of the enormously powerful force of development when it is experienced as being too much to handle, when the experience of reality contains overwhelming trauma and there is insufficient support from the external world to contain it and to continue one's development."

Concluding Considerations

Finally, we would like to add an excerpt from a letter dialogue about this entire study with Dr. Evelyn Schwaber. She supports the fundamental criticism of this term in a letter to me (March 25, 2007):

> As you may have gleaned from my workshops and writings, I have difficulty with the inherent implication of this concept. It presupposes a basic correctness of the interpretation which is, for a variety of explanations, resisted—even if perhaps the timing and specific wording might be better shifted or in some way refined. Thereby it speaks to a way of listening in which the patient's response is necessarily defensive against some truth as conveyed (however questionably) by the analyst. That to me suggests a fundamental outlook, a perspective, in which the analyst might refine or rethink his or her technique so as to help the patient see or better accept what the analyst already sees—the analyst, that is, as guide, rather than as one who has yet to learn something not before seen. I have found that, in the clinical instance, when I finally come to recognize whatever it is the patient may be struggling with or trying to convey, *therapeutic action takes hold*. Resistance to my interventions takes place for reasons inherently legitimate—something in the patient's experience yet to be discovered by me, which, for what may be my own resistance, can evoke great struggle on my part. "When you understand the way my mind works," a patient told me, "without saying it should work another way, that lets me experience more about how my mind works, and remember more." "Getting it"—"without saying it should work another way"—that is, without feeling or believing it should work another way, however difficult on our part, I have found will not lead to a "negative therapeutic reaction," and will, I believe, fundamentally alter its implication, if not eliminate it from our lexicon.

We very largely agree with this. For us the NTR is a very frequent *phenomenon*, but not an *explanation*. What Dr. Schwaber responds with is an alternative explanation to the ones given by different authors, one that is eminently plausible and similar to the one given by several other authors, especially Anna Ornstein, but really not far also from Fenichel's (at least, if we understand that the patient's "defense" means that the analyst has not understood something and has interpreted it at least imprecisely, if not wrongly).

Rightly she counters that she refers to more than an alternative explanation, but rather to a different way of listening, to one where no theoretical supposition is imposed on the patient. I am completely in agreement with her when she says in an earlier article: "And what of preferences we had not recognized in ourselves, unseen assumptions—how do we discover them without turning defensively to theory-based rationalizations ('The patient put those feelings into me,' 'The patient is in the grips of an unconscious fantasy')?" (Schwaber, 2005, p. 790).

It also makes a lot of sense when she claims that

> there is a fundamental difference between listening in an attempt to guide the patient, Socratic fashion, to chart a direction we may prefer, or to see psychic meaning we believe we already see, and listening to learn what we don't *yet* know, to linger with a nuance that might not fit our course, that might indeed reveal to us that we were not listening, despite its espousal, in this latter, open-ended effort. (Schwaber, 2005, p. 791)

She continues: "This is not simply an endemic dilemma confined to our own discipline or our own time. 'All over the world,' Milan Kundera (1980) has written, 'people prefer to judge rather than understand, to answer rather than ask' (p. 237)" (p. 791).

We encounter the phenomenon very frequently, both with our own patients and with those heard about in supervision, often in an almost intractable way. Sometimes Dr. Schwaber's explanation of it is to the point, sometimes even the best understanding in really very severe neuroses does not change the reaction—an almost immovable determination to destroy the best one is, one gets, one wants, one has. From less severe cases I know exactly what she describes. The better, more effective and experienced we become the less likely it is that we encounter this phenomenon. The case Dr. Jarass and I have written about (see chapter 5 of Wurmser & Jarass, 2007) is a very good example for the latter. With her, the real, solid relationship to the therapist that over many years allowed for trust to grow was crucial for the gradual diminishment of the NTR, but even after 15 years it occasionally broke into the course of treatment and eventually contributed to her breaking off the therapy. Much of this we witness in the case Dr. Jarass describes in chapter 5 of this book.

Insight is one thing; a deep sense of dialogue in Buber's understanding of the term, the *real* relationship is another. Both belong together to reduce the appearance of this phenomenon.

Is it perhaps not so that the concept of NRT expresses an objectification of patient and relationship, and that Evelyn Schwaber enters much more into the relatedness to the "you" (*Du*) of the Other and the deep legitimacy of such reactions, legitimation because of the analyst's insufficient empathy. There is no question that the concept of the negative therapeutic reaction stems from the world of I-It (*Ich-Es*), and so does all theory. The "listening" and the missed understanding and encounter in such reactions Evelyn Schwaber so persuasively describes refer to the world of the "I-You" (*Ich-Du*). In our view the two perspectives essentially complement each other. Both ways of understanding need each other lest we succumb to oversimplification (see Wurmser & Jarass, 2011).

One of us (HJ) told a patient: "You become who you are in the relationship, not in studying psychoanalytic books." The patient responded: "You just gave me a piece of gold."

Notes

1. The greatest victory is defeat, /Forward to victory in downfall!
2. I thank Professor Walter Stephens for this reference.

References

Arlow, J. A. (1984). Disturbances of the sense of time, with special reference to the experience of timelessness. *Psychoanalytic Quarterly*, *53*, 13–37.

Bergmann-Mausfeld, G. (2006). Pathologische Passung, Mentalisierung und "negative therapeutische Reaktion" [Pathological fit, mentalization and "negative therapeutic reaction"]. *Forum der Psychoanalyse*, *22*, 249–267.

Chodorow, N. J. (2003). "Too late": Ambivalence about motherhood, choice, and time. *Journal of the American Psychoanalytic Association*, *51*, 1181–1198.

Danielian, J., & Lister, E. D. (1988). The negative therapeutic reaction: The uses of negation. *Journal of American Academy of Psychoanalysis*, *16*, 431–450.

Eickhoff, F.-W. (1989). On the borrowed unconscious sense of guilt and the palimpsest structure of a symptom: Afterthought on the Hamburg Congress of the IPA. *International Review of Psychoanalysis*, *16*, 323–329.

Eickhoff, F.-W. (2004). Do dead warriors continue their struggle in a higher region? The transgenerational perspective. *Psychoanalytic Inquiry*, *24*, 271–285.

Fenichel, O. (1945). *The psychoanalytic theory of neurosis*. New York: Norton.

Freud, S. (1916). Some character-types met with in psychoanalytic work. In J. Strachey (Ed. & Trans.), *The standard edition of the complete psychological works of Sigmund Freud* (Vol. 14, pp. 309–333). London: Hogarth Press.

Freud, S. (1918). From the history of an infantile neurosis. In J. Strachey (Ed. & Trans.), *The standard edition of the complete psychological works of Sigmund Freud* (Vol. 17, pp. 3–122). London: Hogarth Press.

Freud, S. (1923). The ego and the id. In J. Strachey (Ed. & Trans.), *The standard edition of the complete psychological works of Sigmund Freud* (Vol. 19, pp. 3–66). London: Hogarth Press.

Freud, S. (1924). The economic problem of masochism. In J. Strachey (Ed. & Trans.), *The standard edition of the complete psychological works of Sigmund Freud* (Vol. 19, pp. 157–170). London: Hogarth Press.

Freud, S. (1937). Analysis terminable and interminable. In J. Strachey (Ed. & Trans.), *The standard edition of the complete psychological works of Sigmund Freud* (Vol. 23, pp. 209–253). London: Hogarth Press.

Grunert, U. (1979). Die negative therapeutische Reaktion als Ausdruck einer Störung im Loslösungs- und Individuationsprozess [The negative therapeutic reaction as a sign of disturbance in the separation-individuation and individuation process]. *Psyche*, *33*, 1–28.

Hirsch, M. (1997). *Schuld und Schuldgefühl* [Blame and guilt]. Göttingen, Germany: Vandenhoeck & Ruprecht.

Hirsch, M. (2001). Negative therapeutische Reaktion als Objektbeziehungsgeschehen [Negative therapeutic reaction as an object of relation]. In E. Mayr (Ed.), *Wenn Therapien nicht helfen: Zur Psychodynamik der "negativen therapeutischen Reaktion"* [When therapy doesn't help: The psychodynamics of the "negative therapeutic reaction"] (pp. 25–51). Stuttgart, Germany: Klett-Cotta.

Horney, K. (1936). The problem of the negative therapeutic reaction. *Psychoanalytic Quarterly, 5*, 29–44.

Ibsen, H. (1991). *Brand: Et dramatisk dikt* [Brand: A dramatic poem]. Oslo, Norway: Gyldendal. (Original work published1866)

Jarass, H., & Wurmser, L. (2007). "Evil eye" and "searing look": Jealousy, envy and shame in the magic gaze. In L. Wurmser & H. Jarass (Eds.), *Jealousy and envy: New views about two powerful feelings* (pp. 149–178). New York: Analytic Press.

Kernberg, O. (1975). *Borderline conditions and pathological narcissism*. New York: Jason Aronson.

Klein, M. (1957). *Envy and gratitude: A study of unconscious sources*. London: Tavistock.

Klug, G. (2000). Negative therapeutische Reaktion [Negative therapeutic reaction]. In W. Mertens & B. Waldvogel (Eds.), *Handbuch psychoanalytischer Grundbegriffe* [Handbook of fundamental psychoanalytic principles] (pp. 478–483). Stuttgart, Germany: Verlag W. Kohlhammer.

Kohut, H. (1971). *The analysis of the self*. New York: International Universities Press.

Levy, J. (1982). A particular kind of negative therapeutic reaction based on Freud's "borrowed Guilt." *International Journal of Psychoanalysis, 63*, 361–368.

Limentani, A. (1981): On some positive aspects of the negative therapeutic reaction. *International Journal of Psycho-Analysis, 62,* 379–390.

Maguire, J. G. (1990). Notes on stalemate: A particular negative reaction affecting therapeutic outcome. *Annual of Psychoanalysis, 18*, 63–83.

Maldonado, J. L. (1989). On negative and positive therapeutic reaction. *International Journal of Psychoanalysis, 70*, 327–340.

Mayr, U. (Ed.). (2001). *Wenn Therapien nicht helfen: Zur Psychodynamik der "negativen therapeutischen Reaktion."*[When treatments do not help: The psychodynamics of the "negative therapeutic reaction."] Stuttgart, Germany: Klett-Cotta.

Olinick, S. L. (1964). The negative therapeutic reaction. *International Journal of Psychoanalysis, 45*, 540–548.

Olinick, S. L. (1970). Negative therapeutic reaction [panel report]. *Journal of the American Psychoanaytical Association, 18,* 655–672.

Orgel, S. (2007, January). *On negative therapeutic reaction*. Report for American Psychoanalytic Association Panel Winter Meeting, New York.

Ornstein, A. (2007, January). *When analysis makes patients worse: The negative therapeutic reaction revisited.* Paper presented at the American Psychoanalytic Association Winter Meeting, New York.

Plenker, F. P. (2000). Zur Konzeption der negativen therapeutischen Reaktion bei Sigmund Freud und Joan Rivière [On Sigmund Freud's and Joan Rivière's concepts of negative therapeutic reaction]. *Psyche, 54*, 619–641.

Pontalis, J.-B. (1980). The negative therapeutic reaction: An attempt at definition. *Bulletin of the European Psychoanalytical Federation, 15,* 19–30.

Renik, O. (1991). One kind of negative therapeutic reaction. *Journal of the American Psychoanalytic Association, 39*, 87–105.

Rivière, J. (1936). A contribution to the analysis of the negative therapeutic reaction. *International Journal of Psychoanalysis, 17,* 304–320.

Rosenfeld, H. A. (1975). The negative therapeutic reaction. In P. Giovacchini (Ed.), *Tactics and techniques in psychoanalytic therapies* (Vol. 2, pp. 217–228). New York: Jason Aronson.

Rothstein, A. (1984). Fear of humiliation. *Journal of the American Psychoanalytic Association, 32,* 99–116.

Sandler, J. (1980). The negative therapeutic reaction: an introduction. *Bulletin of the European Psychoanalytical Federation, 15,* 13–18.

Sandler, J., Dare, C., & Holder, A. (1973). *The patient and the analyst.* London: Allen, Unwin & Maresfield.

Schmithüsen, G. (2004). "Die Zeit steht still in rasender Eile": Psychoanalytische Einzelfallstudie zu frühem Trauma und Zeiterleben ["Time stands still in a tearing hurry": Psychoanalytic single case study of early trauma and experience of time]. *Psyche, 58,* 293–320.

Schubart, W. (1989). Bemerkungen zum Konzept der sogenannten "negativen therapeutischen Reaktion."[Comments on the concept of so-called negative therapeutic reaction].*Psyche, 43,* 1071–1093.

Schwaber, E. A. (2005). The struggle to listen: Continuing reflections, lingering paradoxes, and some thoughts on recovery of memory. *Journal of the American Psychoanalytic Association, 53,* 789–810.

Schwaber, E. A. (2007). The influence of theory on empathy. Unpublished manuscript.

Valenstein, A. F. (1973). On attachment to painful feelings and the negative therapeutic reaction. *Psychoanalytic Study of the Child, 28,* 365–392.

Wurmser, L. (1981/1994). *The mask of shame.* Baltimore: Johns Hopkins University Press. Republished: Northvale, NJ: Aronson, 1994

Wurmser, L. (2000). *The power of the inner judge.* New York: Jason Aronson.

Wurmser, L. (2007). *"Torment me, but don't abandon me!" Psychoanalysis of the severe neuroses in a new key.* Lanham, MD: Rowman & Littlefield.

Wurmser, L., & Jarass, H. (2007). *Jealousy and envy: New views about two powerful feelings.* New York: Analytic Press.

Wurmser, L., & Jarass, H. (2011, September 1). *Buber und die Psychoanalyse: Die heutige Psychoanalyse und Buber* [Buber and psychoanalysis: Psychoanalysis today and Buber]. Lecture presented at the Buberhaus, Heppenheim, Germany.

1

NEGATIVE THERAPEUTIC REACTION AND THE COMPULSION TO DISAPPOINT THE OTHER

Léon Wurmser

We all know patients who seem to be driven by a compulsion to awaken ever new hopes just to have them cruelly disappointed, to annihilate all expectations, to devalue everything good by action, though not by words, and all this just as much within themselves as in their relations with others: They are most profoundly disappointed about themselves. In the following chapter, I shall try to get closer to an understanding of this phenomenon which is a central feature, I believe, of the negative therapeutic experience.

Theoretical Background

In many earlier works, I have spoken about the omnipotence of responsibility: "These horrible things are all my fault; if I were better my parents would not fight with each other, they would not abuse me, they would not be so sad and despondent; it is all my fault," and along with that the severity of moral masochism: "I have to be punished because I am all-guilty."

Conjoined with that, we may specifically find the splitting of the superego. Besides its meaning as a defense against traumatic reality, this splitting occurs above all as the result of a rift between irreconcilable loyalties or between overwhelming shame and equally overwhelming guilt, leaving the self to negotiate a very narrow path between these two abysses of (largely opposite) types of self-condemnation. Demands are taken as absolute; when these demands conflict with one another or with outer reality, no solution is possible. This absoluteness of expectation and demand, directed against the self and others, is, therefore, a guarantee for massive self-condemnation and constant disappointment in the other. "Then I cannot get any more out of this world of black and white," complained one patient (Karin; see Wurmser, 2011). *Omnipotence of responsibility* is another expression of this absoluteness: "It is my task and the justification for my existence, to reconcile my parents, to prevent all abuse, to undo all the disasters. Though guilty, I am at least not altogether helpless." Or, as it is said in certain forms of mysticism: "Everybody is accountable for everybody else. Everybody is guilty of everything" (e.g., Staretz Zosima in *The Brothers Karamazov* and in the Lurianic Kabbala).

As a consequence of this absoluteness and omnipotence vested in the superego, we very often witness a compulsion to keep disappointing the other: Every promise, every expectation, every commitment is raised to an absolute degree and thus must become unfulfillable. Every new task undertaken turns into a new opportunity to be humiliated once again, to be shown up as a fool while fooling the other as well. If analyzed more carefully, these are ideals and obligations that contradict each other and make disappointment inevitable. Or, as will gradually become clearer in the following case, there are prominent double-bind messages that lead to massive acting out of this kind. But here, too, it is the self-condemnation due to the demand for absoluteness, especially in regard to loyalty or to contradictory obligations, that makes it dynamically so extremely potent. Thus every success, every experience of goodness, is by itself already disloyalty and betrayal and thus has to be sabotaged. The negative therapeutic reaction is a special case of this phenomenon. Another consequence may be the doubleness of resentment and entitlement: "So much injustice has happened to me. Now I am permitted to cross all lines of what is proper and possible." It is the arrogance of the martyr.

I would like to share a case where this phenomenon has been dramatically and devastatingly effective in a patient who has posed great problems of technique for me in terms of transference and countertransference. I will begin with a quotation from the German comedian Karl Valentin, which serves as a fitting heading for the next section.

"This Would Go but It Does not Go" (*Das ginge, aber das geht nicht)*

For about 8 years I saw a student, Fiona, who was working toward her doctorate in public health; there were long interruptions in the treatment.[1] When we began the work she was 27 years old, and she came to me because of a most traumatic incident, a rape—which turned out to have been one of several she suffered. She was the middle of three daughters from an Irish-American family—her father was an authoritarian, extremely opinionated, obsessive-compulsive character, a retired businessman; her mother, who was severely obese, skillfully engaged in her role as martyr, a dynamic rather easily fulfilled with her authoritarian husband. One sister, 3 years older than Fiona, was always, and still is, very bossy and in regard to her mother confrontational, hateful, and blaming. The younger sister, 2 years Fiona's junior, like her mother, had a severe eating disorder with episodes of life-threatening anorexia and bulimic vomiting that required repeated hospitalization, including an operation to remove her parotid gland, and the development of a "chipmunk face" as a consequence of her induced vomiting. This sister's facile ability to lie and to manipulate was phenomenal, her abuse of drugs and alcohol was sometimes evident, but most of the time it was well-camouflaged.

Fiona herself had episodes of gorging binges, but without vomiting, and was then, often for months, so vehemently ashamed of her weight gain that she barely dared to show herself. Actually, she was very slender and at times engaged in extreme sports, climbing huge mountains, partly alone, agreeing to a skydiving dare, and training for several marathons that she eventually had to cancel because of muscle tears. She was very shy, very ready to adapt and submit, very masochistic, and very conscientious. In her childhood, her sisters always proved ready to have her do the house and garden chores they themselves despised. The older sister was especially jealous of her. Fiona did everything in her power to be loved by everyone, perhaps most of all by the two sisters. Thus it became readily apparent when one listened to her history how prominent a defense the reaction formation is against all forms of aggression, in particular jealousy and envy, by self-condemnation and ostensible submission, which of course only deepens the individual's restrained resentment. She was and is therefore also very sensitive to any real or perceived slight and in her sessions easily burst into tears, laments, and accusatory yelling, much in contrast to her very subdued and demure demeanor much of the time. I also observed quite often that she reworked remarks of mine after our hours so that their reinterpretation tormented her as signs of betrayed trust or putdown.

Yet, the dominant problem for a long time had been that, just like her father, she had great difficulty tackling major tasks and carrying them through; she was a very accomplished procrastinator. The more pressure there was from the outside, the more she postponed what needed to be done.

Fiona was in college when she had her first sexual experience. Drunk after a party, she visited a male friend in his room. She does not remember anything of what occurred then. When she awoke, she was naked and bloody and saw photos of his fiancée in front of her.

In spite of all her apprehensiveness, Fiona could also be very capable. Under difficult circumstances she spent 2 years in the Peace Corps in West Africa in order to advance a public health campaign, specifically the treatment of infestation of parasites—a task that was to become the core of her dissertation. While there, during her own birthday celebration, she was invited by a colleague into his room under the pretext that he would give her a present. With lightning speed he overwhelmed and raped her. Other than this, she had no other intimate relations.

Yet, the reason for her coming for treatment was related. A few weeks earlier, on New Year's Eve, in a remote vacation spot where her parents owned a winter home, she had attended a party with some girlfriends, at the urging of her younger sister and against her own preference. Despite her resistance and better judgment, she allowed her sister and one of the men to pour her more drinks (she drinks only rarely). She could remember that they all went to the apartment of one of the girlfriends. After that there was broad amnesia. When she woke up the next morning she found herself injured in her genitals and her anus, with pieces of condom and tissue in her anus. She was deeply disconcerted and confused, but found little understanding or help from her sister and only bits of information. She suspected that her drink had been spiked with some drug. Without informing her parents about what had happened she returned to the East Coast. Not long thereafter she noticed that she had been infected with genital herpes. She sought medical help but, as she experienced it, was not taken seriously; the nurse in the doctor's office minimized the occurrence, and Fiona felt ridiculed by her. Deeply upset, in tears, she was referred to me by the psychiatric student health service. Since that time I have seen her, as already mentioned, with major interruptions in analysis, beginning early on the couch, since my view was that her very profound masochistic personality disorder was the major problem and could be treated effectively only by analysis. We began this analysis in session 14, four times a week.

The work on the acute trauma soon receded, and the disturbance of her ability to work and study soon became the major content, especially in connection with several exams that she failed on the first attempt. After about half a year (after session 95) she returned to Africa to carry out the major part of her dissertation research and came back intermittently, seeing me several times for a few sessions. While in Africa, she engaged in an intimate, longer lasting relationship with a local health care official who pretended that his marriage was only pro forma and not really consummated and who also hid from her that he also tried to give such bliss to other partners. Several times she brought him to America at her own expense and helped him professionally in other ways until she finally discovered how massively she had been lied to and to what extent she had herself been a colluding master of denial.

About 3 years after beginning treatment (session 105), she contacted me again in order to deal with that catastrophic disappointment. For the following 4 years, I saw her in analysis 4 to 5 hours per week, after which I saw her once a week for the following half year. Soon after restarting this analytic work she underwent several local operations for a melanoma and several threatening-looking nevi.

In spite of Fiona's self-sabotage, her intense obsessive-compulsive blockage of work, and generally depressive mood, she was acknowledged for her accomplishments, often achieved at great sacrifice of sleep and leisure time. Under very great inner difficulties she concluded her studies, except for her dissertation. She broke with the overseas friend and engaged a few more times in very unhappy, humiliating friendships with other men. One of these was intimate and again ended with a rape; she states that out of five sexual relationships, four were connected with rape.

For long periods she was very lonely, full of shame about her aloneness, and expressing a mixture of humble submissiveness and a hidden grudge about having felt exploited and offended. In connection with the many forms of denial, it soon became possible to talk with her about the ease with which she resorted to *lying*, often under circumstances where it would not have been very difficult or embarrassing to be honest or simply diplomatic. She followed in this a venerable family tradition. Often it had to do with attempts to evade her father's intrusive questions and his reproaches. At other times it was her fear of exposing herself in front of her advisor, of other persons in authority, or of friends, or she wanted to avoid directly refusing a request. It is also characteristic that until now she has still not been able to share the trauma of that New Year's night with her parents. She also observed how often she was tempted in treatment not to mention embarrassing things to me. All in all, this tendency to hide and lie has changed very much in the course of the analysis.

During our work her blockage against fulfilling a written task and the accompanying obligations became markedly worse. All her preparations for exams and proposals were very much impeded. She delayed them again and again and then failed several times because of insufficient preparation, losing herself in side tasks or compulsively watching TV, feeling completely paralyzed, and engaging in overeating and the ensuing massive self-condemnations. Most of all, however, she wasted much time helping friends (she was steadily expanding her circle of friends) while neglecting the task at hand.

This work disturbance went far back into Fiona's childhood. Already in grade school, Fiona was repeatedly unable to finish major projects; there were no consequences at that time because she was otherwise a very good student, although much more often so because her father stepped in, writing for her what was needed. To her great embarrassment she was rewarded for something she had not achieved herself: the publication of a school composition in a student newspaper. In college, her graduation had to be postponed for 2 years because she could not finish the work of one course, and she was only able finally to do so when her entry into the Peace Corps forced the issue.

For about 2 years prior to treatment, Fiona had been laboring on her thesis, claiming that she was only some months or even weeks from completion, telling this to friends and to her advisor—and to herself. Yet, the writing of it became insurmountably difficult for her.

Five years into our work, she was asked by a former colleague if she was interested in a certain position at the World Health Organization (WHO). After some reluctance and with much insecurity she applied for it. She had to give the assurance that she would have finished her thesis before starting there. With many interruptions, she kept working at it, but was dissatisfied, once with this statistical preparation, then with that analysis, and never broached the writing itself. When she met her future boss, he expressed his concerns about her procrastination and also criticized her quantitative analysis. Still, he granted her an extension of 2 months. She fixed the date of her defense, and gave up almost all her other obligations. Nevertheless, she realized a few days before the date of delivery of the thesis draft that she still did not have everything together. She had not started writing at all. She wanted to postpone the exam by a few weeks. Assuming she had met her deadline, the WHO invited her to come to Geneva for 2 weeks. She went and admitted that she had been obliged to defer the defense by a few weeks. She returned from her stay there full of enthusiasm, having also formed a deeper emotional attachment to the colleague who had invited her and already counting on a valuable and durable connection with him, although she refused him a kiss. Upon her departure from Geneva, she was asked to write a brief report about the literature on the prevention of eclampsia, which was due the following week.

Fiona then labored on the task for the following 4 months, reading about 200 papers and writing excerpts, but never progressing beyond drafting the introduction. With all that, she did not communicate with her presumptive boss or her friend there, except for asking at the beginning for a brief extension. She was tormented by this and felt profoundly ashamed, especially when confessing her failure to me and to her advisor. After about 3 months, her advisor obligated her to send him a daily progress report; with me, she stopped talking about her work on that report and her blockage. It seemed to her that the more she reported to me about her failings or new plans for the work's conclusion, the more she felt compelled to fail even more. Of course, during all that time she did not touch her thesis. She hid from her girlfriends and gave only evasive answers to her parents—they continued financing her studies. After 4 months she put that unfinished report aside and returned to working on her thesis, adding an entirely new type of research data from the field along with their analyses. She organized that with much zest and gratifying yield, but, while trying to analyze the results, started helping another equally stymied male colleague from abroad, soon devoting all her time to piloting him through the completion of his thesis and his defense. She became physically involved with him although she knew that he was not free (he was in the process of divorce and in the middle of a custody battle) and was to return to Asia after completing his doctorate.

Due to her negligence, her debts to me kept accumulating until they exceeded $7,000. The bills were to be paid half by insurance and half by her father, but she often failed to submit them. When I confronted her more insistently, she abruptly decided (6½ years after beginning treatment) to come for the time being only once a week until she had finished her thesis. And even those hours she often canceled or replaced with telephone sessions.

Now I would like to report something from our analytic work, as much as it was not drowned out by the depiction of her daily tribulations and her experiences of failure and victimhood, or the daily dilemmas about how to deal with some new emergency or problem. It is noticeable to what extent her transference reflects her masochistic disturbance. I should also mention that, as with several other patients with severe neurosis, Fiona almost never remembered or brought any dreams; those recalled were also mostly about her victimhood. First, though, I have to talk about a childhood phobia that cast its shadows well into the present.

Vampire Fantasy: "I Want to Suck Your Blood"

Only about 5 years into treatment (session 468) did I hear for the first time about a strong anxiety in her childhood: being assaulted by Dracula. She brought it up in the context of how lonely she was, feeling attracted to a gentle colleague who showed mild interest in her, and attending the weddings of her younger sister and of a girlfriend. The fantasy came up a few sessions after she had had one of the very rare dreams (461) where her African lover had reappeared and was about to leave and she was furious at him and gave him the silent treatment. Her older sister supported her in it. In another part of the dream, another former friend whom she had loved (and who had quickly rejected her) was ignoring her in favor of a ball game.

But in the current session (468), she thought of the cotton blanket usually at the foot of her bed but that she uses now under her head, and it reminded her how throughout childhood she would protect herself against Dracula's assault by winding her security blanket around her neck in order to give her time to call her mother for help. Outside her bedroom there was a terrace sheltering bats under its awning. She thought they would transform themselves into the threatening person with fangs and collared cape.

Her father had once participated in a theatrical production of the Dracula story, and a big poster for that performance was stored in the closet. That picture evoked such panic in her that she refused even to get her father's hat from the closet. *The image had been magically transformed into the thing itself.* Her sisters had quite a bit of fun in posting themselves in the darkness at both entrances to her bedroom and whispering to her: "I am Dracula; I come to suck your blood." Or her father would sit in the living room, staring at her without blinking, and suddenly break the silence with a whispered: "I want to suck your blood." Often she had nightmares with similar content and sought help from her parents. When at her mother's suggestion she tried to imagine good scenes, these quickly turned into scenes of horror. Thus, even as an adult she used a blanket as a kind of pillow to shield her neck. The malicious laughter of the vampire reminds her of her father's laughter at others' expense. "I think of fangs, neck, blood, cape, and the evil laugh." She remembered how scared she was to stay with her father alone after dark: "Part of me is afraid that every man could be a Dracula type." It did not surprise us that this had really, in a way, repeatedly happened. Several men were, metaphorically speaking, blood suckers, exploitative, and I asked myself if I do not myself belong in this series (which also included, by the way, the topic of her scientific research—a blood-sucking parasite).

She added that in the story Dracula is an ordinary person by day and only transforms himself into a monster at night: "He had his hidden side." And the same was true for her father and also for other men. Just as then (through much of childhood, beginning from about age 4), she would lie in bed petrified by fear, unable to run across the room to the light switch because somebody might be hiding under her bed ready to grab her, she was nowadays paralyzed by anxiety in her social interactions and very often in her professional work. She compared this terror with the panicked anxiety she observed in a nephew, who feared that his older brother did not love him anymore. He had been sick and hospitalized, and when he returned home to convalesce, worried that his brother did not look at him anymore, so he ran after the school bus demanding reassurance from his brother that he still was "his best buddy."

Her father laughed: "[Your older sister] was so mean to you when you were younger. When you were very young you were the cutest child, so happy and laughing." Everything changed when she went to school, "because the children were so mean." What she described about her nephew was a repetition of what she had feared with her sisters, but also her parents—thus her massive inhibition of aggression and the panicky fear of bloody aggression coming from the outside, from vampires. Fiona complained in tears how she changed from a happy little girl into an intimidated unhappy child. Throughout her life she had turned all her aggressions against her own self and to the outside world appeared to be completely unaggressive. She had to be the "perennial victim": "I don't know how to triumph."

"It is so dangerous to triumph that you preemptively accept defeat," I said.

"And in its place I complain about it all day long."

"And then appeal to the rescuer: K [another boyfriend who had recently left her], me, your father, and especially your advisor." She had to be very careful not to show any jealousy or envy.

I believe that the vampire simultaneously represented many things in Fiona's life, including her intense yearning to be close and loved, especially by her father; her violent disappointment and shame about the felt rejection; her fear of being devoured by the beloved (the overwhelming and controlling power of her father in particular); and her fear of being devoured by her own consuming feelings and desires, in particular her gnawing feelings of jealousy and envy against her sisters, her anger at all four members of her family, and the bites of her conscience (*Gewissensbisse*)—all this in a dramatically projected way, as compromise formation.

But I suspect that other contents were hidden in the nightmare image as well, most of all images of being sadistically overpowered by her father, first experienced as fascinating and pleasurable, then as terrifying, and similarly images of the primal scene—all condensed into this emblem for her masochism in three forms: sexual, moral, and relational.

Countertransference as Clue

I would like now to review excerpts from the analysis before the partial interruption I mentioned, by which point most of the productive analytic work had been carried out. At this time, she was tormented by the work on that little WHO report that had ballooned into a giant nightmare, and she apparently felt more motivation to reflect analytically on inner issues, than to be consumed by what appeared to be outer exigencies.

One would, of course, immediately think of my countertransference. It was a very important element: As if on a roller coaster, I kept feeling assured and encouraged in my hopes and then ever again disappointed and discouraged. An inner image pushed itself to the fore, especially during those months when she was endlessly reworking a few sentences and paragraphs of the introduction to that report (in fact, she never went beyond it): It seemed to me as if she were cleaning and polishing the doorknobs for the bathrooms on the *Titanic*; I mentioned that image to her. At the same time I was annoyed, feeling in myself the conflict between a very strong work ethic and the inner resistance against it—irritation that she was abandoning herself to such an extent to her passive strivings. It was as if she *actively put her passivity into the scene* and as if she did not have enough of a work conscience, and most of all an insufficiency of honorable behavior toward the people to whom she had promised work and obligated herself. Thus I kept being tempted to intervene as a scolding or devaluing superego figure. But woe, if anything of this rang out (or came out); it made it all worse, because it was very clear that she did not suffer from any absence of a superego at all but rather from an excess of it, from its absoluteness demanding the highest claims of perfection. Out of this stemmed another metaphor that she had also adopted: that of the locomotive running at full power while the brakes are applied to the maximum so that it does not move from the spot.

I had persistent doubts about the quality of the analytic work because so much remained on the surface, that it was less an "analytic process" in the proper sense than a supportive-protective acting out of a rescue fantasy on both sides. Perhaps unconsciously, I was particularly careful not to intrude, not to "penetrate," not to fall into the role of her father and of the rapists.

For years I had been following the detailed recounting of daily events, of the errors and terrors and failings of her very limited social and professional orbits. I lacked an overview of these dynamics, except for the stereotypical feeling that she could not allow herself any success in order to avoid exciting the envy of her sisters and surpassing her parents who had not achieved what they had wanted in life (more about that later). The solution for her conflicts around competition would be the masochistic self-exposure: "I am no rival; please, do not be jealous or envious; I am a failure, as industrious and conscientious as I otherwise am in life. I am already destroying myself." What became decidedly added to this was my recognition, cautiously imparted to her, of how aggressive against others this inaction really was: She not only made a ridiculous fool of herself; everybody else who put stock in her came to feel like a fool. She excited in the other person the rage that she usually suppressed in herself or at times rationalized by her victimhood: "Injustice has happened; I have been treated unfairly"—the hidden resentment. I saw this rage that I felt within myself more and more strongly as an important indication for how she skillfully embarrassed and angered the other in order not to be embarrassed and angry herself.

Contradictory Identifications and a Double-Bind World

F: What I find so scary: We saw how my motivation, my goal is to raise high expectations and then to shatter them. I see this as a pattern. But is it my goal?

A: The Why?

F: I am not getting anywhere with the Why. It made me feel like an evil person.

A: A compulsion?

F: Exactly.

Evidently it is a compulsion deeply anchored in unconscious processes, and we have found many meanings, but not its core that would make the difference. How could we move forward? An important insight during that period was that there was at home a real double bind message: "Be successful for us, but remain dependent on us! Prove yourself in life, and we shall be proud of your accomplishments, but do not be autonomous, stay passive, listen only to us! We are always right!" With Fiona's father it was impossible to present one's own opinion. He insisted that he never made a mistake and was always in the right. Nevertheless, he himself had a great problem with delays and procrastination. It was always a hair-raising adventure to go on a trip with him because everything happened at the last minute and they often actually did miss planes or trains. Years earlier he had earned a great deal of money through a computer company, then fought with others and sold the business. He had lived for many years on that money and now, during the recession and stock market dip, those resources were rapidly shrinking. He had been living on the income from stocks for a long time, yet for the last 20 years he had planned to write a grand play, a world changing piece, which had remained so far only a plan—just as Fiona was stuck at the introduction to her report and to her thesis.

Until now he had been very generous toward his children. By the way, he had never physically mistreated Fiona. As long as she needed his help she had his sympathy and his financial and even moral support. He was a former marine and the countervailing demand existed in him not to show weakness, not to yield to pain: "Don't be a wuss!" When the older sister fell off her horse one day and fractured her pelvis, he did not recognize the seriousness of the accident and forced her to continue riding in spite of severe pain.

At the same time, and I believe very crucially, Fiona feared that with her every success he would take the credit for himself, and she assumed the same for her overly patient advisor and her equally overly patient analyst. But this insight did not seem to lead any farther. I suspect that behind her insistence on this fear of credit claimed by the other hid a deep but strongly fended-off envy: She did not want to permit me and other father figures to take part in her success, for which she would have to feel grateful.

Her mother stood in constant struggle with the father and tried to devalue him, even in front of strangers. She punished him as well by her massive eating addiction. Her life's role was apparently victimhood and martyrdom. Fiona describes her as very egocentric and chronically depressed. Often when the children came home from school she was still sitting around in her pajamas, or she picked them up much too late from ballet or other lessons and then excused herself with lies. She chronically showed her disappointment and in turn had to disappoint and dismiss her husband and children when they felt any joy—whereas she was always more than supportive and encouraging when things did not go well. Because she was ashamed of her appearance and the disorder in the house, it was only rarely possible for the children to bring friends home.

For Fiona's mother, in contrast to her father, lying was almost second nature. In her own family of origin she had not been able to express herself honestly. There it had only mattered to keep up appearances, not to be real.

On the other side, Fiona felt guilty about her wish to run away from the family while not wanting to relinquish her dependency on them. She sensed that there was something to it that with this behavior she secretly and unconsciously took revenge on them, and felt at once guilty for such vengeful thoughts: that she was an ungrateful and spoiled brat. "I do not even know what I would like to get back at them for. My conflict is their needing me to need them."

"So that it is revenge and submission at the same stroke," I added.

"I am in a prison and I am holding the keys," she added in the following session. In three separate spheres (work, intimacy, transference) she was reliving her family life. How so? She experienced each as if to avoid being heard or seen by her family. She assumed that everybody had an individual agenda, and everything was veiled: "I am so trained to find alternate meanings. This is the *communication at home: Nothing is direct.* You always have to infer what is being communicated from facial expression and body language. What people really say is misleading … I overinterpret things." The response at home to another opinion or a disagreement was, from her mother, mostly a defiant silence and pouting; her father was also a master at that.

> To my father we are the reason why he could not write his play, and my mother is miserable with my father, but she says she only stayed with him because of me; because I had pleaded with her not to leave him. She holds that over my head. Everybody falls short of their potential and blames it on the other. I have nobody else to blame but me. But I do what they do.… This strong prohibition against wanting something and stating it, against defining a goal and expressing it: That was a very selfish thing to do, and you were not supposed to do that. Why should one person be allowed to excel when everybody else is handicapped?

This is particularly true for her mother's broader family. Fiona was thus partly but strongly identified with this chronically disappointing and psychosocially paralyzed mother while she at the same time endeavored to be the opposite of this hated identity. Yet, "I could not leave them. Both would be miserable. For a long time they were focused on D [the younger sister] instead of on their problems. Perhaps I am trying to do that now: get them to focus on me as the problem child."

F: And if it's not them, it is people like me or the advisor or the boss or friend in Geneva: Look, how sick I am! It was so with K [the boyfriend from about a year ago who quickly lost interest in her]: [I showed him:] "What a loser I am. I have to be fixed."

A: Pleading to the other: "Be my rescuer!"

F: And I do not let them, and I resent them if they try. It is all right to bring negative attention to yourself, but not positive attention. To portray myself as the victim is all right. But when I am competent and moving ahead, it is a no-no, and it breeds resentment. [Again this was clearly played out in the transference as well].

The Reward of Victimhood

In the following session she deepened the purpose of this victim role: "I have to be the glue that binds my parents together. They come together for the crisis when I need their help."

I say: "'Come and rescue me in spite of my anger when I break all my promises. Forgive me all my anger!'" It is a powerful defense against her own anger at her parents.

At this point she remembers an image from her childhood. She was perhaps 5 years old: "My seat was beside my father's. I poured myself a glass of milk, from half-gallon-or-so jug. I was small. It was full. I felt his eyes on me: You are going to spill it. Sure enough! I doubt myself, and I spill it. If somebody doubts me, I panic and prove them right. And at the same time I resent it. It was the same when my father finished my school project: there was relief on one level, satisfaction for his satisfaction. On another level, I was full of resentment and anger because he told me with that action that I could not do a good job."

A: So it was your own identification with failure, and if we look at both your parents they failed too.
F: My father felt that about himself, and he overcompensated for it. But he feels that something is missing: that he did not accomplish success.
A: And you cannot permit yourself to be successful. And with your mother this is perhaps even more strikingly so. And if you were successful, you would feel guilty.
F: It is even more the case when I visit my mother's family: nobody there has a career.
A: And you go full blast to make it impossible to have a career.
F: And I always thought having a career was unsatisfactory. I always saw myself as a mom first....

She talked at length about the imbroglio of a girlfriend of hers who was successful in her career but had a disastrous marriage and was about to give birth to a child. Then she returned to her father: how he had failed to get his college degree and how he had sabotaged his own success.

I added: "So that you blame it on the apprehension by someone else [father, the boss in Geneva: their doubting her ability] while the real content is: *'It is too dangerous to be successful. I ought not to compete'*... Toward your father: 'You have the power and the control? I have the power by destroying it.'"

She confirmed it: "'You think you can control me? You cannot do that.' It was almost conscious at the end of college. The more he hounded me, the more defiant I was."

"And the same now: You are at the cusp of the doctorate and of a promising job, and you are hell-bent on destroying both. It is a sublime revenge: Let them pay for God knows how many years, and at the end you destroy it."

She immediately saw this as a reproach:

F: I feel that was a potshot, a malicious hint that I am supposed to feel guilty.
A: Of course you feel guilty and ashamed, but the revenge is more important, and the defiance and the need to disappoint.
F: More than the competing?
A: Can you connect the dots?
F: It is better to think that I am afraid of success than that I manipulate my parents. That sounds evil, that I am a bad person.
A: Could they be connected?
F: I do get resentful and angry when my father doubts whether I can do it. Like with the milk or the orals. The more nervous he was the angrier I got. And the more nervous I get, the likelier it is that I will fail.
A: Perhaps the bridge is: The more incompetence on the side of the parents, the more their need to have power, and the more important for you to defy them.

In short: open submission, secret defiance, revenge, and finally guilt feelings that thwart all success.

Double Bind in the Family and Split Loyalties

We asked ourselves in the following session anew: "Why this compulsive need to disappoint? How can we understand this need to humiliate myself in front of everybody who is important to me?" She always feels like a fraud, that she would not do a good job, even as she presents herself as if she would do so.

A: You expect the humiliation and rejection anyway, and so you bring it actively about. And that both [being disappointing and being rejected] are almost identical: that others would be disappointed anyway.
F: It is so scary: I let everybody down.

I enlarge the interpretation (of turning passive into active) a little later: "You very much wish to be successful and the best, better than your parents and your sisters, and at the same time you are very deeply afraid about it and prohibit it to yourself.... It is a very deep double bind: Be better than we are but do not be better than we are,' and this is an unsolvable conflict. Therefore, you always have to make them proud of you and at the same time to disappoint them."

F: I can see that with my mother: A part of her is happy for me, and a part of her resents me.
A: And with your father: He wants you to be a successful adult, but he cannot tolerate your independence, that you have your own opinion. I would suspect that this holds true for their own lives as well: that they have been raised with a similar double bind: "Be independent, but don't think on your own."

Fiona immediately confirmed this, first for her mother, then for her father: Her mother had a very authoritarian father who told her she could either go to college (move out) or take a job, have a car, and stay home. She chose the latter. On the day she married, her father told her: Now she was "out" and would never be allowed to return except for visits; she had chosen her bed, and she had to sleep in it—even if there were problems in her marriage, which actually soon began to happen. The decision was final. "She would be punished if she went her own way: 'If you go we slam the door shut.'"

As for her father, the story went that he had an alcoholic father and a very compulsive mother, a worrywart: "His father, a banker who did not live in a socially conscious way, never praised him. Certainly, he [the grandfather] wanted to be proud of his sons but did not want them to outdo him and make him ashamed of who he was." So her father started out with great ambitions. He tried to prove himself by buying a large house in a prestigious neighborhood although he did not have the means for it. Even now he is very much set on winning, even in games with his grandchildren. "He was jealous when I went to the Peace Corps: 'Make me proud, but don't surpass me!' He had applied to it himself and had had to write an essay about why he wanted to enter, but he never wrote it."

A: Exactly the same as what you do with the WHO.
F: How is that similar?
A: He had the ambition, and at the same time it was forbidden to fulfill the ambition. He tried to fulfill it, and yet he sabotaged it.
F: And I got weird vibes from him about WHO: that he would be proud, but I also sensed that I would be doing something that he wanted to do himself.
A: And that you would leave him: "Be independent, but woe to you and to us if you left us."

F: I had that feeling when he visited me in Africa. The day before his departure he told me that as a father he could not leave me there. I told him: How dare you?! I could come home and go to the post office and be hit by a car.

A: And deeper: that separation is dangerous.

F: Separation is dangerous, and I would be completely apart.

Merger and separateness, dependency and independence, submission under autocratic authority and autonomy of will—each duality suggests an encompassing and basic polarity, a central conflict not only intrapsychically, but also rooted deeply within the whole family and family tradition. Separation was experienced as unfaithfulness, as a breach of trust which Fiona compulsively now reenacted in her promises and their breach—as a compromise formation between the opposites. A concrete form of it was the constantly simmering loyalty conflict: She always tried to do right both by her father and by her mother, and what pleased the one, of course displeased the other. She confirmed that both parents kept trying to win over the children in the battle against each other. This is in itself a paralyzing conflict: the support of the one was seen as betrayal of the other and as disloyalty, inevitably entailing a broken promise. Her mother had always reproached her that she was like her father, meaning this of course negatively: "I never found a way out; it was so engrained in me that I am bad, that she does not like me. Now I see that she loves me and misses me."

Part of this conflict is that every success can turn into disloyalty. To say it more broadly: feeling good, feeling better has to be undone. This is also true for her own heterosexual relations. "Only as a victim, could you be acceptable."

F: My father always had to be the best; he felt threatened as soon as anybody came close.

A: And your mother was resentful.

F: I heard her voice in my head: 'You little brat!' if anyone bragged about anything. Where they allowed us to excel was in the domain of horseback riding; there was no competition because neither of them rode.

A: And yet it is competition too: you are able to do something that the parents could not, as is now the case with the doctorate.

F: There the conflict is tangible. My father would be proud, but insulted.

Of course, the therapy itself was a cause for intense loyalty conflicts between me and her parents, and hence for the negative therapeutic reaction. She kept asking whether it was not harming her more than helping her. Everything good she had to unmask as something bad, as if she did not deserve it. She could not allow me, just as she could not allow her advisor and her father the success; she had to defeat us by her own failure. Here again it is a compromise formation between submission and defiance, between seeking acceptance and her own envy.

She called her father in her childhood "My Valentine, nobody could be as great as him, nobody that perfect on the whole earth. I did believe the nonsense when I told him that no-one could equal him; that he set the standard for a boyfriend so high that I would not find anybody with such great qualities as his. The point came where I did not believe this anymore."

Later I commented: "You are bound to him as beloved, and at the same time you hate him so much and rebel against him. It's a trap."

With her father, all was perfection and control, even grandiose self-expectation, and with mother everything was failure. She added: "I feel how I am embarrassed about them and disappointed, but I cannot say it with all they have done for me, and how I have had a better childhood than most other children."

"It is so difficult to be grateful when you feel at the same time that an injustice has been done and you hope to hear from the other that he is sorry."

The Dangerous Bull

It was also around this time (session 661) that she brought in another noteworthy dream: "I was with [my younger sister] and her girlfriend swimming …" [*She interrupted recounting the dream and explained that the girlfriend is also a bulimic, and that she lost her baby, and always saw Fiona's sister as her ideal because she had allegedly conquered her eating disorder.*] "The joke was that we would swim very deep and then come up as if we were sharks." She again interrupted the narrative of the dream: It reminds her how she had, as a small child, fallen backward into the pool and gone under, and how her father had rescued her. And when she was less than one year old she had diarrhea and vomiting. The mother called the doctor who told her to wait. When her father came home he made the mother rush her to the hospital. "Otherwise I would have died of dehydration. So it happened twice that he saved my life. My mother downplayed the seriousness of it. My father wants to be needed." Then came the second dream where she was in Africa, followed closely by the horse of her childhood. In the dream he (her horse) was kind, curious, supportive, but he could be angry when she did not pay attention to him. There were mud huts, shambles, friendly and curious people, and a wall of plywood. "Then I was with [my older sister]. A bull was running by. [The sister] said: He cannot see you if you do not move. I said: That's true for hippos, for rhinos. We jumped up, and he slammed into the plywood. Then he walked away and was looking at me over his shoulder. He gave up. She was wrong, and I was right." She repeated: "Somebody was mad at me and gave up and walked away, a peaceful understanding ... getting special treatment: 'Had I known it was you, I would not have charged.'" The immediate precipitant of the dream was a call from a girlfriend who talked about some special treatment she got and successes she was enjoying. Fiona mentioned examples of how her younger sister is spoiled by her future husband: "Everything is just for show."

I summarized: "You are angry about their self-display, their exhibition: 'Look, how good I am, how special, how generous I am.' And it arouses envy in you. It reminds us of what you said about not wanting to give me or your advisor credit."

"And I fear that they will steal it from me and that they do not recognize my contribution."

"It is an image where the other *gets*, but you do not get. He [the advisor] gets the prize or the award, but you do not, and that makes for envy."

"And resentment." Reminded by me, she talked then about an incident where a school friend had tried to get Fiona off the honor role at graduation and succeeded in being seated herself on stage, although she had not earned the credits for that honor: "I was troubled about the apparently arbitrary distribution of credit and praise," but also how she herself got an award in school that was undeserved because she had performed some hand signal on a bicycle the wrong way. She was so troubled that she might *not* get the prize that she cried, felt humiliated, and succeeded in getting the prize at last: "That too felt wrong. I got special treatment that I did not deserve."

A: Which means arousing the envy of others. Very importantly, both are in you: anxiety about your own envy, and anxiety about arousing the envy of the others, as it shows again in the work blockage, and we have both sisters in the dream where this is so much the case.

F: In the first dream I had not outdone [my younger sister]. She encouraged me to be like her. And I made myself look inferior.

A: That is exactly it: not to arouse her envy. Perhaps something similar happened in the second dream?

F: When he backed off, it was like a secret between us. I did not advertise it.

A: You put [your older sister] in the wrong, but it could not be shown. You had to hide that.

She then spoke about the cold, resentful way in which the older sister treated her own husband and children, indicating especially also envy about his professional success. I suspect that the bull himself is Fiona's own feared aggression, mostly in the form of envy and jealousy.

"Help Me, but Don't Help Me!"

Yet those double-bind messages appeared increasingly to be all-encompassing and determining, as already stated: "Be independent, but obey and submit to us; be the best but not better than we are. Be loyal to your mother, but also be loyal to your father. I expect from you perfection, but you cannot achieve anything anyway." Perfection as well as failure are simultaneously expected. And in turn, in the transference, it is directed at me: "Help me, but do not help me!"

Only at that point did Fiona recognize how her taskmaster at the WHO resembled her father: "'I am always right; I am in charge; I control you. I tell you what you have to do.' So it is partly my rebellion against it: 'I have power too. Watch this: You cannot force me to do this!' My power is through inaction.... Like my sister with her anorexia: She only had power by refusing to eat, and he [the father] got madder and madder. The more he tried and the angrier he became the more she dug in her heels: Watch me not do what you say." What bothered Fiona most in her presumptive boss was his lack of humility: "He is this established research guy, is more accomplished, knows more than I do, but he was not admitting that he could have any flaws—exactly as it is with my father."

A: And as with the glass of milk when you were a small child: "You cannot do it anyway." He [the boss] had expressed his concern at their first interview because of your procrastination with your thesis.
F: Right. And my expectation that he wants the perfect write-up, but it is me who put that on it.
A: It is the critical voice of the future boss, whomever or whatever he stands for, that keeps you from writing.
F: This critical person who needs to assert that he is better than everybody else and who wants people to jump when he says jump! And when they do not jump he seeks his revenge.

It is felt as a *countervoice*, she says—in Freud's early formulation: a *counterwill*—that lets her blow this wonderful opportunity: "You will screw it up anyway." This is exactly what she feels when she sits at the computer, "a repulsion, it makes me get up and leave; it is a split part, like an angel over one shoulder, and a devil over the other. The one says: Do this! And the other: You cannot. Don't give it to [the boss], he will make fun of you anyway. Like in cartoons."

When her advisor asked her how it was going she very accurately replied: "'Most of the time I'm perfecting the art of self-sabotage.' He put his arm around me and said: 'Too bad your thesis is not on self-flagellation.'"

On the one side, she is very capable and has engendered much respect by her work in Africa (and also in some statistical work here) as well as by her demonstrated great competence in dealing with very difficult situations, and yet she disappoints everyone with whom she comes into contact. She relates it herself that way:

F: When my friends look at me they see a competent person.
A: This is the tragic thing: Both are true, and you are both to the hilt. Like many people in history who show this tragic doubleness.

She inquires whom I have in mind, and I mention Nixon and Clinton. She agrees: "I saw a documentary on Clinton: how after every success he had to screw it up. As soon as he had a political success he had to have another woman.... The same is true with me. I talked with my girlfriend and was tearing up when I saw how I prevent myself from being successful. When I came back from Geneva I felt so encouraged: great job, great people, I liked the city, the friend—and now I have actively screwed it up. I was in tears, and she [girlfriend] had tears in her eyes...."

A: It is in the truest sense tragic—a tragic character, this need to destroy yourself. [She quotes her girlfriend who said her therapist had told her: "You deserve happiness."] There is a deep sense in you that you don't deserve it.
F: Exactly.
A: The deep riddle for us is: Why? [brief pause]: There must be a deep sense of guilt, and my hypothesis is that it stems from the loyalty conflicts and the double bind messages where you always have to end up feeling guilty.
F: I explained that yesterday to [my girlfriend], about the traditional family, that it looks right, but if they had split up they both would have been happier and we more adjusted. Their staying together did not help the children. They fought all the time, and there was the issue of taking sides. I hate to confront, and I tried to avoid it: by defending Mom to Dad and Dad to Mom, and so both thought I was against them.
A: And so you inevitably became guilty, and felt the responsibility to hold the family together."
F: As if I had that power.
A: The omnipotence of responsibility.
F: I learned in my psychology class that children whose parents have died function better than those whose parents got a divorce. They think it is their fault.
A: And that fighting without divorce has the same impact.
F: I knew for a long time that I had a say in the outcome, and my mother said I did: she had stayed only because I had asked her to stay. She strengthened this conception, this idea ...

A: … of responsibility.
F: That it was up to me.
A: And with that the inevitable sense of guilt.
F: That her present misery is my fault.
A: And for that you punish yourself for every success.
F: Because I am supposed to be miserable too.
A: This may be the answer to the Why.

The Testing and the Hidden Jealousy

A few sessions after this important dialogue and shortly before my departure for Europe, Fiona gave a very persuasive interpretation, manifestly referring to her boss in Geneva and to her friend there, but of course also to the transference and ultimately and explicitly to her father: "I tried to be the person I thought he wanted me to be. It points back to my father and his perfectionism. He has such high standards for himself and for others. This is what I do with him: I deliberately screw up: 'Look, *I am not perfect. You still like me anyway.*' It is unconscious. When [the boss in Geneva] spoke with my advisor about me he shocked him by asking if I was studying for the Nobel Prize, if I was so top-notch that only perfection would be good enough. Hence my need to show up that fantasy: 'Take me or leave me!' It is the same thing I did in sixth grade when I did not finish my project. I was the teacher's pet and she watched the deadline pass. I needed her to know that I was not perfect, and I had to know that she liked me anyway. And it worked. And it was not the last time that I pulled this routine."

A: I wonder if the same happens between you and me?
F: It would make sense, but I cannot see it, session by session. It would be an innovative application of this tendency. (She talked then more about how she was referred to me and asked herself: "Perhaps I am testing you to make sure that I deserve it"—my caring, support, and kindness, which the referring physician had named).
A: Or is it not more: "I want to make sure that you still like me even if I constantly disappoint you"?
F: Right. And I show it when I constantly come late or don't come and don't call. It is not conscious and deliberate. What I'm hearing now in my head is something I have heard before: "Just be the best Fiona that you can be"—instead of pleasing this or that or disappointing this or that.

On the day before my departure for more than a week in Europe, she did not refer to the impending interruption, but discussed her various friends and how she was afraid to commit herself to one person, because someone else might come whom she might like more: "I regret the choices I have made in many connections. I hesitate to close doors." She went on to talk about her deep fear of separation. "As long as I still have this base with my advisor and his family and you, the thought of leaving it all is counterintuitive. People are more important for me than a job. But I know that as an adult one does that."

"But it means closing doors, and there is such a tremendous fear of separating."

"I hate good-byes. As a child I ritualistically said good-bye whenever we went away, for instance to visit my grandparents: good-bye house, good-bye trees, good-bye to the mail box, to the grass, but most of all to the other car that had to stay behind; I thought they would be angry at me and take revenge on me when I came back, or they would not be there anymore. I felt such sympathy for the other car that I tried to console and reassure it. I thought the house was hearing me, the trees were hearing me. I was afraid the family would leave me behind, and that I would not be missed if I were not there."

Her thoughts wandered then to her position in the series of siblings and how she was hypervigilant to see whether she got the same amount of birthday cake as the others. I said: "So the question of separation lastly is a jealousy issue: 'I am left out or left behind.'" She confirmed it. She then went back to the issues with her study and work plans, the question of living up to the plans of termination that her advisor had, and of sending a provisional report to Geneva after all, and all the indecision with which she had opened the session.

Confrontation

Fiona spent the summer developing a new approach to part of the underlying research, undertaking that additional work with great excitement, but also experiencing several setbacks. Parallel to this, she became more intensely and intimately involved with the colleague who had the same problem with completion. She cut down our sessions to once a week after I had confronted her that I could no longer accept that the bills were not being paid because she had failed to submit the bills to insurance and to her father.

Upon hearing that she abruptly wanted to cut back on analysis, I said at first: "We have to address how much hatred and resentment against me is in this. It is a direct assault on me and my work, like the failure to pay." She talked more about how she had once again broken every plan, every deadline, every task her advisor had set. I found the interruption, just at this point, very ill-advised: "All this is not only very self-destructive, but also very aggressive against me, against the advisor, and especially against your father." I asked her point-blank: "Why are you so angry at me?"

> In all sincerity: I am not. I am mad at myself and taking it out on you. I don't want to come back for the daily humiliation to say that I have made no progress on the thesis, and that is all I want to be dealing with. I don't want to talk about it, how I am blocked, like with the report, how I kept coming and describing how I was stuck, and I never got on with it. It only increases the pain and does not help the problem. It is an oversimplification. I can guess why I am mad: I still have the same problem and cannot deal with it effectively. That sounds as if you were expected to solve it for me.

Her father had told her for years that the analysis did not accomplish anything: "What I do is not working. I cannot imagine that someone else [another analyst] would do it differently. It is me. I am resistant to it."

"This may be a key: that it is not so much aggression against him as that you have to prove him right, or better: It is both: You are aggressive toward him by being defeated along the whole line, and at the same time you are his loyal daughter by confirming that he is always right."

In the following session I tried to summarize: "'I am always testing punishment; I disappoint you, I court punishment, and especially shame, but I want forgiveness and acceptance.'"

She said, "I clearly see this as a pattern that repeats itself the whole time, but have we discussed what is behind this?"

"Discussed yes, but not fully worked through."

"What?"

I summarized for her the main points from the work of the preceding months: feeling inevitably guilty in the face of the double bind and loyalty conflicts and the ensuing omnipotence of responsibility, always falling short before the absoluteness of expectations and the profound shame about this, the rage at and desire for revenge for the power and self-centered expectations of others, the wish to turn around, from passive to active, the disappointment. Above all, there was the issue of not allowing me, the advisor, or her father to get any credit for any success of hers, thus hiding her own envy from herself, so that she was constantly looking for forgiveness. She had a powerful envious wish not to allow the other, especially the authority, to claim any credit: "I am failing so as to show you that you are no hot shot," but at the same time she censored this wish strongly: "It seems so malicious, so evil." It is an explicit wish to punish the other fueled by envy that can only very grudgingly be admitted.

It was extraordinarily difficult to recognize and to tackle her fear of her envy and her jealousy and the use of self-punishment and self-loathing to conceal them. Nevertheless, even in that regard she made progress, and spoke at times on her own of these feelings in regard to various people in her life. All this has to be seen against the dominant family dynamics:

guilt for separation/separateness and success, shame for weakness, dependency, and failure, and the vicious circle of these two equations.

Peripety[2]

I will now briefly tell the nightmarish story of what happened when we reached the deadline for the defense of her dissertation, a kind of culmination of her traumatophilia. The defense had been postponed until March 24 (a little more than 7 years after the beginning of analysis), because she had not been able to meet any of the previous deadlines for submitting the paper. The committee needed the text 3 weeks in advance in order to review it. Yet only on March 22, the day she had to present her research to faculty and students, did she deliver the first six of eight chapters to the committee. She worked through the whole night and, in the morning she still had to struggle with several practical problems because she had forgotten to bring the cable for her Power Point presentation. It was impossible for her to review the old part of her work, which she had prepared years earlier for her preparatory exam: "Zero sleep, zero preparation," she said. The lecture in front of the whole audience therefore started about 10 minutes late. She stumbled badly through the first part and only toward the end regained some fluency. According to Fiona, her report was not received well, and feedback was mixed. The following night she again worked through the night in order to pull the two final chapters together. The evening of the 23rd the chairman of the examination committee informed her that the exam could not take place the following day and that she would have to find a new defense date at the end of April, which she would have to coordinate with each of the members of the committee, all of whom were often abroad.

I myself had trouble not becoming gripped by a sense of catastrophe. I kept asking myself: "What had I missed? What could I have done better? Which mistakes did I make?" It was in those days that, with the help of three papers, I had an additional important insight.

The Compulsion of Being Late: As If Time Were Frozen

In the light of these three papers, which I will briefly describe below, the psychopathology of Fiona's experience of time and the extreme peculiarity of how she was dealing with time almost punched me in the face.

One is a 2003 paper by Nancy Chodorow in which she draws a connection between women who, in spite of a strong wish to have children, seem to keep thwarting its fulfillment until it is too late, with the denial of time and thus also of change. Other generative activities, like writing and a doctorate, are held up as if there were no passage of time, as if time were frozen. Behind this pathology of the experience of time (i.e., living in quasi-timelessness), she sees early unconscious fantasies about the mother–child relationship that would be full of destruction rather than generativity:

> [T]he timelessness of the early mother-child bond that a woman takes with her into her own reproduction of mothering has acquired a deadened and imploded quality, rather than that of an emerging chrysalis. Cyclical time, rather than being active and in movement, becomes stopped or repetitively circular; monumental, eternal time freezes. The psychological time stops as age and time stand still, time is repetitive or circular, and the biological time is eliminated. (p. 1189)

All this seemed to fit Fiona. Yet we might be able to say still more about this deadening of time. The second paper, an earlier work by J. A. Arlow (1984), deals somewhat more broadly with this significant issue. About a patient he says:

> [H]e would have liked to remain a child forever. For him the flight from the tyranny of time was a flight from death. He felt he was a dropout from time and wondered if the college dropouts were not in their own way seeking to escape death. If time could be made to stand still, nothing would ever change. There would be no advance toward death; life would be one perpetual pleasant afternoon. (p. 31)

With this patient it was the return to the protective mother, in others a union with God, the father. Time meant for them frustration on various levels of development, the limitation by reality and the limitation of life by death:

> Time thus becomes the representative of realistic necessity, and the inevitable frustrations experienced at all subsequent levels of psychosexual development intensify the connection between time and reality. Thus the roots of the rebellion against the tyranny of the clock go back far into the individual's early development. (p. 15)

I would add something essential to this topic: Namely that time is a symbol both for the superego and for the traumatically experienced separation, for Fiona, from the beloved and hated mother in particular. Both might very well be equated with annihilation and death. This denial of time has huge destructive power; I think of explosives, and Chodorow used the metaphor of "imploding," a kind of inner explosion.

The third paper was an early version of Gerd Schmithüsen's paper which, in an expanded form, appears as chapter 3 of this volume. There he states that "the everlasting present serves as a defense against the awareness of loss, separation and death"; it reminded me directly of what I experienced with Fiona: I felt as if time itself were to be eliminated. (It reminded me as well of Kirillov in Dostoevsky's *Demons*).

To pursue these connections in greater depth: Fiona was strongly identified with both parents and bound to them in contradictory loyalty. In this checkmate situation it was impossible for her to become herself. Time must stand still in order to arrest growth, change, and the passage into adulthood and responsibility. The inevitable separation was experienced as too painful. Thus blocking time can be understood in her as a defense against separation, against incest, against murder and death, and finally against the superego—all issues dealt with in the preceding sections. This timelessness or standing still of time means that limitations are erased and mortality is denied.

Indeed for Fiona, time stood peculiarly still: It struck me again and again how vague she was with time determinations, how often she failed to say yesterday or tomorrow, but rather Tuesday or Thursday, leaving it unclear in which week. In nearly 800 sessions, there was hardly one to which she came on time. Everything to do with deadlines she had to cancel, to break, to deny, to undo. It was also conspicuous how she turned night to day, yet mostly without also turning day to night. She worked in school until 6 a.m., keeping herself awake with caffeine, then went home, maybe slept restlessly and with interruptions for 3 to 4 hours, and then tried again to work. The value of such work for 12 hours was perhaps, she said, only that of 2 hours.

In Fiona the compulsion to be late and thus to break every promise and to disappoint everybody was first a wish fulfillment: to erase all boundaries in behalf of an *archaic merger*, to achieve with mother and father an early union and total acceptance, in short, to be a child again. Second, it was a resolute defiance against reality and against the superego, against all commitments and restrictions, a protest against having to live a separate and limited existence, against growing up and overcoming sadomasochistic sexuality. Third, it was a form of self-punishment and a triumph of moral masochism, and thus also a fulfillment of sadomasochistic wishes in all relationships and presumably also in sexuality itself: She presented herself as the victim of malign forces outside and within herself, and the mistreatment of time and the mistreatment by time was an expression of this sadomasochistic compromise formation.

Moral masochism is expressed by the inability to let anything good stand. Every good session had to be destroyed immediately, very much as part of the negative therapeutic reaction. At the end of a good hour I said once accordingly: "And now should I say we had a bad hour?" Laughing, she responded: "With nothing good in it."

It seemed to me that Fiona's guilt stood like a huge elephant in the middle of the room. As we have seen it had a whole series of origins, including the loyalty conflicts outlined; the dilemma of separation guilt and dependency shame; guilt derived from double-bind situations, where it was inevitable for her to feel guilty; her feeling of omnipotence of responsibility as would-be savior of the torn-apart family, connected with her helplessness; the massiveness of her aggressions against both parents, alternating in intensity; and above all, such profound feelings of guilt most likely originated in the entire family attitude of blaming, of accusing, of assigning guilt, and the pervasive cruelty connected with it. As with other patients with such a devastating sense of guilt and shame, with this *guilt throwing*, a heavy weight appears to be the lasting influence of religious constraints against pleasure, joy, and sexuality in a family history where everybody feels disappointed, dissatisfied, and frustrated: "I have been short changed." This feeds a venomous feeling of envy, jealousy, and resentment. Behind the chronic attributions of guilt, we find this unholy trinity. In order to hide this triad and not to name it, one blames the other. Rather than "Thou shalt love thy neighbor like thyself," it is "Thou shalt judge and condemn the other like thyself."

One lets the other feel guilty in order to express in veiled form in particular one's own envy. This has a massive effect upon the countertransference as well. The dense fog in which I find myself and grope around hides my own guilt feeling: that I have done something wrong and failed her once again. She lets me suffer what she herself suffers. This seems to be the most important thing in the transference. And yet there is more to it.

The Power of Negativity

Fiona's inability to work even under extreme pressure reminds me of an essay by Stanley Coen (2003) about how the negativity in transference and countertransference evokes both fear and fascination: "Fascination with the negative preserves the exciting, perverse, magically omnipotent illusion that one can control what is uncontrollable—an enormously reassuring power indeed" (p. 465). In regard to technique he writes about the importance of playfulness. Humor does play an important role in our sessions, as just noted, especially about this negativity.

Yet this use of humor in therapy has to unfold against the backdrop of very specific understanding, as in the last sessions during Fiona's desperate attempts to finish the thesis once and for all. This is an understanding of the displacement of guilt, defiance, and shame, and certainly also of the omnipotence fantasies. Thus I also tell her: "In this negativity lies a lot of power." She mentions that she anticipates how we will devalue and condemn what she has achieved. I think it is rather the *perverse power of triumph by defeat*: "Manifestly you are the one who suffers, but there is omnipotence hidden in this suffering." She confirmed it: "Everybody who has grown up in a household headed by my father was made helpless."

To this is added a component of sexualization, built upon the premise: Love means pain and disappointment. There is no love without suffering and humiliation and victimhood.

Fiona described how frightening the terrible fights between her parents were and how she interposed herself between them, crying. She grew up in a family where love and sexuality meant pain and shame. Chronic traumatization, the conflicts of conscience about separation and dependency, and sadomasochistic sexuality were intimately conjoined. Yet she resisted such an insight.

She could experience it more readily when I offered the following more comprehensive interpretation: "There is no doubt that you were severely traumatized, and we may best understand this traumatization as consisting of mutual humiliation and blaming, of the incessant fights between them ending with pleas for forgiveness. These scenes are accompanied by the threat of the family's collapse and separation. With each deadline you reenact the danger of a new trauma, but this time it would be brought about actively by you. You build up the threat not in order to repeat the trauma itself but in order to come very close to the precipice of guilt and shame and then to plead for forgiveness, and thus the catastrophe would be averted once more."

The patient finally passed her exam and finished her studies, but not without risking another similarly catastrophic end. She left soon after for Africa. After a few delayed and very partial payments of my fees, I have not heard anything more from her.

Concluding Comments to the Theme of What Is Tragic

Fiona was, as I told her in one of our dialogues, *a tragic character* in the absoluteness of her inner demands, in the guaranteed failure before these conflicting ideals and duties, and in the inevitably ensuing condemnation and self-destruction. She reminds us of the tragic side of us all and opens the view into an abyss of human existence.

The tragic worldview—Weltanschauung—sees something essential about the human soul in irreconcilable conflict, and therefore brings us again and again against (or to) the ambiguity, the paradoxical nature of ethical life. Thus it inquires into the reasons for suffering, seeks their meaning, and finds answers in the basic conditions of human existence. It sees the origin of tragic experience in such unappeasable, unsolvable conflicts, especially in the conflict between one good and another good, between one value and another value, such as the conflict between right and duty where it is not easy to determine which should have priority. It is the "struggle of morality within itself—*der Selbstentzweiung des Sittlichen*," about which Hegel has written (1807/1952). In the deepest sense it is what Peter Szondi has called the "reversal of one thing into its opposite" (*Umschlag des Einen in sein Gegenteil*)—the dialectical and insoluble contradiction where one brings about that very thing that one fears most and tries most to avoid, and where the rescue itself inescapably turns into annihilation, or where paradoxically the highest value tips over into a non-value, a good into an evil.

Patients like Fiona who are suffering under severe neuroses with a strongly masochistic nature evoke in us this tragic consciousness. This makes the countertransference so especially cumbersome. In such situations, I am often reminded of Schiller's words: "Who could rejoice in life who looks into its depths!"—"*Wer erfreute sich des Lebens,/ der in seine Tiefen blickt!*" ("Kassandra") and "Woe to whoever approaches the Truth through guilt! It never will be delightful for him"—"*Weh dem, der zur Wahrheit geht durch Schuld! Sie wird ihm nimmermehr erfreulich sein*" ("*Das verschleierte Bild zu Sais*").

Still, we must maintain that this represents only one side of these patients, one part of Being that we are called upon to transcend. We can find a counterword to this in Ibsen: "It is the eye that transforms what has been done. The reborn eye transforms the old deed"—"*Det er øyet som forvandler handlingen. Det gjenfødte øye forvandler den gamle handling*" (John Gabriel Borkman, 1889/1966, p. 550).

Not all conflicts and tragic entanglements are principally unsolvable. As we know from Freud, "where id was there shall ego be." This is a call to shape into words what has hitherto been unspeakable and unsolvable, to let inner freedom arise out of compulsion, and to transform conflict, as far as possible, into complementarity.

Notes

1. For discretion's sake I had to omit the direct time references which made the case presentation particularly cumbersome since the factor of time was essential.
2. I purposely chose a central term in the theory of tragedy, *peripeteia* in Aristotle's *Poetics*, for the crucial tipping point.

References

Arlow, J. A. (1984). Disturbances of the sense of time, with special reference to the experience of timelessness. *Psychoanalytic Quarterly*, *53*, 13–37.

Chodorow, N. J. (2003). "Too late": Ambivalence about motherhood, choice, and time. *Journal of the American Psychoanalytic Association*, *51*, 1181–1198.

Coen, S. J. (2003). The thrall of the negative and how to analyze it. *Journal of the American Psychoanalytic Association*, *51*, 465–489.

Hegel G. W. F. (1952). *Phänomenologie des Geistes* [Phenomenology of the spirit]. Hamburg, Germany: Hgb. J. Hoff meister. (Original work published 1807)

Ibsen, H. (1966). John Gabriel Borkman. In *Nutidsdramaer 1877–1899* (J. W. McFarlane, Trans.). London: Oxford University Press. (Original work published 1889)

Schmithüsen, G. (2004). Die Zeit steht still in rasender Eile [Time stands still in a tearing hurry]. *Psyche, 58*, 293–320.

Stern, J. (2003). Cyclones, bicycles, and psychoanalysis: The witch-of-us? Complex and *The Wizard of Oz*. *Journal of the American Psychoanalytic Association, 51*, 1241–1261.

Szondi, P. (1978). *Versuch über das Tragische* [Essay on the tragic]. Frankfurt: Suhrkamp (Original work published 1961)

Wurmer, L. (2011). *Scham und der böse Blick. Verstehen der negativen therapeutischen Reaktion* [Shame and the evil eye. Understand the negative therapeutic reaction]. Stuttgart: Kohlhammer.

2

ON NEGATIVE THERAPEUTIC REACTION[1]

Shelley Orgel

In my work with patients, my technical approaches and theoretical assumptions concerning negative therapeutic reactions have evolved in several respects beyond Freud's original descriptions. In *The Ego and the Id* (1923), Freud wrote about a group of analysands:

> Such people cannot endure any praise or appreciation.... Every partial solution (given by the analyst) that should result in improvement produces in them ... for the time being an exacerbation of their illness; they get worse instead of better.... [The] greater part (of this resistance) reveals itself as the most powerful of all obstacles to recovery, more powerful than the familiar ones of narcissistic inaccessibility, a negative attitude towards the physician, and clinging to the gain from illness. (p. 49)

We see, Freud wrote, "that an unconscious sense of guilt finds satisfaction in the illness and refuses to give up the punishment of suffering" (p. 49). In Freud's view, the locus of the battle is between the patient's sadistic superego and his masochistic ego. The relatively neutral analyst is a weak outside bystander to this energy-absorbing intrapsychic struggle. The patient's unavailability, Freud (1924) wrote, "thwarts our educative aims ... our attempts to exert an influence" (p. 166). I think he meant here that the analyst is unable to use the suggestive power of the physician's authority to mobilize a wish in the suffering patient to get better as a way of attaining the analyst's love. One weapon was available to those inclined to use it, Freud thought. Such an analyst, enacting the part of the patient's primitive ego ideal, assumes the omnipotence attributed to the original parent. What is sacrificed is the psychoanalytic principle that mandates giving "the patient's ego freedom to decide." This analyst famously plays "the part of prophet, savior, and redeemer to the patient."

The analyst's conflict in these circumstances exemplifies an often debated issue about how analysts work. Does the analyst strive to be essentially a neutral, objective interpreter of manifest derivatives of the repressed, including the unconscious superego? Or, do analysts also attempt to offer what they believe the patient, because of deficiencies of nature or nurture, has lacked, and must incorporate from *another*, in order to grow and get well? Different versions of the latter position have included: becoming a model that replaces earlier objects of identification; an empathic participant in necessary, therapeutically helpful enactments; a mirroring or idealized self object; a reparative object; someone who offers a "corrective emotional experience" with a new, long-wished-for version of past objects, and so on. Whether and by what means it is possible to integrate these newer models with the so-called classical one remains a subject of exploration and controversy. But now I'd like to discuss a few instances in which negative therapeutic reactions proved challenging and stimulated fresh insights into this ubiquitous and complex phenomenon.

The first is an experience many years ago that made a lasting impression on me. A male patient had for several years of analysis railed against his mother whom he described as cold, critical, and the dominant parent. We had, by this time, constructed his unconscious fantasy that his father, who had died suddenly a few years earlier, had for many years surrendered his masculine potency and ultimately his life to the patient's mother in a relationship that had at its core a violent version of a sadomasochistic primal scene. To avoid his father's fate, to "save his life," he built a persona as different as possible from his father whom he had despised for weakly yielding his parental authority, his body and soul, to the patient's mother and to others including his bosses for whom he had slaved. The patient had been deeply blocked from mourning for his father. In the beginning of his analysis, he even derogated as a weakness the latter's sentimental, adoring attitude to him as a little boy.

My patient was married to a woman he felt superior to. She was kind, accepting, and forgiving, although he often spoke to her condescendingly, often neglected her sexually, and excluded her from his busy outside social and professional lives.

We had considered many interpretations that centered on his fears of and antagonisms toward women, and on their power as sources of his hypochondriacal dread of illness and death. Much of our work focused on his conflicted wishes for a close male relationship. He sought someone whom he could not dominate, a worthy rival with whom he could contend in struggles which both would survive, and from which he could feel strengthened. He often spoke bitterly about how his mother had "poisoned" his ability to love and trust others. On a Friday, I made an interpretation believing that my patient could benefit from it, that he was warding off an awareness of his strong identification with his mother, with the result that his freedom to feel and act was constricted in his life generally, and in his relationship with me. Although he consciously idealized me, at the same time he provocatively demonstrated by his unchanging behavior that I was failing to help him progress. I believed, but did not interpret then, that he was strongly identified with his mother as the phallic survivor and aggressor in his primal scene fantasies. This identification also constituted a path toward gaining the love of the formerly idealized oedipal father of his early childhood, among other meanings. What I hoped was that he could find relief from the incessant pressures of his internal war between his masculine and feminine identifications and object choices; these were complicated by his images of his mother as a phallic aggressor and his father as feminized and weak. He responded to my interpretation with what I thought were confirming associations.

On the following Monday he told me he had been profoundly depressed all weekend, and had resumed some old ways of acting out self-destructively, including endangering his health. He despaired of ever getting better. We came to understand during that next week that as a result of following the interpretation, he had "lost" the mother he hated and needed, and he felt deeply alone over the weekend. He had felt motherless as well as fatherless; she and I were gone, and he was unable to feel connected with his wife. He dismally foresaw further losses that would surely come in time, including his own premature death.

I did not think this negative therapeutic reaction happened mainly because of his unconscious guilt, a need to suffer, although he *did* feel guilty about his hostile derogation of his father, especially in his adolescence, and about his verbal attacks on his mother. And with me, he could dramatize the depth of his suffering manipulatively. But mainly, I believe my interpretation disrupted an equilibrium and that he then suffered from a fresh loss of the maternal object that he had retained through his warded-off identification with her. His aggressive tirades against her also worked to keep that essential relationship alive. Our understanding this sequence of responses was helpful in this patient's ongoing analysis.

It's an axiom that all change involves loss. Psychoanalysis confirms this inevitability as it exposes the hidden meanings that determine an individual's life. We ask our patients to face, with the courage of responsible consciousness, the series of losses which the progressive journey through life and through analysis demands. Shengold (2006) has written extensively on this subject: "The at-times ecstatic happiness of children is increasingly shadowed and even transiently eclipsed by the impending separations and losses that maturation and individuation involve—losses that threaten to leave us parentless and alone in the universe" (p. 882). The analyst who assumes the role of the child's ego ideal makes it temporarily possible for the adult patient to deny these facts of life, and thus serves to revive the illusory belief, which had been necessary for the young child's intact psychic survival, that a parent—omnipotent, omniscient, benign—will always be there. What has been labeled a negative therapeutic reaction, then, expresses a resistance (defense) against accepting the imperative cost of the wished-for aims of analysis itself.

Living acquires meaning as we face the necessity of separations, including, in adults, the realities of aging and death. One purpose of negative therapeutic reactions, in some patients I have worked with, is to stop time, to keep the illusion of eternal youth, to refuse to grow up. For some, the unfolding bodily and mental changes time brings seem too narcissistically wounding to bear. But for most of these people, so are intimate, close attachments, because desperately needed others can never truly be given up, mourned, and eventually internalized. When one owns as truth and integrates a narrative that joins one's individual past to the present and anticipates an unknown future, the everyday irretrievable present is endowed with a richness enhanced by the poignant knowledge of its transience. But one also learns that the future implacably comes, and we face it essentially alone, without magical protection. And we also face our inner lives alone—the peremptory power of drives always impinges, and the always present internal conflicts we attempt to resolve, to mediate better solutions for, always necessitate the deprivations of compromise. Can patients' struggle against their conscious goals in analysis ever be absent, even beyond its ending?

What we call negative therapeutic reaction expresses in more intense but qualitatively identical ways an inevitable, universal resistance to change, and therefore, to the very instruments analysts employ to enable change. Interpretation in general signifies a psychic and human coming together; simultaneously, it signals inevitable loss and the reality of separateness. Therefore, "good interpretations," by their very effectiveness, mobilize, in some degree, resistances that mitigate the power that the "positive transference" gives to strengthen the patient's motivation to endure unpleasure in order to achieve the illuminations of unexpected discoveries. Perhaps the seeming benefit of inexact interpretations comes about because the so-called positive transference, aiding the "push" of suggestion, remains undisturbed. A lively analytic process destabilizes those fought-for equilibria that usually represent the outcomes of a virtual lifetime struggle. Clinging to the status quo, as I have illustrated in my first vignette, is a way to hold on to internal object representations and relationships, narcissistically endowed self-representations, and the analyst as the object of transferences and of identifications. I would contend that the analyst is also a "real" present-day person in the patient's life with emotional meanings to both, enriched from years of living their lives while doing analytic work together. Rather than representing withdrawal, many instances of negative therapeutic response I have seen are attempts to *hold on*. And rather than a single response to an interpretation, these reactions often coalesce into patterns that may develop into stalemates, often perpetuated by the bond of sadomasochism that ward off depression.

Here is a second source of negative therapeutic reactions that I believe is not uncommon. If the correctness of an analyst's interpretation seems to be proven *because* progressive change follows it, some patients—analysts, too—conclude that the analyst's understanding has successfully made the patient's mind an object that can be seen into, penetrated. These patients feel violated. For them interpretation is an invasive action, one that is often eroticized in fantasy. The analyst has breached the "walls" containing and safeguarding their subjective possession of living substance, of internality. When a patient responds with a "No!" in word or *action*, it can mean an assertion of separate identity. This response is rooted in the earliest of self, the "I will not swallow that!" articulated in Freud's "Negation" (1925) and Spitz's "No and Yes" (1957). These patients assert: I am I because I control what is me, mine, what enters me.

I believe this response is present in all patients to varying degrees. This variability, which reflects the nature of the balance of power between defense of boundaries and wish to merge that is evoked by the interpretation, determines what the patient "shows" in response. Several patients have acknowledged that they don't want me to be right, especially when my interpretations sounded generically "analytic" in tone and content. I understood them to mean they heard me as a masculine authority whose self-regard was invested in his proud possession of and ability to impose a potent body of psychoanalytic knowledge. I will condense the reactions of several patients, mainly, but not only, women, into a single example, namely, Freud's (1937) bedrock; the male's resistance to a passive relationship to another male, also applies, I think.

This patient has said that if she "accepted" *my* insight, it would reveal to both of us that I "*knew*" what was hidden inside her. Her fantasy was that I would have shown I *can* use my phallus to penetrate any or all of her body orifices—mouth, anus, vagina. Her acceptance without protest, without resisting new ideas coming from outside represented submission, and meant she acknowledged that she lacked and wished for a penis. Further, it may have been an enacted consummation of oedipal wishes that would dictate punishment. The results, in some instances, have included a shutting down of active sexual desire or guilt when she felt sexual desire and pleasure; suffering physical symptoms of unconscious fantasies, manifest as spastic contractions of libidinized bodily openings; and inhibitions of creative thinking. Imaginative capacities, especially in individuals with artistic talents, are animated by the inner freedom to allow their open, unshielded senses to take in the astonishments of a seductive object and part-object world. I believe Greenacre's (1957) delineation of the phase and concept of the child's love affair with the world is genetically related to this.

Such meanings can enter into the negative therapeutic reaction to what we analysts might call "good" interpretations. Insofar as analysands feel interpretations are instruments of the analyst's (male or *female*) phallic power, taking them in, absorbing them becomes dangerously exciting, infuriating, terrifying, and guilt ridden as they light up a network of connections with a virtual lifetime of erotic and rageful fantasies and activities. Some patients fight against yielding to such interpretations also to keep the analyst undamaged, emotionally present, and alive in the outside world. They must remain resistant to what they see as *our* analytic goals in order to preserve a viable relationship with us. In this sense, this pattern of meanings is connected with the need I spoke of earlier, to stop time, to hold on to the illusion of the innocence of childhood, to freeze the analysis in order to preserve it. Parenthetically, when patients catch our technical errors, a moment in which we show anger, evidence of our narcissistic vulnerability, they sometimes look back on the event as a turning point after which stubborn stalemates and negative therapeutic responses gave way to progress.

The essential elements of progressive change in analysis include alleviation of suffering from the consequences of neurotic conflict; gaining pleasure in living; and leading an examined life. Since the analytic process itself is always embedded with instinctualized meanings, and the aims of analysis are equated unconsciously with satisfying pre-oedipal wishes and winning oedipal triumphs, can any psychoanalytic treatment escape completely from some conflict-laden mixture of positive and negative therapeutic reactions? Is what we call a negative therapeutic reaction a compromise formation that restores a balance when the price paid to get what the patient wants feels greater than what the result is worth? Some patients—not necessarily sicker ones—especially those with more unruly drive endowments or more powerful, sadistic superegos, exert greater pressures to keep "serious conflict going," as one patient put it, in order to ward off the forbidden gratifications that a successful outcome would signify unconsciously. The analyst's interpretive success, which results in weakening defenses against drive derivatives, is more threatening to such people both intrapsychically and interpersonally. However, I do not believe we are seeing a violation of the principle that the individual's aim is to balance the wish for the greatest possible pleasure with the least possible unpleasure. In other words, I don't think that it contradicts the pleasure principle, as is suggested by Freud's early formulations relating negative therapeutic reactions with melancholia, for example.

I would like now to illustrate this point by describing a patient who from childhood on believed he was different from others in that he was more driven, that he suffered more intense feelings, including rages and overwhelming unidentifiable internal pressures that made him feel trapped within his body, in his family, within the confining walls of his childhood house. This vignette will also illustrate the idea that defeating the analysis and the analyst restores a delicate intrapsychic balance. This patient struggled against being undone by success, which meant, most obviously, victories over age-old rivals, his father and a younger sibling. Not getting better in analysis represented thwarting the analyst's success in the transference. But such a pyrrhic victory for *him* also insured *my* physical survival, if with narcissistic wounds, and it promised a timeless continuation of our relationship. Professional successes eventually ushered in conscious feelings of unworthiness, feelings of depression, and hypochondriacal concerns that included almost delusional beliefs that he was about to die. And he had a compulsive need to reduce his accomplishments to nothing. He'd say things like "I'm a total failure, a piece of shit, and so is what I've done with my life." Although I don't believe his "regressions" were precipitated by particular interpretations, it was clear that since I hadn't helped him, I, too, was a failure. After sinking into this state of self-loathing and inexplicable guilt for a period lasting from hours to weeks, he seemed to have suffered enough. It was as if the bad shit had been expelled and he was now clean, good, renewed. Typically he began to reevaluate work he was doing more positively, and it began to go forward. He became again an attentive husband and father, and he would become hopeful that analysis, too, would work.

Here is a clinical moment I found enlightening: My patient had been collaborating with a good old friend, A, on a piece of work. He told me the following fantasy: He learns A has killed himself after sending my patient some material he has worked on for their joint project. My patient said, "I wish I had loved it and told him so; this would have given him redemption and he could have lived. But I couldn't say this because my giving 'approval' would in itself always express my superiority. What I can't do that *would* save him, would be to convey to A that he has done something I *can't* do, that he has gotten beyond me."

It seemed to me that A represented my patient in analysis with me, and that he also was playing with a transient identification with me, while A represented *him*. What saves A would be what my patient wishes I would say to *him*. His fantasy expressed his close-to-conscious awareness of a dynamic configuration of the very conflicts which enter into our subject today, the negative therapeutic reaction.

If my comments "helped" him, it would mean that I am superior to him. His vengeful "failure," displaced onto his friend who commits suicide, thwarts my "encouragement and good intentions" by which I convey my "superiority." In this sense, his failure in analysis as well as his proclaiming himself and his work to be shit constitute victories over rivals representing his father and his sibling, and are paid for by self-punishment. The latter, in turn, is erotized and clung to until he reaches a kind of climax of self-abuse, in which he "accepts" the prospect of imminent death. He said at other times: "If I am willing to accept death, surrender to (an omnipotent version of) my father, to God, I can be redeemed and fulfill my creative vision and ambition; I can be reborn." During the dark phase, the patient felt he must remain exiled from gratifying connections with his family, friends, and his analyst. He must wait patiently and alone for his self-condemning inner voice to quiet its clamor, and to begin to feel the onrush of a *wish* for the return of the suspended longing for reunion with loved ones, for an infusion of conscious fantasies that fueled his sexual desire, and for an appetite for work. It is as if he has reached the ending of a masochistic orgy of pathological mourning of the death of his "bad" self-representation.

This situation seems very close to what Freud described as a conflict in which a powerful, harsh superego defeats a masochistic ego. But there is a meaningful difference. In the periods of masochistic suffering, his unconscious erotic and aggressive transference relationship to me remained strong. The patient *wanted* to tell me about his failure and mine. There was sadism in the telling, and exhibitionism, too, but strong, less instinctualized desires to be heard and understood competed with these wishes. He believed that his benefitting from my protective presence and concern for him gave me narcissistic satisfaction, but meant more than this to both of us. He was also appealing to me as a parent—father and mother—who remained relatively steadfast, could ride out his "hysterical storms," and would remain with him in the world of his mind as he ventured forth less fearfully into more distant realms, including elaborate worlds he made up that found their way into in his work. These transference wishes were similar to those I described in the first male patient.

The interaction he sought with me also represented a reliving of his early relationship with his mother, especially from about ages 4 to 9. As a child, when he came home, he would report the events of his day to her. They shared gossip, and complained about others, including his father. He performed as a good talker and expressive actor for her as his audience. These interludes gave them a special closeness, an erotized bond, from which others, especially his father, were excluded. The situation of two people talking intimately about everything was exciting, forbidden, dangerous—feelings that entered into the analysis. The erotic wishes the situation aroused were not to be consummated on pain of death. He had come to include hatred in his feelings about his mother, seeing her as using him for *her* narcissistic gratification. When he didn't give her what she needed, she would be critical where she'd formerly praised him, seemed indifferent, and was also irritatingly self-critical. He had come to believe that his mother was chronically depressed for many years, and therefore could easily "disappear" and abandon him if he failed to "manage her emotional responses." Reestablishing what became in his fantasy an apologetic self-demeaning relationship to her became a pattern in many other relationships, and was a significant dimension in the transference. As he put it: "Having a masochistic relationship to a narcissistic person is my way of keeping my mother from turning her face away from me. She didn't want me to do well. She envies my success—away from her."

And so, bemoaning his failures, especially at times when the successes he achieved were recognized by others, meant to him he was offering his mother the sacrifice she wanted, and was avoiding the worse fate of empty aloneness, choked by drives that had no outlet for discharge. By identifying with her projected self-loathing and marshaling reasons to hate himself, he felt trapped in a recurring pattern in which he alternated between reveling in an exciting, even grandiose expectation of glory and immersing himself in a bitter self-hatred he could not change or dare to relinquish. He said, "Instead of amusing her, I became a reflection of her. I couldn't save her (note how this echoes his fantasy about A). And I can't escape her. I can't love her. I feel deprived of an ability to love her. If I had overcome her, I could forgive her, and love her again."

In our work together, my slowly helping him to think that his efforts, personally and professionally, could be good enough, that he could aim for and be relatively satisfied with achieving the best he could do, gradually took hold. His grandiose fantasies and his idealizations of me in both the maternal and paternal transferences, each always accompanied by the reverse, and the storms of aggression that struck me and him, were slowly tamed. He felt less need to monitor my responses, to "manage" me in order to judge if he was successful in keeping me present, involved. The cycles became shorter and consumed less of his life and of our relationship. His view that his success gave me narcissistic pleasure and therefore diminished him, a dynamic emphasized by Karen Horney (1936) and Melitta Schmideberg (1938) was present, as it was in all the patients I have referred to, but with time and patience we were able to get beyond it.

The negative therapeutic reaction did not announce a limitation or an end to our work, but was an inevitable and valuable part of an ongoing psychoanalytic process.

Note

1. This chapter is based on a contribution to a panel on "The Negative Therapeutic Reaction," at the American Psychoanalytic Association Winter Meeting, January 20, 2007.

References

Freud, S. (1923). The ego and the id. In J. Strachey (Ed. & Trans.), *The standard edition of the complete psychological works of Sigmund Freud* (Vol. 19, pp. 1–68). London: Hogarth Press.

Freud, S. (1924). The economic problem of masochism. In J. Strachey (Ed. & Trans.), *The standard edition of the complete psychological works of Sigmund Freud* (Vol. 19, pp. 157–172). London: Hogarth Press.

Freud, S. (1925). Negation. In J. Strachey (Ed. & Trans.), *The standard edition of the complete psychological works of Sigmund Freud* (Vol. 19, pp. 235–242). London: Hogarth Press.

Freud, Sigmund. (1937). *Die endliche und die unendliche Analyse* [Analysis terminable and interminable]. In J. Strachey (Ed. & Trans.), *The standard edition of the complete psychological works of Sigmund Freud* (Vol. 23. pp. 209–253). London: Hogarth Press.

Greenacre, P. (1957). The childhood of the artist: Libidinal phase development and giftedness. *Psychoanalytic Study of the Child, 12*, 74–72.

Horney, K. (1936). The problem of the negative therapeutic reaction. *Psychoanalytic Quarterly, 5*, 29–44.

Shengold, L. (2006). As August approaches. *Psychoanalytic Quarterly, 75*, 879–886.

Schmideberg, M. (1938). "After the analysis..." *Psychoanalytic Quarterly, 7*, 122–142.

Spitz, R. A. (1957). *No and yes: On the beginning of human communication*. New York: International Universities Press.

3

"TIME THAT NO ONE CAN COUNT, ALWAYS BEGINS ANEW"

Thoughts Concerning the Function and Meaning of the So-Called Negative Therapeutic Reaction from the Perspective of Time Standing Still[1]

Gerd Schmithüsen

The purpose of this chapter is to address a phenomenon that often arises in the negative therapeutic reaction (NTR), to recognize the value of that phenomenon, and to make it more accessible for analytic work. I will describe a dialectic in NTR which manifests itself in a tension that develops between the defenses of refusal, negation, retreat, and the feeling as if time were standing still and the simultaneous hope of finding a way out despite all previous disappointments and fears ("a hopelessness not empty of hope," Schneider, 2004, p. 58). In NTR a highly complex dynamic is at work between a desire to make contact and at the same time an impulse to retreat. The movie *Dances with Wolves* (Kostner, 1990) illustrates this dynamic impressively and directly in the scene where the protagonist, who has been posted to a place in the Wild West that is on the frontier between the European controlled territory and the Indians' lands is confronted by a hungry wolf and offers it a piece of bacon. Tempted by the smell, the wolf strains its entire body toward the meat, yet at the same time hesitates, every muscle taut, ready to explode into action if need be so it can run for its life.

I will illustrate the constructive sides of this phenomenon without ignoring the destructive power. This is no small undertaking because we are dealing with a conflict that takes place between different ways of experiencing and behaving, which, at first glance, appear to be paradoxical and exclusive. This conflict is difficult to understand theoretically and causes serious problems in clinical settings, often leading the analysis into blind alleys and an abrupt termination.

The majority of colleagues who have written on this confusing phenomenon appear to agree that NTR becomes manifest during the course of the psychoanalytic process in patients' paradoxical reactions. Patients decide to undergo psychoanalysis to understand their mental illness, symptoms, behavior, and personality that are at the root of their suffering and prevent them from living a satisfying life. Consciously they want to free themselves from the constraints, symptoms, and negative character traits to gain greater personal freedom in their inner and outer worlds. However, if, in the course of analysis, patients gain constructive insight (i.e., if their condition improves), their reactions cause their condition to get worse and whatever helpful insights that had been achieved are attacked and devalued. Patients actively undermine the "success" of the treatment for unconscious reasons. This also applies to the therapeutic relationship: When patients experience the relationship as being helpful, they attack it, thus risking the success of the treatment.

Freud first mentioned this paradox in his paper in 1918, in which he reflected upon and reevaluated his theory in his clinical work with the "Rat Man." This patient "attempted to contradict the effect for a short while by an aggravation of the symptom which had been cleared up" (1918, p. 69). Already in this description the central characteristic of the negative therapeutic reaction is tacitly implied. During the analytic process, the patient gains insight, he gets closer to the analyst. This is negated, his symptoms get worse, and he tries to escape. After achieving insight, the patient attacks the analytic process. "The negative therapeutic reaction is the paradoxical reaction of a patient who initially feels relieved by the analytic work and has expressed this but who then reacts in a negative way and, in so doing, destroys what has already been attained" (Von Susani, 2010, p. 490). I will not list the impressive literature on this subject here but refer to the overview Wurmser provides in this volume.

A phenomenon similar to the NTR can be found in patients who bring the analytic process to a standstill by inducing a feeling in the analyst as if "time were standing still," as I have already described in 2004. These patients also come for analytic treatment because of their subjectively experienced—usually intensely felt—distress in the hope that the analyst will be able to help them with their inner or external distress, their psychic illness. They accept the analytic setting, come regularly to each session, pay the fee agreed upon, and appear to cooperate. However, the way in which they talk is quite remarkable: They often talk nonstop, without slowing down, without a pause. Their speech is a continual flood of words, which causes the analyst in his or her evenly hovering attention to feel powerless, helpless, disinterested, empty, and as if time were standing still. Although these patients are extremely reliable and punctual, the analyst experiences these sessions less and less as a meeting between two persons and feels him- or herself less and less a listener and more and more as a disturbing element that the patient tries to eliminate. This dynamic arises quite frequently and often comes to a climax after sessions which the analyst feels have been "good sessions," and during which he or she had the feeling that a meeting had taken place with the patient which led to substantial insight. Such "good sessions" are often followed by a flood of words from the patient that paralyze and virtually cut off the analyst. One of my patients put it like this: "Your consulting room is like a big dock, and I am a huge ship that pushes enormous quantities of water to the side. Between the sides of my ship and the sides of the dock there is only a millimeter of space for water. And that space is left over for you."

Although such statements and similar phenomena of a standstill in time seem like a radical negation of the analytic process and the analyst, calling to mind concepts like the death drive and also thoughts about the discussions around NTR, I prefer not to concentrate on this aspect of radical negation. What is important to me is the recognition and appreciation of the constructive aspect of this phenomenon even when, at first glance, this appears to be a paradox. I agree with Wurmser (2009) that the concept of NTR only describes a phenomenon and does not prevent any explanation for this. In this chapter, I will explain my own views of NTR based upon the phenomenon that I call "time standing still" (2004) and I will illustrate this with a clinical example to provide a basis for discussion. The phenomenon of "time standing still" in my opinion seems to be a central aspect of NTR, to which Orgel refers in chapter 2 of this volume.

I first noticed this phenomenon in my analytic work with patients who have been extremely traumatized when they were very young.[2] I am convinced that there are certain circumstances when working with such patients that the analyst cannot avoid experiencing the feeling that time is at a standstill. Although the patient has actively caused this experience, he is not consciously aware of having done so because it takes shape solely in the countertransference, often for long stretches of the analysis.

In contrast to the phenomenon of timelessness, I think that the phenomenon of time standing still[3] is brought about due to a radical defense. Through this phenomenon defenses are actively, albeit unconsciously, brought into play which prevents any further development of the catastrophic fear that developed when the child was separated from the maternal object at a time before the ego had been consolidated (Von Susani, 2010); later on this fear is brought into the analytic relationship and becomes available for analytic work. This fear of reexperiencing a traumatic psychic breakdown derives from a severely traumatizing experience which took place in the past at a time when the immature psychic apparatus was overwhelmed with anxiety that was then internalized.

> The final theory of anxiety permits us to reopen the question of the relationship of trauma or fantasy ... from now on it is important to understand the interest in a conception of internal trauma created by the inevitable, but quantitatively and qualitatively variable failure of the object to provide mothering. The *Hilflosigkeit* leaves the baby powerless in face of the demands of his primitive

> drive impulses, with no possibility of moderating the imperious nature of their demands for satisfaction, which create serious disorder in which all the sense giving structures collapse and give way to a disorganization of the ego, which is as yet incapable of putting defences to work which might avert the intolerable anxiety. (Green, 1977, p. 138)

This standstill in time is, therefore, simultaneously the result of a defense against an underlying, nonsymbolized, and as such incomprehensible fear of annihilation or fear of psychic death, and at the same time it is a precise repetition of this earlier experience of psychic annihilation that takes place in the transference relationship. The standstill in time is an attempt to deny the reality of circular, cyclic, as well as linear time and therefore to negate dependence upon which the existence of the subject relies, including development, separation, and death. These patients can only imagine separation unconsciously as a repetition of the catastrophe of the absence of the existentially needed object, and is experienced as psychic annihilation. Therefore, they not only defend against separation but also against the ability and necessity to experience separateness, or basically against any development at all—Bion (1959) has contributed much to this topic with his thoughts about "catastrophic change."

I think that the experience of time is actively interfered with to avoid a reconfrontation in the present with a breakdown from the past. In order to survive, time is brought to a standstill, the trauma becomes encapsulated, and therefore cut off from experience, but the agony never ends.

The Phenomenon of Time Standstill

A Clinical Example: Mr. P

> There was a dark room beneath the earth shaped like a piece of cake. At the tip of the piece of cake there was a grate. An insect, perhaps a butterfly, sat on the grate and got caught. It sat there in the dark … I don't know how long, with its feelers stretched out towards the sun shining outside. After a long time it began to quiver, first it stretched out its feelers, as if it were longing for something, then the quiver spread out through the wing; it looked as if it were being snuffed out.

Mr. P was an amiable, young-looking analysand around the age of 50. He described the way he felt in his dream and his associations to it, of feeling simultaneously imprisoned in an unbearable enclosure (Meltzer, 1981), and isolated and protectively enclosed in a cocoon (Steiner's "psychic retreat"; 1987). He sits in the dark in a dramatic scene, disoriented, disconnected from a libidinally or aggressively cathected object. The dream work and his associations give the analyst the impression that this condition was endless, as if time were at a standstill. At the same time, Mr. P feels absolutely great in his rigid inaccessibility. He imagines himself to be the only one who can survive this.

Simultaneously, he expresses hope in his dream in the pleading feelers and the way the feelers stretch out yearningly and at the same time a fear that a—hopefully—benevolent object is just outside his reach. Yet the quiver looks as if it were being snuffed out and had to be snuffed out in order to control and prevent a repetition of the existential fear of annihilation in the transference.

His ability to produce this kind of a dream, to remember it, and to bring it into the analytic session has been preceded by years of analytic work in which I, as his analyst, often felt like the butterfly he described in his dream: torn between the desire to feel alive during the sessions and the need to understand something of what was going on between Mr. P and me and the reason why that wish had to be snuffed out. The analytic sessions were characterized by phases of an unbroken chain of Mr. P's words and his sentences spoken without a pause to think, with little affect or modulation in his tone of voice. Frequently, he focused on meticulous descriptions of scenes on the street, scenes in films or bits of literature which fit these stories, rambling on, elaborating, making comments, and then remarking on his comments. Generally speaking, on these occasions I was unable to make any sense of what he was saying nor did I know what he was referring to, and lost my own feeling for time as well. This often happened at breakneck speed, which often made me feel very uncomfortable and dazed, as if I had been put into a trance or hypnotized, somewhere between waking and sleeping, as if I had been paralyzed or poisoned. In his paper from 1997, Baruch referred to a similar phenomenon which he called "seamless speech," a manic way of talking which tends to destroy any space between the analysand and the analyst, which attacks the ability to think, and at times makes thinking impossible for them both. In his paper on the formation of idylls, Gerisch (2002) implicitly deals with this phenomenon as well. In her paper on NTR, Von Susani (2010) describes a similar phenomenon used as a primary, manic defense. One of my analysands refers to this way of talking as "magic talk," which she describes as feeling as if time were at a standstill.

In the sessions with my patient, I lost my sense of the passing of time. Shortly before the end of a session, I would often look at the clock, which served me as a triangulating object that saved me by helping me to regain my sense of the flow of time and helped me end the session and reexperience circular, cyclical, and linear time. Before I go into the psychodynamics of time standstill in greater depth, I feel it is important to present a short overview of this complex topic and the development of the way time is experienced from a psychoanalytic perspective (i.e., the subjective, inner experience of time). Furthermore, I would like to differentiate between the related concepts of timelessness, cyclical and linear time, the duration of time, and—as a result of a radical defense, the arrest of time, time standstill—work out the essential differences between timelessness and time standstill.

Excursus: The Psychogenesis of the Beginning of the Experience of Time from a Psychoanalytic Point of View

In psychoanalytic literature (Colarusso, 1979, 1987; Gaddini, 1998; Gutwinski-Jeggle, 1992; Häflinger, 1990; Hartocollis, 1983; Loewald, 1972), there seems to be agreement on the brief state of timelessness in the experience of the newborn infant. Loewald (1972), for example, describes this state as one without desire, memory, or anticipation. There is no separation between past, present, and future, only the experience of an inseparable mother–child unit free from tension or desire.

As infants begin to "surface" from this primal state of timelessness, their subjective experience of time begins, depending upon the experience of some kind of deficit or tension connected to their physical experience of essential (drive) needs. This presupposes the existence and the subjective experience of a need-satisfying or tension reducing object relationship.[4]

After having previously experienced the satisfaction of his or her needs, any deficit thereafter will evoke a rudimentary memory of this past, satisfying experience, which will, in a further developmental step, later be hallucinated. Freud refers to this already in 1900, in *The Interpretation of Dreams*: "The first wishing seems to have been a hallucinatory cathecting of the memory of satisfaction. Such hallucinations, however, if they were not to be maintained to the point of exhaustion, proved to be inadequate to bring about the cessation of the need or, accordingly, the pleasure attaching to satisfaction" (p. 598).

Based on the repetition of fulfilling experiences, an inner response develops as a reaction to the deficit; this leads to the ability to remember the previous satisfaction, to project this satisfaction into the future, and in this way to anticipate satisfaction. This ability to be able to anticipate satisfaction internally presents for the first time a perspective of time aimed at the future.[5] The repeated experience of cycles of satisfaction, hunger, anticipation of satisfaction, and satisfaction in its circular course constitutes the first experiences of cyclic, circular time and shapes its experiential core.

The infant experiences waiting for his needs to be fulfilled: for example, the span of time between becoming aware of hunger and its satisfaction within the framework of this cyclic experience of time, which is experienced internally as being short or long. Depending upon whether the experience of waiting was felt to be of "shorter or longer" duration, a specific element of circular/cyclical time takes shape. The 1-year-old child, for example, is able to experience a span of time only as long as he is able to maintain an inner picture of a need-fulfilling object. If this internal picture falls apart, the ability to experience present and future and the internal connection collapses.

In this case, the child is exposed to an internally traumatic situation: Time has fallen apart. This traumatic experience, however, does not lead to a state of timelessness but rather to an unbearable, catastrophic experience of a meaningless, eternal "now," without continuity, without end; it is an experience of fragmenting, when the world falls apart and nothing makes sense: This experience is equivalent to the experience of time standstill. In my opinion this is essential, from a theoretical as well as from a clinical perspective.[6] In timelessness and time standstill, both qualities are actually real representations of states beyond time, as Loewald expresses it. These are very different from each other. He thinks that timelessness refers to a basically normal, albeit fleeting, primary experience of being unseparated, with minimal tension or desire, from which the categories of time as described above are developed. However, in my opinion, time standstill is a twofold phenomenon. According to Loewald, this results from a (genetically earlier) breakdown in the ability to anticipate due to a (singular or usually cumulative) traumatic experience which overwhelmed the still immature psychic apparatus.

At a later stage, time standstill is actively used, as I see it, however unconsciously, for defense purposes on the basis of a more maturely developed sense of time. Time is arrested in the experience of the object in order to avoid being confronted again with the fear of breakdown, which has already taken place in the past; the new experience of the breakdown is phantasied as a (deadly) catastrophe, because the subject is confronted with either an intrusive or an unavailable, psychically absent object (i.e., an object that is unable to contain the fear). Winnicott (1974) calls attention to this twofold character in his thoughts on psychic breakdown:

> [T]he breakdown has already happened, near the beginning of the individual's life. The patient needs to "remember" this but it is not possible to remember something that has not yet happened, and this thing of the past has not happened yet because the patient was not there for it to happen to. The only way to "remember" in this case is for the patient to experience this past thing for the first time in the present, that is to say, in the transference. This past and future thing then becomes a matter of the here and now, and becomes experienced by the patient for the first time. This is the equivalent of remembering, and this outcome is the equivalent of

> the lifting of repression that occurs in the analysis of the psychoneurotic patient (classical Freudian analysis). (p. 105)

The second aspect of the experience of time is linear time with its dimension of the passing of time when the split between good and bad becomes integrated; this is only possible when the depressive position has been reached and takes place genetically at a later stage of development (Klein, 1935, 1940). Therefore, I conclude that the subjective experience of circular, cyclic, and linear time is inconceivable unless there is an object capable of containing the affects and is libidinally or aggressively cathected, or can be cathected.

Sheldon Bach (2001) emphasizes the existential meaning of the psychic availability of the early mother. In his article, he describes patients who are not able to feel completely alive in the present because in the past their parents failed to consciously maintain a vivid memory of them when they were children. His (Bach's) patient described not having been remembered by his mother and continually getting lost in reality. His mother had been present, but he could not really feel connected to her at all. The emotional connections as well as the feeling of the continuity of time were missing, both of which are necessary in order to connect the isolated bits of experience and that become a memory.

The Psychodynamics of Time Standstill in Psychoanalytic Literature

There is little psychoanalytic literature which explicitly deals with the phenomenon of time standstill as a clearly defined, clinical phenomenon. I will present the psychoanalytic contributions to the psychodynamics of time standstill in chronological order from the perspectives of the drive theory and ego psychology as well as from the perspective of the theory of object relations.

Drive Theory and Ego Psychology

Jones (1927) uses the Greek term *aphanisis* in relation to drives to describe the fear of being completely annihilated. According to Jones, this fear results from the complete and continual destruction of the ability and the possibility to enjoy sexual pleasure due to unconscious feelings of guilt.

> We cannot, of course, expect that the unconscious, with its highly concrete nature, will express itself for us in these abstract terms, which admittedly represent a generalization. The nearest approach to the idea of aphanisis that we met with clinically is

> that of castration and of death thoughts (conscious dread of death and unconscious death wishes). (p. 461)

This results in a sense of absolute desperation and the withdrawal of cathexis from the outer objects and redirects the libido toward one's self. Here Jones postulates an idea which Rosenfeld as well as Green take up later.

According to Schilder (1936, quoted by Hartocollis, 1983), the depressive experience is the result of a defensive procedure caused by aggressive drive impulses and the fear that movement, action, and a flow in time will cause the self to commit a murder, during which time is experienced as racing and the self, in contrast, is felt to be immobile and existing in time as if it were standing still.

In reference to the psychology of depression, Hartocollis (1983) describes how the psychoanalytic exploration often discloses murderous phantasies toward love objects, which are frequently warded off by an incapacity to move and a standstill in the subjective experience of time while the outer reality is experienced as changing at an absurd pace.

Loewald (1972) mentions the phenomenon of time standstill in relation to the defense against fear and pain, which are felt to be too much to bear for the immature ego. He emphasizes that the experience of fragmentation makes the quality of past, present, and future meaningless, which, in my opinion, results from a traumatic experience which overwhelmed the immature psychic apparatus. This experience of a meaningless "present," a standstill in time, is not a "present" in the sense of an element in the continuity of time which holds the world together because the reciprocal relationship between present, past, and future has dissolved. As a result, each moment in which one feels disconnected from the other is experienced as being empty (void of meaning); it can only be experienced for oneself alone and as such, feels as if it were nothing (e.g., the object relational concepts of the "attacks on linking," Bion, 1959; and the considerations of Gaddini, Rosenfeld, and Green as stated below). This is what Loewald means by "time standing still."

Modell (1996), too, expressed similar thoughts when he referred to Winnicott's ideas about manic defense. Painful memories of the past, above all those related to loss, are disavowed with the help of manic defense. It seems as if the individual were very effectively cut off from memories of the past and worries about the future: "He is in a world of the everlasting present" (p. 80). Modell precisely describes how the present is represented in even the smallest detail in a concrete manner and cut off from all affective associations. In this way, it looks as if there is a lack of emotional depth or a disturbed sense of psychic experience (psychological mindedness). The everlasting present serves as a defense against the awareness of loss, separation, and death.

Object Relational Theoretical Approaches

Gutwinski-Jeggle (1992) explicitly refers to the role of trauma in the development of the phenomenon of time standstill. This is the equivalent of a psychic fixation on trauma:

> When we speak of a psychic fixation on trauma (Freud, 1920), we are usually unaware of the double meaning in a spatial-time sense, that is to say, that there is not only the tendency to adhere to the trauma in the unconscious as a "place," so to speak, but there is also a tendency to adhere to the time (during which the trauma took place), which means that time stops at that moment, thus making time something that is endless. (p. 176)

Gutwinski-Jeggle explicitly calls attention to the importance of the necessity to undo trauma in a transformational object relation, which means containment, and emphasizes that: "Trauma is eternal as long as it has not been understood" (p. 176).

What Laplanche (1997) calls "the creation of time" is of great importance, according to Gutwinski-Jeggle: The ability to tolerate the absence of the object is possible only when the potential return of the absent object can be imagined and can therefore be anticipated. In connection to this idea, the separation from the object, I recall the origin of the word *time*, in German *Zeit* (Old and Middle High German *zit*, meaning: "separated into parts"; *Brockhaus-Enzyklopädie,* 2002), and in English *time* is distantly related to *tide*: a rhythmic pull of water back and forth, in German *die Gezeiten*!

If this period of waiting for the return of the object cannot be tolerated, severe distortions in the perception of experience in and with time will develop. "Because this type of personality can only experience a 'now' or 'never,' there can be no 'later'; he cannot imagine that there is an end of the unbearable situation but can only think there can be no end" (Gutwinski-Jeggle, 1992, p. 210).

In my opinion, Gaddini describes implicitly the mechanisms of the psychic retreat which result in a standstill in time at a bodily level. He considers the premature perception of a boundary when experiencing something "foreign" at the stage of development he calls the psychosensory self, which leads to a more or less radical retreat from the world of objects and to a refusal to develop. Gaddini conceptualizes two areas of psychic experience which he sees as deriving from bodily experience. The first and older derives from the primitive perception through the soma; the second is connected with the step-by-step perceptive acknowledgment of external stimuli, stimulated by oral activity.

In the earlier stage that Gaddini (1998) calls the "psycho-sensoric," it is impossible to recognize the fact that that the object is "different from the self" (p. 139). The original perception is, according to Gaddini (1969), exclusively physically imitative:

> Early identifications can be distinguished from imitations by the important fact that a reality, even though fragmentary, becomes introjected and assimilated. In this sense Jacobson uses the term "realistic identifications." I would like to suggest that this realistic element represents, right from the beginning, something which permits us to speak of identification proper. Early imitations, on the other hand, represent and are concerned only with unconscious phantasy. Furthermore they seem to follow a process of their own, which apparently has a distinct role in the development of the ego. (p. 476)

This physically imitative perception, for example the early "dialogue" of baby and mother of the wide-open eyes or the open mouth, leads in a next developmental step to a hallucinatory image, a phantasy of a fusion by means of a magical identification with the object and somewhat later on to the first imitations. This results in a sense of "being" one with the object (i.e., to deny its existence outside of oneself and separate from oneself):

> Imitation seems to be connected, originally, with perception, in the sense that primitive perception is physically imitative. At first the infant perceives by modifying his own body in relation to the stimulus. In this way, the infant does not perceive the real stimulus, but the modification of his own body. Perhaps the differentiation of the systems of perception and systems of memory has its beginning in this community of physical perception and imitation. (Gaddini 1969, p. 476)

Gaddini calls this complex experience "the total self." At this psychosensoric stage of development of the "total self" there is no spatial and no temporal experience but only something like a common surface.[7]

According to Gaddini, the premature experience of "extraneous," "not-self," and "change" are avoided, because they are associated with feeling threatened and unbearable anxiety: the fear of catastrophe, the catastrophic loss of the "total self" (i.e., the fear of complete annihilation). In the psychosensoric stage the child can regress and retreat from conflicts which arise when it is still dependent on the object and can also exclude the external object (see Green's thoughts on disobjectualization below). This means that the cathexis is withdrawn from the object and the object seems to have been destroyed because in a magical way of thinking, the child him- or herself becomes the object via imitation of the satisfying object: "One can define the imitation as the mechanism of psychosensoric activity through which the childish self creates a magical identity with the object" (Gaddini, 1998, p. 142).

The second, very early area of experiencing the object, which Gaddini refers to as the psycho-oral stage, results from the gradual realization that there are stimuli that exist outside of the self. Psycho-oral experiences in which the self is unavoidably confronted with the reality of the object are based upon physical experience that provides a basis and makes this realization at all possible. This makes it possible to remember desires, conflicts, and frustrations as well as to anticipate having to wait for a shorter or longer period of time, and in so doing, to convey a sense of time in the self as well as in the object.

In my opinion, this first elementary defense (i.e., the withdrawal of cathexis and the formation of an ersatz experience via phantasied fusion and imitation) seriously disturbs[8] the experience of time—of circular and later on also of linear time—and as well the formation of psychic structure. On the other hand, it is exactly the implicit—psychic—annihilation of the object that induces the experience "as if time were standing still" in this very object.

Self-idealization plays a central role as a mechanism for withdrawal according to Rosenfeld's theory on destructive narcissism. The omnipotent-destructive parts of the self are idealized, including those that are opposed to positive libidinal object relations as well as those that oppose the libidinal part of the self, thus preventing dependent object relationships and permanently devaluing external objects.

Rosenfeld (1971) thinks that some people have destructive-narcissistic parts of the self connected to what he calls the psychotic structure or organization, that are split off from the rest of the personality. "This psychotic structure is like a delusional world or object, into which parts of the self tend to withdraw. It appears to be dominated by an omnipotent or omniscient extremely ruthless part of the self, which creates the notion that within the delusional object there is complete painlessness" (p. 175).

Basically, what Rosenfeld is referring to is an "actual withdrawal" of the self from the libidinal object cathexis. This withdrawal takes place in a narcissistic state similar to what Freud (1914) called primary narcissism. In this state, the patient appears withdrawn, is unable to think, and loses all interest in the outer world.

In my opinion, the results of this attack on the object's libidinal cathexis lead to an experience as if time were standing still during the analysis. By depriving the object of all meaning, including the cathexis of the object, the analyst feels dead, the contexts of meaning are torn, the temporal and syntactic structure of the language is destroyed, and in consequence the present becomes absolute and eternal.

Green's thoughts on disobjectualization fit in here and link this concept to Winnicott's ideas to what he called "psychic breakdown." For Winnicott (1974), psychic breakdown is brought about when the subject experiences "too much" (an impingement), or "too little" (an emptiness); that is, the absence of an object that is alive and resonates. Where something should have been or should have taken place, in terms of containment, there was nothing:

> Death, looked at in this way as something that happened to the patient but which the patient was not mature enough to experience, has the meaning of annihilation. It is like this, that a pattern developed in which the continuity of being was interrupted by the patient's infantile reactions to impingement, these being environmental factors that were allowed to impinge by failures of the facilitating environment ... In some patients emptiness needs to be experienced, an emptiness that belongs to the past, to the time before the stage of maturity made it possible to experience emptiness. In order to understand this it is necessary to think not of trauma but of nothing happening when something good might have happened. (1974, p. 105)

Like Freud (1920), Green (1975) understands this kind of phenomenon on the basis of a destructive force that opposes all attachment and the mixture of drives (i.e., it aims at overcoming the libidinal cathexis and to go "beyond the object"). Green agrees with Winnicott when he states that the specific characteristic of the destructive drive is caused by an environmental failure, either an overabundance or a lack, which is unable to lessen the strength of the destruction drive.

Green sums up all the processes working against the cathexis of the object in his concept of the "function of disobjectualization." This is the equivalent to the homeostatic principle, the final goal of the psychic apparatus to maintain a zero-point of excitation. Green (1975) emphasizes how radical decathexis in negative narcissism actually is; in other words, decathexis applies to everything: the object, the body, affects, the ego, representations, thinking, ultimately even to the cathexis of cathexis itself, "to attain a state of emptiness and ... non-being and nothingness.... The analyst feels himself identified here with a space devoid of objects, or finds himself outside it" (p. 7).

Through what Green calls the "negative hallucination," not only does the representation of the potentially need-satisfying and the tension-reducing object and the self get snuffed out or annihilated, but the relationship to a bad inner object is maintained at any price. The patient's central, fundamental dilemma can be summed up with the choice: "delusion or death" (p. 7).

This radical conceptualization of decathexis conceals a fundamental and implicit explanation for the origins of the experience of time standstill. When the object's cathexis is destroyed, even if only the cathexis of the cathexis itself is attacked and all connections are negated, including the connection to the libidinal parts of the self, only one—possibly idealized—void or nothing exists as a perpetual Present. When there is no imaginable end to this state, the object stops existing psychically, both in the experience of the destructive self as well as in the object's experience. This results in the object's experience "as if time were standing still," which, in my opinion, is a central aspect of NTR which has not yet been explicitly discussed in psychoanalytic literature.

Hypotheses Concerning Time Standstill

I will now summarize my arguments and the conclusions I have drawn from the above mentioned theoretical postulates in the following hypothesis.

When phenomena of time standstill, as illustrated in the case study, occur repeatedly over a longer period of time during the psychoanalytic process or dominate it, I assume that this is a defense against the fear of experiencing something that is expected to lead to an acute psychic breakdown (i.e., a fear of repeating an earlier breakdown in the present). At first, this can only be detected in an acting out on the part of the analysand, and becomes manifest in a specific countertransference. In agreement with both Winnicott and Green, I consider this earlier breakdown to be a defense against a severe trauma or the result of deficient containment (Bion, 1959); in other words, there was a chronically intrusive and at the same time inaccessible psychically dead object.

Via projective identification, the analyst experiences a state in which "time is standing still," as illustrated in the way my analysand acted out in the transference-countertransference. In this way the analysand wards off the fear of having to reexperience the original, nonsymbolized and, by that, unthinkable fear of annihilation (i.e., fear of psychic death),[9] which is actually part of his unconscious experience (see Gaddini, 1969; also Bion, 1962).[10] Yet, at the same time the experience that has been induced in the analyst is the repetition of the psychic experience of having been annihilated which the patient experienced in the past. Through projective identification the analysand has become the intrusive object (i.e., in a reversal), the trauma that was passively suffered in the past is now actively inflicted. This dynamic makes the analyst into the inaccessible, psychically dead object[11] for periods of time, which results in his experience of time standstill. However, it is only through this repetition, first in the countertransference, that the fear of annihilation (i.e., fear of psychic death) becomes accessible for working through, preceded by work in the countertransference.

Von Susani (2010) comes to a comparable conclusion in her work on

"Identity Dysfunction and the Analytic Process," in which she mainly and explicitly deals with the concept of the NTR: "When earlier deprivations caused by experiences of helplessness are reactivated in the transference, the patients will try to annihilate any relationship which might revive the loss of the indispensable object" (p. 489). She calls attention to the fact that the experience of alterity is unbearable:

> All these patients have the transference situation in common, in which the earlier traumatic failure becomes activated. They fear the analyst-object as a potentially traumatizing other that will repeat the original, non-represented traumatic experience. In the psychoanalytic process radical defenses emerge to keep this early, traumatic experience of discontinuity split off in the unconscious. (p. 489)

More explicitly, this leads to an acting out in the sense of purging, a noncommunicable function which I refer to in the metaphor of "racing time," and the NTR succeeds by destroying any understanding/knowledge. Von Susani introduces one central theoretical concept of NTR in the image of autistic defense as a "pathological auto-sensual activity" which is aimed at creating a standstill in psychic processes:

> The pathological auto-sensual activity is … a defense against the development of an emotional attachment which characterizes the autistic defense. When these activities appear in the therapeutic process, they aim to bring the psychoanalytic process in the transference and countertransference dynamic to a standstill, which means, in this case, to prevent becoming aware of the fact that the object is not a part of the self. (p. 492)

Moreover: "The function of this defense construction is to paralyze the positions and to prevent a repetition in the here and now of the loss of the primary object, i.e., the primary traumatic experience which threatens the feeling of cohesion of the self" (p. 494). Von Susani, referring to Winnicott (1974) on psychic breakdown, continues: "The patients tend to [turn to] psychic isolation and to retreat from the object for fear of being hurt again, for fear of 'losing their skin' with a new failure. This defense construction contains the risk that the transference object and, by that, any change will be excluded" (p. 494).

Case Study

I will now illustrate the theoretical and above all the clinical value of my hypotheses drawing from the material in Mr. P's analysis. For this purpose, I will describe a session from the last half-year of treatment in great detail, focusing on the following aspects:

- In a session, Mr. P brings the analyst's experience of time in the transference and countertransference to a standstill.
- Mr. P does this repeatedly just at the moment when he longs to be close in the transference (i.e., when he comes into contact with his longing, his desire, and at the same time with the existential necessity for a libidinal-aggressive object cathexis).
- Mr. P brings time to a standstill because the transference wish immediately triggers a death-fear in him which he experiences as an existential threat. To be more specific, the fear of coming into contact with an object upon whom he feels existentially dependent, that is physically but not emotionally available, and the fear of being confronted with an intrusive, destructive object that threatens to destroy his inner space.

To better understand and to place the session within a frame of reference, I will provide some brief information concerning my first impression of the patient, a few biographical details, and a summary of the process before the session presented here.

The first time I met Mr. P I noticed that he moved like a zombie. He was wearing an old-fashioned looking, gray knitted jacket, brown corduroy trousers, and clunky shoes and carried a plastic bag. He looked as if he came from another time, slightly unkempt and disoriented, like a homeless person. Later I found out that he was wearing his father's trousers and that his father had committed suicide 3 years before by shooting himself in the back of the neck with his old army pistol. He sought treatment because he was unable to deal with his feelings after a separation after which he felt completely alone, obviously confused, and without any orientation.

In contrast to Mr. P's indifference and emptiness, I immediately sensed within myself there was a horrible, unspeakable need and also something paralyzed, almost frozen. After I decided to take him into treatment, I had some doubts and was afraid that the analysis might end with my death or his.

According to Mr. P, already in his early childhood his mother was psychically odd and exhibited bizarre behavior. Unpredictable in her style of mothering, she was from one moment to the next alternately physically rough, almost violent, and completely absent psychically. She had recently been diagnosed as clearly psychotic. When Mr. P was between the ages of 4 and 10 his grandmother took care of him. She lived in the same household of the well-to-do, upper middle-class family. She saw in Mr. P her own son, his uncle, who had died at the age of 12 years, even to the point of sometimes calling him by his uncle's name. His father, who had been very successful in his professional life, seemed to be a weak figure in the family, and was incapable of making his son feel secure. He was largely absent from his family, rather resigned, and preferred to remain on the sidelines. However, it seems that Mr. P felt secure in his relationship to his grandfather, a retired manufacturer, who lived with the family as well, and who maintained an optimistic attitude toward life despite his physical illness.

At the beginning of the four times per week analysis, Mr. P filled the sessions to bursting point with his manic style of speaking which seemed to serve several functions: on the one hand, to establish intimate contact with me and assure my undivided attention, to bind me, so to speak in every sense of the word, to the point of paralyzing me; on the other hand, via projective identification, to get rid of his intolerable inner states by projecting them into me. He did this in hopes of attaining momentary relief, but also because he, as he himself admitted, was convinced that I would only be able to understand him if I could see, feel, and think the way he did. This reflects an unconscious phantasy of a fusion with the analyst, of destroying the analyst through imitation, as defined by Gaddini, and the idealization of the destructive-omnipotent parts of the self, from Rosenfeld's point of view (1971), as well as the creation of a kind of second skin, as Bick (1968) describes it, by holding himself together with incessant talking. On the other hand, he intended to keep me at a distance because, in his phantasy, he felt that I was the dangerous, potentially violent, penetrating, and intrusive object that he needed to control with incessant talking, as if he were pelting me with bullets. In this way he himself became the intrusive object which he feared to find in me and that he defended against by paralyzing me. He described this violent penetration with these words: "Words and sentences come out of my mouth as if from the head of a hydra, from whose mouth two heads protrude and from each mouth again two heads and so on. And the words are coming out of all these mouths."

I thought that we had reached a turning point in the treatment when I became able to connect the material which emerged in the session to my feelings in the countertransference, feelings of emptiness, being psychically dead, and as if time were standing still. I was forced to experience these feelings throughout the treatment of Mr. P; I then connected them to my inner world and explained this to Mr. P. In this way I gradually became able to sense the unbearable experience that Mr. P was warding off by projecting it into me. The following daydream image proved very useful and allowed me to understand this when, after years of analytic work, he was finally able to communicate on a symbolic level something of his inner state related to the early stage of his analysis: It is about an astronaut who is thrust into outer space with a severed supply line. The last thing that he thought was that he would now be adrift for all eternity as an empty shell unnoticed by the team on the supply ship. The connection between this daydream image to my concordant as well as complementary countertransference allowed me to say to Mr. P that he was afraid to realize that, although he was in the same room as I and he was talking to me (i.e., I was physically present), I was completely absent emotionally and therefore could not be reached (a state in which I frequently found myself in the years of the analysis). This, I said, must feel very familiar to him and probably reminded him of scenes when he was together with his mother and grandmother. This interpretation shocked him deeply. At the same time, based on what had been worked out in the analysis at that point, it seemed to reach him in a way, so that he did not immediately have to destroy it but could hold it within himself and continue to work with it in the analytic relationship. It seemed as if we both had consciously come in contact with a major part of his inner world and his past, at least to the degree we had been able to reconstruct it from the analytic material. The further development in the process seems to indicate that this was a major turning point.

After that, Mr. P began indirectly to describe his inner experience of time standstill in his relationship to me and to his state at the beginning of the treatment, first in a fragmentary and later on in a more symbolic form. This also meant that he had become increasingly able to reclaim the feelings that he had excessively projected into me. In order to illustrate the extent of his difficulties, I would like to present an example of a fragmented description and then an example of a more symbolic description of his experience, both of which I was very familiar with throughout the analysis in my countertransference.

> Shocked … staring into the abyss. The final salvation. One just stands there. Kept me from falling, drunk without alcohol or dope. Had sometimes the idea of fainting, went to the table at night, couldn't judge the distance, swayed, then ran past or ran into. It can't go on like this. Fell asleep. Completely fell over. Had to try to lift the right arm. Heavy as lead. Disintegrated into meaninglessness. Heard my voice. It's drowning a bit. Came to me in an image. No knowledge there, forgetting that spreads. That's something that one can't simply ignore. I am like molten lead. Something like a funeral. The frozen cadaver of a rabbit that begins to thaw. One can't eat it, it's disgusting. It's a kind of disgust that's related to embarrassment. One just stands there, all of a sudden, like a madman….

> Yesterday, after an argument with my girlfriend, I wanted to go back to my apartment. Then I found myself on a bench. I just sat around. I didn't know why, didn't know where I'd come from and didn't know where I wanted to go anymore. I just sat there and stared into space, didn't even have the energy to think about standing up. I felt completely wasted, like some homeless guy.

Background of the Session

To better illustrate this phenomenon, I will present a detailed description of a session from a more advanced period of the analysis (a Tuesday session, the second session in the week in February of the last year of the analysis) to answer the question posed at the beginning of this paper: how and at what specific point in time and why did Mr. P bring time to a standstill in the analyst's experience. In order to put this session into context I will briefly summarize the session from the preceding Monday and the events of the week prior to these two sessions.

During Monday's session I could follow Mr. P for 20 minutes. He spoke, although indirectly and in a convoluted manner, about his difficulties during the weekend break. While I was listening to him, I got the impression that he had felt bad over the weekend and had missed the session as something necessary for his survival and that the weekend had been an excruciating period of waiting for him. That fit to the previous week. I had canceled the first two sessions of that previous week, which I had informed him about 3 months before. Mr. P hesitated when he told me in the Wednesday session of that previous week, how he had waited for the session in the park near my office. His descriptions of the cloud formations, the way the light shone, and his anticipation of spring in the air, gave me the impression of something that for years had almost been extinguished: a mixture of budding hope and a revelation of a yearning for a living other. At first he spoke about how he had greatly wanted to express and share his intense feelings with someone while he was waiting.

As if the renewed rush of wishes for libidinal cathexis in the Monday session had been too much for him and confronted him too undisguisedly with his existential dependency upon an object that would be capable of containing them, Mr. P began to destroy the developing contact with his inner desires as well as with his analyst. He changed the topic, and as he spoke more and more quickly, it became increasingly difficult for me to put the material into a context. The way he elaborately and in great detail described the disconnected events of the weekend gave the impression of someone who was being hunted. Then when he told me about a film he had recently seen it felt as if he unconsciously wanted to increase the confusion and the speed. While he spoke, the grammatical structures of his increasingly convoluted sentences got mixed up, the conjunctive, present, perfect, and past tense got confused. I was not able to relate to him in a reflective way but could just manage to hear what he was saying without being able to remember what he had said before that. In the truest sense of the word I felt "faint": my hearing got fuzzy, my sight blurry. I stared at one spot as if hypnotized and as if increasingly paralyzed, and I was becoming cold. I could not imagine that this would ever stop. It was as if, once again, I had gotten drawn into the experience of unbearable eternity.

As had so often happened, during this Monday session I finally emerged from this state shortly before the end of the session, looked at the hands of the clock on the table, and recovered my ability to think: "Just five more minutes!" and then was able to end the session.

Tuesday, Second Weekly Session

Mr. P arrived on time. After I opened the door for him, he quickly walked to the couch. As soon as he lay down, he began the session.

P: I think that others can deal with feeling lost or lonely or feeling isolated better than I can.

Then he talked so fast and in such great detail and just as concretely as he had spoken in the session before, talking about events from the weekend, about arguments with his girlfriend and her children, a phone call from his mother, a radio program which he describes in great detail, jumping back and forth between the different times, commenting on what he just said by referring to what he had read over the weekend and then making further comments on that as well.

I could just barely manage to remember the comment he made when he arrived, as if it were a "musical theme" which I had kept alive inside me by connecting it to something from the week before. However, I felt increasingly disconnected from him, losing my sense of time and the meaning of what he was saying, and finding myself sliding into an unpleasant mood, as if I were "hovering."

Mr. P sounded as if he had been listening to himself while he was talking, and he said:

P: The way I talk here someone could think that there would be no difference between you and me. I just barely veer away, so to speak, from your periphery, and then I also think that I might have hit you.

A: It sounds as if you're saying that when you speak, you circle around me as if you wanted to exclude me. And when you repeat this, you turn round in a circle.

P: [*Sounding very angry*] I go in circles around you, I spin my web around you, then I pierce you like a spider, and then I devour and digest you and perhaps I triumph because I've succeeded. But after that there's a stale aftertaste in my mouth. [*He pauses and seems to reflect.*] Then I circle around myself. That's terrible in its obstinacy. If it goes on like this you might even say: "Let's give up, Mr. P. We're going to stop, I can't stand it anymore." Then, what I wanted in good moments has been buried.

A: When you encircle me again and again and spin your web around me and then suck me dry and imagine that you leave me behind as an empty shell, then you are the only one left. You are everything, like God. As a result, you bury what you wanted in good moments, like you said before, when you begin to accept my help and see a possibility to escape from the vicious, repetitive circle of not being able to have a true relationship. You began the session with your thoughts about feeling abandoned and feeling lonely.
[*Longer pause. Mr. P seems to reflect upon this*]

P: It's often so awful that an emergency plan gets switched on. I'll do absolutely anything at all to get rid of that unbearable feeling of not being able to stand it anymore. But when it's very bad, I can't even lift a finger. Then it feels like I'm sitting immovably in front of a wall. This becomes a state where I just sit there in a stupor. It can last for a few minutes, and after that I come back. One could say that it gets dark, not just metaphorically. Then I've got to get out. [*Very long pause*] I can only stand it when I feel I've still got (in my back) something to say. But there, where nothing's left, where language fails me, like just before, then something surprising or terrifying happens ... [*He talks very fast again, as if he were on the run*]. Then there's just this feeling of being left alone. [*Pause.*] That woman who left me ... she was a devil. She said: "When you don't have me anymore, no one else will ever want you." One can say something like that and sometimes it just goes in one ear and out the other. But that time it really hit me. I had a devilish fear that I would never get away from her.

A: I think that you also feel this devilish fear that you will never get away from me and the analysis if you really encountered me as a partner in dialogue [*Gegenüber*] and you don't just encircle me with the intention of making me disappear, especially when you begin to feel that you're existentially dependent on this partner.

P: That's right.

A: When you encircle me as you said before, again and again, capture me in your net and dissolve me, then I'm not there anymore and there's nothing left but you. You're all alone then, but you don't feel as if you need someone or are lonely. Then you feel free but in a perfidious way, because there's no one left who could leave you or who is beyond your reach.

P: But there is also no one whom I can leave. Then I can't go away anymore. Then it just goes on and on. It's endless. [*Pause*] It feels like that now. It's unbearable. [*Pause, then I tell him that time is almost up. Mr. P sits up very slowly, hesitantly, and remains immobile for a moment while remaining seated, all churned up inside, and seems to reflect.*] I'd rather just sit here like this. It's so hard for me to leave here today.

Then he stood up and hesitated as he left the consulting room after I had shaken his hand and said "'til tomorrow."

Discussion

I will use a microanalysis of the Tuesday session to illustrate and connect the complex dynamic in my patient's struggle to simultaneously come near me and to pull himself away from me by reflecting on their background and consequences. In so doing, I will focus on his cumulative, early childhood trauma and his fear that it will be repeated in the transference, on his defense mechanisms, and on the phenomenon of time standing still which results from this but which was considerably weaker in this session due to the years of analytic work.

Mr. P immediately brought the theme from the week before into play, which seemed to have occupied him ever since: his feelings of being existentially lost, lonely, and isolated. But he had to bring his budding hope toward an object and his feelings of neediness, which was the outcome of the analytic work thus far, quickly to a standstill with his further comments, to "freeze" them so to speak (i.e., his hopes and desire about being understood by an object that he seems to existentially need and is able to contain his fears). It is precisely this budding hope and neediness that automatically evoked in Mr. P his fear of coming into contact again with the inner trauma he experienced as an infant and being overwhelmed by it, which Bohleber (2000)[12] calls "automatic fear," in reference to Freud. The fear is that the existentially needed object is physically present but psychically absent and can be completely inaccessible or overwhelming or intrusive. This would be a repetition of his early childhood experience in cumulative, traumatic situations, which he would be exposed to again in the transference and made to reexperience the psychically dead, intrusive, and completely unavailable mother and grandmother who were unable to contain his fears. He would be at the mercy of his overwhelming archaic fears and his abject despair, and he would suffer the hopelessness and the destruction of all structures that provide meaning and coherence. Finally, he would be reconfronted with an unbearable agony because to him this meant being subjugated to an eternal "now" (i.e., a standstill in time). This corresponded to the inner state which Mr. P forced me, his analyst, to feel again and again in the way he talked and in the transference-countertransference, although in the session presented here in a somewhat milder form than at the beginning of his analysis. This took place in the following manner.

Very soon after the beginning of the session, Mr. P evoked a feeling in the analyst "as if time were standing still" in the fast way he talked, jumping randomly from one tense and one topic to the next and thereby destroying the temporal and contextual connections. He no longer used his furious speech as he did at the beginning of the session as a means to communicate his thoughts but as a means to evacuate what seem to be unbearable contents, which he projected via projective identification into the analyst, as it were at breakneck speed. In this way, he switched the analyst off in his function as an analyst, paralyzing him and simultaneously drawing him into the same state that he himself feared. Switching from what was passive suffering into active harming, he became the intrusive object which penetrated the analyst "at breakneck speed" and in so doing, attempted to destroy the analyst's inner world. This was probably what he himself experienced as an infant, a toddler, and as a small child in his relationships with his (intrusive) mother and later on with his (intrusive) grandmother.

In his statement "there isn't any difference between you and me," Mr. P gave himself a very apt interpretation by referring to his way of talking and showing his intention to fuse with the analyst. He seemed increasingly able to realize what he was doing to the analyst, snuffing him out as an inner and an outer object and trying to "make himself the analyst" by imitating him.

At this point in the session, the following aspects described above converge dealing with how the analyst's experience of time is brought to a halt: On the one hand, via introjective identification (Gaddini, Bick), Mr. P withdraws the (libidinal-aggressive) cathexis from the object "analyst" by imitating his analytic function and by that making himself the (pseudo-) need-satisfying,(pseudo-) understanding object that can (pseudo-) contain his fears. This means that, from Gaddini's point of view, via an unconscious fantasy, the patient regresses to a psychosensory stage of development in which he fuses with an object when only a "total self" existed but no object. In so doing, he avoids being reconfronted with the trauma of experiencing an existentially needed object that is physically present but psychically absent. Second, he idealizes this procedure of withdrawing cathexis from the object and investing it in his "self-sufficiency," which corresponds to the idealization of the omnipotent destructive parts of his self as described by Rosenfeld (1971). Consequently, this leads to a negation of the analyst in his analytic function and finally to a radical withdrawal of cathexis: the withdrawal of cathexis from the analyst as someone who tries to understand the relationship between patient and analyst as a transference figure as well as the withdrawal of cathexis from parts of the self that are identified with gaining insight.

In *this* session the analyst was able to maintain the cathexis of the analytic function, the wish to understand. Among other aspects, Mr. P's repeated attempt to eliminate his and my wish to understand, as above illustrated, is "a withdrawal of cathexis from cathexis itself," which Green calls disobjectualization. I am convinced that this is a major aspect of the phenomenon of time standstill and the NTR, which, finally results in an experience of an eternal now which corresponds to the analyst's experience of time standstill.

Later on in the session, when he depicted how he encircles the analyst, spins his web around him, stabs him, and digests him, Mr. P very convincingly described the intrusive object that he fears—in the transference—as being existentially threatening. He tried to prevent any confrontation with the repetition of the early childhood experience that he feared by becoming himself the "racing" intrusive object which induces in the analyst a feeling of time standstill.

My interpretation ("When you encircle me again ...") made it possible for Mr. P for the first time in the analysis to explicitly describe the inner experience of time standstill and to relate it to himself. This was an inner state that he had, understandably, felt to be unbearable and for this reason had to relocate in the analyst via projective identification.

His statement "I can stand it only when I have something behind my back that I can say," brought the (defense) aspect of "breakneck speed" back into play. Mr. P clearly expressed that he was in the process of understanding that his racing tempo in his way of talking did not have the function of communication in a discursive sense, did not serve to communicate his thoughts to someone who was capable of thinking, being empathetic, and understanding him. He could not imagine this other person psychically because he thought that person was inaccessible, psychically dead, or threatening because of being intrusive, and so had to be destroyed.

For this very reason, he was at this point not yet able to develop an inner picture of what might happen if he would separate himself from his primary object—in the transference, his analyst. This was his current transference fear which he expressed in a surprisingly clear way and which obviously belonged to the core of his fear of breakdown: Because he unconsciously could only imagine that every separation was a repetition of the catastrophe of an empty room without any existentially needed object—that means psychic annihilation—he defended himself not only from separation but also from the ability and the necessity to experience separateness (i.e., basically from all development). This was the reason for his understandable fear of not being able to get away from the woman—who stands for the primary object—and the analyst in the transference. It is as if he were under a curse that said: "If you leave me, you will degenerate, become a homeless bum, socially isolated, and despised. Shut out of human society. You will never find anyone else."

Mr. P confirmed my transference interpretation of this remark not only verbally but he also internalized it. His reactions later on also showed that he understood the interpretation intellectually as well as emotionally and that he was in the process of understanding that he was the one who actively made time stand still to avoid separation.

At the end of the session I reintroduced (cyclical and linear) time by ending the session and by saying goodbye and reminding him that we would meet again for the next session ("until tomorrow"). In this way, I implicitly told him that there was a progression of time in the process, including the linear and the cyclic aspect of time as well as a developmental aspect. I implied that there would be a future after the separation from the analyst as the current transference of the primary object; the probable return of the absent analyst could be internally imagined, libidinally cathected, and could therefore be anticipated, which meant that development was considered possible and separation tolerable. At the end of the session, the reality of the analytic setting helped me refer to the future and the possibility of imagining the analyst, of libidinally cathecting him, and by that to anticipate him in his analytic function.

Conclusion

I have identified, described, and theoretically classified a specific experience "as if time stood still," by using a clinical example and psychoanalytic literature. This phenomenon presents itself, usually over a long period of time, solely in the countertransference and in the analyst's experience which has been actively but unconsciously induced by the patient. I have vividly described the dynamic at work in this process (i.e., at which specific moment in the relationship and why the analyst's experience of time is brought to a standstill). I have explicated its significance for a deeper understanding of the dialectic of the NTR as described in the introduction and based it on psychoanalytic theories, and I have arrived at the following conclusion.

The phenomenon of a standstill in time in the analytic process—and in my opinion the NTR as well—is caused by the dynamic between patients' unconscious transference wish that motivates them to seek analysis and at the same time by transference fears: their seemingly absurd hope of discovering in the analyst an object that can understand them, is emotionally alive, is capable of containing their feelings, and is existentially important, and also their fear of discovering their unconscious, existential transference fear. The kind of fear that is meant here is the "nameless dread" of being subjected to a repetition of the past breakdown again in the analysis. I understand this breakdown as the result of an unconsciously feared repetition of traumatic experiences (understood as inner trauma) in the transference with a primary object that behaves erratically, vacillating between being intrusive and inaccessible, an object that is simultaneously "overly full" and psychically dead. Patients try to avoid being reconfronted with their transference fear of being annihilated and the resulting intense hopelessness by actively but unconsciously projecting a standstill in time into the analyst, the feeling "as if time stands still" as described in the case material. In this way, they induce a state of deadness in the analyst, who over long periods of time is present physically but is psychically inaccessible for the analysand as well as for the analyst him- or herself. In my opinion, this is a central aspect of the NTR although an appropriate appreciation of this aspect is lacking in the analytic literature on NTR.

This "procedure" is twofold: On the one hand, it serves to excessively evacuate by projective identification the analysand's inner tension, death fears, agony, and feeling of nothingness into the analyst, so that the analysand no longer needs to feel the "nameless dread" of the abyss of hopelessness and fear of annihilation. This aspect of negation has been extensively discussed in the psychoanalytic literature in relation to the NTR.

On the other hand, the ability to work this existential problem through is only made possible via the projection of these states into the analyst. However, it is crucial that analysts do not reproject those states by (premature or unsuitable) interpretations for their own defense. But analysts should be able to allow themselves to be used as a container and to work on their countertransference, using their understanding of the transference–countertransference relation. It is this aspect that is constructive and one that potentially gets the therapeutic process going again. As noted earlier, it has been completely disregarded in the literature on the NTR, causes serious misunderstandings between analysts and patients, and can lead to retraumatization and the abrupt termination of the analysis.

I have elaborated on the theory and illustrated in the case study how and by which mechanisms the experience is induced in the analyst "as if time were standing still": by the withdrawal of the libidinal-aggressive cathexis from the object and the self, disobjectualization, the phantasized fusion with the object, imitation, and the idealization of the omnipotent, destructive parts of the self. The interaction between the mechanisms described here leads to the destruction of the relation to future and past, which results in the breakdown of the ability to imagine and to anticipate an end of the unbearable state or condition with the help of an object that is capable and willing to act as a container. However, if an end to this state remains unimaginable, then the experience of time standing still remains immutable.

It is precisely through phenomena of time standing still that "that past which"—to paraphrase Racher's words "never really became past" (de Simone, 1997, p. 19), but also a past that cannot be remembered is brought into the present in the analytic relationship. Only in this specific present can this past be interpreted and made available for analytic work, symbolized, and returned into the natural flow of time, but only if it has been understood in the transference.

Above all, it appears that the constructive aspect has been disregarded in the discussion of the NTR, which is already evident in the term *negative therapeutic reaction*. Perhaps this expresses the therapists' understandable disappointment and often enough their resignation because they can only understand the phenomenon they observe and the experiences they often suffer exclusively from the perspective of refusal and negation instead of seeing the constructive, hopeful side of this phenomenon, which patients unconsciously hide from therapists as well as from themselves—for very good reasons. These thoughts concerning the positive aspect of time standstill are my contribution toward a better understanding of the phenomenon known as NTR.

Notes

1. This chapter appeared in an early version as "Time Stands Still in Tearing Haste: A Psychoanalytic Case Study on Early Trauma and the Experience of Time," *Psyche, 58*(4), 2004, pp. 293–320. Translations by Regina Hermans, Dipl. Psych.
2. In this chapter, I do not explicitly deal with thoughts concerning the effects of real traumatizations on the way in which time is experienced. As a rule, victims of severe traumatizations can consciously describe how time stands still with respect to the experience of a traumatic intrusion. However, in cases of severe, early traumatizations during a period of development prior to the consolidation of the psychic apparatus, the experience of time standing still remains unconscious and as such presents itself during the analytic process as a phenomenon which is experienced as a blockade and is very difficult to access.
3. For the sake of brevity, I will now refer to this phenomenon as *time standstill*, although I am aware of the fact that time as such cannot stand still, other than perhaps in the unconscious idea of one's own death, which is quite possibly symbolized in the standstill in time (e.g., self-portrait by Edvard Munch, in which he portrayed himself as an old man next to a clock without hands).
4. For the sake of simplicity, I will from now on refer to the experience of satisfaction and deficit, tacitly including the reduction of tension and the condition of tension.
5. Häflinger (1990) points out that, in this context, future represents the earliest perspective of time.
6. Hartocollis (1983) emphatically points this out by referring to Loewald's thoughts pertaining to this problem.
7. Bick (1968) expresses similar thoughts: "The need for a containing object would seem, in the infantile unintegrated state, to produce a frantic search for an object—a light, a voice, a smell, or other sensual object—which can hold the attention and thereby be experienced, momentarily at least, as holding the parts of the personality together. The optimal object is the nipple in the mouth, together with the holding and talking and familiar smelling mother" (p. 484). From Bick's perspective, this "protecting object" is experienced concretely as a kind of skin. When the original "skin function" is disturbed, a "second skin" is developed, "through which dependence on the object is replaced by a pseudo-independence, by the inappropriate use of certain mental functions, or perhaps innate talents, for the purpose of creating a substitute for this skin container function" (p. 484). With my analysand this second skin function is facilitated by his ceaseless, at times almost uninterrupted talking, although one can say that he has a gift in his ability to be "inventive" in a fascinating way.
8. In this context, I think that the thoughts Freud (1925) expressed in his short paper on the *Wunderblock* (Magic chart), about the discontinuous way that the Pcpt-Cs.

system works are of theoretical and outstanding central importance. This is important insomuch as it is through this defense of the complete withdrawal of cathexis from the object that the emergence or development of the concept of time is prevented and under certain conditions leads to a fixation site for regression.

> On the Mystic Pad the writing vanishes every time the close contact is broken between the paper which receives the stimulus and the wax slab which preserves the impression. This agrees with a notion which I have long had about the method by which the perceptual apparatus of our mind functions, but which I have hitherto kept to myself. My theory was that cathectic innervations are sent out and withdrawn in rapid periodic impulses from within into the completely pervious system Pcpt.-Cs. So long as that system is cathected in this manner, it receives perceptions (which are accompanied by consciousness) and passes the excitation on to the unconscious mnemonic systems; but as soon as the cathexis is withdrawn, consciousness is extinguished and the functioning of the system comes to a standstill. It is as though the unconscious stretches out feelers, through the medium of the system Pcpt.-Cs., towards the external world and hastily withdraws them as soon as they have sampled the excitations coming from it. Thus the interruptions, which in the case of the Mystic Pad have an external origin, were attributed by my hypothesis to the discontinuity in the current of innervation; and the actual breaking of contact which occurs in the Mystic Pad was replaced in my theory by the periodic non-excitability of the perceptual system. I further had a suspicion that this discontinuous method of functioning of the system Pcpt.-Cs. lies at the bottom of the origin of the concept of time" (p. 231).

9. A list of primitive agonies (*anxiety* is not a strong enough term to convey the strength of this feeling). Suggested alternatives are:
   a. A return to an unintegrated state (defense: disintegration);
   b. Falling forever (defense: self-holding);
   c. Loss of psychosomatic collusion, failure of indwelling (defense: depersonalization.);
   d. Loss of sense of real (defense: exploitation of primary narcissism, etc.);
   e. Loss of capacity to relate to objects (defense: *autistic states, relating only to self-phenomena* [emphasis added]) (Winnicott, 1974, p. 103).
10. Thoughts on "nameless dread," a nameless terror which the baby feels when the mother cannot contain the baby's existential fear and give it back to him in a processed shape.
11. In terms of "making concrete through acting out," as described by Kogan (1992).
12. Bohleber (2000) refers to "Freud's concept of 'automatic fear.' The difference between this kind of fear and signal fear is that the individual is at the mercy of a nameless fear that cannot be localized. This fear is so primitive that it can only be described in economic terms" (p. 824).

References

Bach, S. (2001). On being forgotten and forgetting one's self. *Psychoanalytic Quarterly, 70*, 739–756.

Baruch, G. (1997). The manic defense. *International Journal of Psychoanalysis, 78*, 549–559.
Bick, E. (1968). The experience of the skin in early object relations. *International Journal of Psychoanalysis, 49*, 484–506.
Bion, W. R. (1959). Attacks on linking. *International Journal of Psychoanalysis, 40*, 308–315.
Bion, W. R. (1962). *Learning from experience*. London: Heinemann.
Bohleber, W. (2000). Die Entwicklung der Traumatheorie in der Psychoanalyse [The development of trauma theory in psychoanalysis]. *Psyche, 54*, 797–839.
Britton, R. (1989). The missing link. In R. Britton, M. Feldman, & E. O'Shaughnessy (Eds.), *The Oedipus complex today: Clinical implications* (pp. 83–102). London: Karnac.
Brockhaus Enzyklopädie (2002). Der Brockhaus multimedial 2002 premium [6 CDs]. Mannheim: Bibliographisches Institut &F. A. Brockhaus AG.
Colarusso, C. A. (1979). The development of time sense: From birth to object constancy. *International Journal of Psychoanalysis, 60*, 243–261.
Colarusso, C. A. (1987). The development of time sense: From object constancy to adolescence. *Journal of the American Psychoanalytic Association, 35*, 119–144.
De Simone, G. (1997). *Ending analysis: Theory and technique*. London: Karnac.
Freud, S. (1900). *The interpretation of dreams*. In J. Strachey (Ed. & Trans.), *The standard edition of the complete psychological works of Sigmund Freud* (Vols. 4 & 5). London: Hogarth Press.
Freud, S. (1914). On narcissism: An introduction. In J. Strachey (Ed. & Trans.), *The standard edition of the complete psychological works of Sigmund Freud* (Vol. 14, pp. 67–102). London: Hogarth Press.
Freud, S. (1918). From the History of an Infantile Neurosis. In J. Strachey (Ed. & Trans.), *The standard edition of the complete psychological works of Sigmund Freud* (Vol. 12. pp. 7–122). London: Hogarth Press.
Freud, S. (1920). Beyond the pleasure principle. In J. Strachey (Ed. & Trans.), *The standard edition of the complete psychological works of Sigmund Freud* (Vol. 18, pp. 1–64). London: Hogarth Press.
Freud, S. (1925). A note upon the "Mystic Writing-Pad." In J. Strachey (Ed. & Trans.), *The standard edition of the complete psychological works of Sigmund Freud* (Vol. 19, pp. 227–234). London: Hogarth Press.
Gaddini, E. (1969). On imitation. *International Journal of Psychoanalysis, 50*, 475–484.
Gaddini, E. (1998). *"Das Ich ist vor allem ein Körperliches": Beiträge zur Psychoanalyse der ersten Strukturen* ["The ego is first and foremost corporeal": A contribution to the psychoanalysis of the primary structures]. Tübingen, Germany: Edition Diskord.
Gerisch, B. (2002). Auch ich war in Arkadien: Der traumatische Einbruch in den idyllischen Raum [I too was in Arcadia: The traumatic drop in the idyllic area]. *Zeitschrift fur psychoanalytische Theorie und Praxis* [Journal of psychoanalytic theory and practice], *17*, 343–370).
Green, A. (1975). The analyst, symbolization and absence in the analytic setting. *International Journal of Psychoanalysis, 56*, 1–22.
Green, A. (1977). Conceptions of affect. *International Journal of Psychoanalysis, 58*, 129–156.
Gutwinski-Jeggle, J. (1992). Trauma und Zeiterleben [Trauma and the experience of time]. *Jahrbuch der Psychoanalyse* [Yearbook of psychoanalysis], 167–214.

Häflinger, U. (1990). Versuch einer Entwicklungslinie des Zeiterlebens [Development of an experimental line of time experience]. *Zeitschrift fur psychoanalytische Theorie und Praxis* [Journal of psychoanalytic theory and practice], *5,* 99–111.

Hartocollis, P. (1983). *Time and timelessness.* New York: International Universities Press.

Jones, E. (1927). The early development of female sexuality. *International Journal of Psychoanalysis, 8,* 459–472.

Klein, M. (1935). A contribution to the psychogenesis of manic-depressive states. *International Journal of Psychoanalysis, 16,* 145–174.

Klein, M. (1940). Mourning and its relation to manic-depressive states. *International Journal of Psychoanalysis, 21,* 125–153.

Klein, M. (1946). Notes on some schizoid mechanisms. *International Journal of Psychoanalysis, 27,* 99–110.

Kogan, I. (1992). From acting out to words and meaning. *International Journal of Psychoanalysis, 73,* 455–465.

Kostner, K. (Director). (1990). *Dances with wolves* [Motion picture]. United States: Tig Productions.

Laplanche, J. (1997). Ziele des psychoanalytischen Prozesses [The goal of psychoanalytic processes]. *Jahrbuch der Psychonalyse* [Yearbook of psychoanalysis], 93–116.

Loewald, H. W. (1972). The experience of time. *Psychoanalytic Study of the Child, 27,* 401–410.

Meltzer, D. (1981). The relation of splitting of attention to splitting of self and objects. *Contemporary Psychoanalysis, 17,* 232–238.

Modell, A. H. (1996). *Other times, other realities.* Cambridge, MA: Harvard University Press.

Rosenfeld, H. (1971). A clinical approach to the psychoanalytic theory of the life and death instincts: An investigation into the aggressive aspects of narcissism. *International Journal of Psychoanalysis, 52,* 169–178.

Schilder, P. (1936). Psychopathology of time. *Journal of Nervous and Mental Diseases, 83,* 530–546.

Schmithüsen, G. (2004). "Die Zeit steht still in rasender Eile": Eine psychoanalytische Einzelfallstudie zu frühem Trauma und Zeiterleben ["Time stands still in a tearing hurry": A psychoanalytic case study of early trauma and the experience of time]. *Psyche, 58,* 293–320.

Schneider, G. (2004). Die narzisstische Gefahr der Veränderung [The narcissistic threat of change] In K. A. Dreyer (Ed.), *Entwicklungen und Veränderungen: Aufgeben oder Aufgabe?* [Developments and changes: surrender or abandonment?] (pp. 47–65). Tagungsband.

Steiner, J. (1987). The interplay between pathological organizations and the paranoid-schizoid and depressive positions. *International Journal of Psychoanalysis, 68,* 69–80.

Steiner, J. (1993). *Psychic retreats: Pathological organizations in psychotic, neurotic and borderline patients.* London: Routledge.

Von Susani, C. (2010). Identitätsstörung und psychoanalytischer Prozeß [Identity disorder and the psycho-analytical process]. *Psyche*, 64, 481–504.

Winnicott, D. W. (1974). Fear of breakdown. *International Review of Psychoanalysis, 1,* 103–107.

Wurmser, L. (2009, January). *"Negative therapeutic reaction" and the compulsion to disappoint the other.* Paper presented at the American Psychoanalytic Association Winter Meeting, New York.

4

NEGATIVE THERAPEUTIC REACTION IN THE LIGHT OF OBJECT RELATIONS THEORY

Mathias Hirsch

The negative therapeutic reaction, as a paradoxical exacerbation of symptoms following a correct interpretation or any other event seen as progress in analysis or therapy, was discovered by Freud (1923). It was attributed by him to unconscious feelings of guilt because, according to him, the patient needed the illness to satisfy his or her need for punishment. This idea is based on the concept of instinctual drive: What requires punishment is the oedipal crime. However, progress in therapy may also be understood as separation from the dependency on internal objects opposing progress and the development of autonomy. Such departure from parental objects also causes feelings of guilt, namely separation guilt. A patient of Modell (1965) was not allowed to feel any better because, as he believed, his mother would otherwise have killed herself. The mother of a patient of mine firmly insisted on continuing to pay the patient a monthly allowance although the latter had long terminated her university studies and was earning a good salary. When the patient refused to accept the money, her mother declared desperately: "If I can't give it to you any longer, my life is without meaning, I will kill myself then." What connects the phenomenon of the negative therapeutic reaction with today's topical issue of trauma is thus the great difficulty traumatized persons have separating from the very objects once responsible for the trauma. Unfortunately, there is the apparent paradox that children receiving sufficient love and respect are able to separate more easily, whereas children who were treated badly remain in greater dependency. According to Bowlby, "bitten lambs stay longer with the mother sheep."

Freud (1916) first spoke of an unconscious feeling of guilt being responsible for "being wrecked by success." Later, on the other hand, when analyzing the "Wolf Man" (Freud, 1918), he observed a negativistic attitude similar to that of a small child's defiant "No," before describing and defining the negative therapeutic reaction in *The Ego and the Id* (1923): In certain persons every partial solution in analysis would paradoxically result in an exacerbation of symptoms. According to him, this is not so much due to defiance toward the doctor and fixation on gain from illness, but mainly to "a feeling of guilt which is finding its satisfaction in the illness and refuses to give up the punishment of suffering" (p. 49). The feeling of guilt is unconscious, the patient does not feel guilty him- or herself; it is expressed as resistance to progress, to recovery. Punishment through illness is needed; today one can add that punishment is imposed by an object (and the corresponding superego) not well-intentioned toward the child and hindering its further development.

Freud, therefore, suggested two possible motivations of the negative therapeutic reaction: on the one hand, the patient's negativistic "No" to the analyst's correct interpretation, and on the other hand, the strange adherence to the illness due to a feeling of guilt emanating from a superego, which the function of punishing is also ascribed to. He therewith laid the foundation for an object relations view. For the formation of the superego is a first conceptualization of the introjective development of internal object representations, precipitates also real characteristics, and influences of external objects, such as parents in particular, as stated by Freud (1924; cf. Hirsch, 1995, 1997).

In line with its double nature, two main trends may be found for the negative therapeutic reaction in the literature, both of which are attributable to Freud: first, the patient's defiant "No" to the analysis, the negativism, which is seen as a desire for autonomy, as defense against dependency (the Wolf Man); second, the feeling of guilt which corresponds to an object relationship internalized through introjection and the dependency thereon. These opposing aims cannot, however, be integrated into a concept. The ability to say "No" would, after all, mean a "success" compared to the earlier neurotic dependency. Or does the negative therapeutic reaction mean a relapse into former dependencies (i.e., the inability to bear progress represented by successful therapy)?

For my contribution to the discussion of the negative therapeutic reaction, I would like to propose a process concerning the change in the analyst's object quality: At first, analysis and analyst are an alternative "good" object from which comes a request to separate from the internalized "bad," clutching, and manipulative object. If this temptation to separate on the one hand and the threat of separation on the other hand get too strong, the analyst assumes exactly the manipulative character of the internalized object; the vehement transference, particularly projection, to the analyst makes him a threatening object from which distancing is necessary and possible because, secretly, a return is intended to the originally "bad" object represented in the symptoms (which are getting stronger), in self-destroying behavior (e.g., addiction, eating disorders) or in corresponding partner relationships. The danger is that at this point through projective identification the analyst can no longer control his or her countertransference feelings which, when acted out, make the analyst in fact a "bad" object.

Negative Therapeutic Reaction as Return to the "Old" Object and as Expression of Dependency from It

Even if the idea of autonomy seems to be at the center of discussion in the literature on the negative therapeutic reaction, starting with Anna Freud (1952), it is for me a clear expression of the dependency on a strong, negative, internal object preventing progress and success (also in analysis) and prohibiting individuation (cf. Mueller-Pozzi, 1985). Progress in analysis means a threat of separation that is met with anxiety. In his paper on the negative therapeutic reaction, Asch (1976) clearly states in this sense: "Such patients respond to this part of their superego as if it were an object. They attempt to maintain a relationship with a special kind of powerful mother by internalizing her" (p. 386). This is also how one has to understand Fairbairn's (1952) observation that the negative therapeutic reaction actually occurs when analysis eases the patient's feelings of guilt (i.e., weakens or does away with the connection to the internal object). Freud (1926) speaks of the "protection of the superego" in connection with object loss anxiety, the superego as introjected object protects against a feeling of abandonment. In contrast to the oedipal tendencies, the unconscious feeling of guilt is directed against and would thus prevent a success in analysis. Asch (1976) speaks of the "pre-oedipal crime" which, in the last analysis, is the wish to give up the close ties with the mother, created by real emotional exploitation, and its object representation; Asch returns here to "separation guilt," first formulated by Modell (1965). To the aspect of the feared separation from the mother object, Kernberg (1971) further adds the fear of its being destroyed by successful therapy:

> The patient identified himself unconsciously with an extremely destructive mother image, and his refusal to improve reflected his fear that improvement meant separation from mother and destroying her. At the same time, he deflected his rage against his mother onto himself and all those who tried to help him. The self-destructiveness was seen as a combination of … an expression of diffuse aggression, identification with a sadistic mother image, envious hatred of all those who were not in such a slave's position, fear of mother's punishment if he tried to free himself from her, and fear for her life if any change occurred. (p. 611)

Several authors view the negative therapeutic reaction as being close to fantasies of omnipotence (Novick & Novick, 1991), narcissistic object relations (Rosenfeld, 1987), and masochism (Valenstein, 1973). Dependency on internalized objects is involved in all of these phenomena; even grandiosity merely gives itself an appearance of independence as compensation. In masochism, pain represents the motherly object and the bond with her, as convincingly elaborated by Valenstein (1973): "The negative affect state representing the missing or pain-provoking primary object" (p. 172). Valenstein also describes the antagonism in masochism between the early objects represented by the pain and possible new or alternative social objects: "Early affects are predominantly painful and as such recur consistently, crystallizing in the direction of attachment to pain and distrust of objects" (p. 178). The analyst would be such an "object."

Clinging to the primary object also protects against the elementary fear of existential emptiness following separation, an emptiness that would arise because a sufficiently good motherly relationship could not be introjected; therefore an alternative, supporting relationship is not conceivable. Fear of emptiness would also explain the great difficulty in successfully giving up the relationship with the "old" destructive object for a new therapeutic one. According to André Green (quoted in Kittler, 1991) "the stubborn clinging to a bad internal object" is expressed "in a negative therapeutic reaction as if what is being feared is the interval between the loss of the bad object and its replacement by a good object" (p. 134). This shows quite clearly that these are object happenings and that the negative therapeutic reaction can be seen as a defensive reaction to commencing a new, alternative relationship. The patient is required to perform two movements at the same time: to separate him- or herself from the old object, and to enter into a relationship with the new object. In a way, this is a paradox: Emancipation (freedom) from the old object is demanded, which may be connected with a new bond, a dependency that is possibly too strong. The analyst would thus be experienced as a kind of seducer who promises freedom but also threatens abusively to devour just like the primary object. This form of relationship disorder, an inability to love, is the anxiety to experience in love a deindividuating union. It causes the subject to stay at home so to speak, which means staying with the mother imago the patient was originally dependent on. Loneliness, pain, and known illnesses are preferred to the new and unknown.

It is exactly in situations where there is a threshold reached in someone's development in life that similar paradoxical phenomena can be found; these are to prevent a person from crossing a threshold that means both separation as well as a fresh start (e.g., examination anxiety and hypochondria; Hirsch, 1997, 2003). Examination anxiety is consciously experienced as the fear of failing an exam; on closer inspection, however, one discovers a similarly great fear of passing the exam and being forced to cross the said threshold, to build up a new identity. Similarly, hypochondria is frequently caused by crossing a threshold such as marriage, an examination, or the building or buying of a house in particular (Hirsch, 2006).

Both symptom complexes can be understood as acting out the refusal to develop further. In all these paradoxical phenomena, the acting out is in the foreground, as pointed out by Olinick (1964); after all, the fact that symptoms get stronger in the negative therapeutic reaction also indicates self-destructive acting out.

An eating disorder symptom was acted out in the following scene from the therapy of a bulimic patient, Melanie; I explained the paradoxical movement of the negative therapeutic reaction the patient had unconsciously succumbed to by means of an example of another patient who had experienced the same issue.

Melanie reported that she was informed by an assistant professor at the university she attended that her thesis was all right so far, that she was on the right track, that everything would be okay. On the one hand, she was glad; on the other hand, she felt like getting ill, she wouldn't do any sports today (actually she did sports every day to feel well, to feel she had achieved something). She knew exactly that not doing any sports would make her feel very bad. She even looked forward to the group (for the first time in 2 years, the group meant something good to her). She had not met her boyfriend in the evening although it would have been possible, and had experienced an eating attack followed by vomiting that she had not had for a long time. She had a terribly bad conscience then, reproaching and accusing herself, but finally said to herself: "You also have to see, Melanie, that it got much less with puking." Two superego voices were thus negotiating.

I pointed out her positive attitude toward the group, but she said it had nothing to do with the group because she had actually looked forward to it. I said that this was the very thing, that she had to destroy something good (namely her successful studies and the group); in order to enable her to realize this, I told her the drastic example of a patient, a diabetic, who through her eating/vomiting attacks endangered her life at a time when bulimia had not yet been a known and common disease. This patient had ruined the first interview, in which I felt that I had understood her, was in contact with her, by which she was able to have feelings and could weep, by going into the café across the street directly after the interview to devour large quantities of cream cake which she had to vomit afterwards. Having told her story without any affect at all, just like an observer of herself, Melanie now started to weep violently and understood: She was not allowed to be good, she was not allowed to be successful, and she was extremely afraid of the end of her studies once she had submitted her thesis in 5 weeks; she constantly thought: "Melanie, I will be proud of you once I have passed the exam, but at night I will be puking...." She is splitting herself: one superego part will be proud of her, but another superego part will destroy everything, as if one part of her mother would say: "Melanie, the whole family and I are so proud of you, of your academic career, the first one in our family so far, but only as long as you are doing that for us and staying with us; as you wish, however, to be independent, you are a bad daughter…." When I said this to her, adding that when her mother says she would be proud of her, she "could puke on it," she replied that yes, in her mother's eyes she was bad, her mother was complaining that she had not seen her (while Melanie was in the exam situation), that she was a bad daughter, and had changed for the negative (through the therapy!). Her mother would not understand her at all; in May when the daughter could not avoid asking her mother for money (after the oral exams, which she had done very well in), her mother had said: "If you need money, stop your studies."

I understand the eating attack after a "good session" as an affront to the therapy and as a return to the ambivalently needed as well as rejected primary mother object.

Negative Therapeutic Reaction as Attempt at Autonomy

It has probably become clear thus far that, in my view, the negative therapeutic reaction is not so much an expression of a step toward autonomy but, on the contrary, a failed separation. Relapsing into stronger symptoms and destructive behavior means returning to equivalents of the destructive internal objects from which the analysis intends to free the patient. Nevertheless, there is quite obviously a "No" in the negative therapeutic reaction against a "bad" devouring object in the transference; "this is the negativism that is a sine qua non of the [negative therapeutic] reaction" (Olinick 1964, p. 540). The second red thread (in addition to the feeling of guilt) running through the history of the negative therapeutic reaction concept is negativism; it starts with Freud (1918) comparing the negative therapeutic reaction to a child's defiant "No." Ursula Grunert (1979) describes the function of saying "No" as serving the attempt at autonomy (Spitz, 1957) and formulates: "The negative therapeutic reaction is the … gesture of disassociating oneself, of 'No,' which corresponds to the different phases of the process of separation" (p. 3). Finally, Pontalis (1980) more or less exalts the autonomy manifesting itself in the negative therapeutic reaction: "The negative therapeutic reaction thus appears as resistance, but in a vital, heroic sense of the expression, so to speak, eye to eye with the one who merely assures us to wish for our best, while we only ask to breathe in fresh air" (p. 36). However, the authors speaking of autonomy and ego strength apparently fail to see that there is something negative in the definition of the negative therapeutic reaction, namely the worsening of the symptoms. There is above all the self-destructive acting out patients feel forced to, patients who in my opinion are not at all able freely and autonomously to decide for themselves a constructive opposition against the analytic object. What seems to be an expression of autonomy could rather belong to the fields of omnipotence and masochism. To me, the patient's "No" does not seem to start individuation in any way (Grunert, 1979); rather, it corresponds to a masochistic triumph along the lines of: "It serves my mother right if my fingers get frostbitten, why doesn't she buy me any gloves?"

Negative Transference and Projective Identification

In the transference at any rate the analyst turns into the omnipotent, threatening, devouring maternal object who prevents the exercise of free will and an independent identity, irrespective of whether the negativist protest, which frequently leads to breaking off the analysis, occurs on the grounds of autonomy or as a masochistic triumph. But neither Olinick (1964) nor Schubart (1989), as advocates of the autonomy hypothesis, mention how the characteristic switch in the quality of the relationship comes about.

I would like to try to explain how the change in the quality of the relationship in analysis can be understood. As I see it, such patients (and their corresponding identity-preventing introject, respectively) cannot bear that an object, letting them have their way, respects their true needs. This is because they feel abandoned as they know only sadistic objects, which they can, however, rely on, so to speak. In their masochistic fantasies, the well-meaning object is therefore transformed into a bad object despising and attacking them because it is not the usual, reliable one.

Moreover, the demand in analysis to separate from the destructive introjects leads to a massive threat of separation. Due to this request for development and autonomy, inherent in psychoanalysis, the therapeutic object is seen by the traumatized, masochistic patient as having a double nature: On the one hand, it promises freedom from the identity-preventing, "old," internalized object; on the other hand, it becomes precisely the same manipulative object in the transference once the separation process has reached a certain stage in the analytic work. The task would be to try to prevent an exacerbation of symptoms and, in the worst case, an imminent breakup of the therapy by an interpretation disclosing the dynamics; this may be successful, or, despite the analyst's extensive inner calm, nevertheless lead to analysis being broken off irreversibly. The danger is that through projective identification the analyst feels an aggressive impulse to keep the patient at any cost (namely at the cost of giving up his or her analytic attitude), wishing to convince the analysand in an authoritarian manner that the therapy is good, that she or he has to stay. It is at that point that the therapist or analyst would in fact become the pursuing, identity-preventing maternal object, rather than the alternative that he or she aims to be, and the patient would be right in turning away. The risk of such a destructive mistake through unconscious "co-acting" as a result of the negative therapeutic reaction is, in my view, the reason why it has been emphasized so frequently in the literature that the negative therapeutic reaction would be an expression of a mutual relationship, that one could not know whether the patient's "No" was constructive or destructive. I believe, however, that one can know or at least guess it from the destructive nature of the worsening symptoms and the premature termination respectively.

An Attempt at Integrating both Hypotheses

Two authors representing the autonomy hypothesis mention the double character of the patient's "No" in passing but without elaborating it. Olinick (1964) believes that the "No" rejecting a correct interpretation would pacify the superego; for me, this is an indication of the binding to the object representation. Grunert (1979), too, cannot apply the autonomy hypothesis to all of the cases presented by her; in one case the author concedes a hidden desire for symbiosis. In my view, a possible way to understand the double nature of the negative therapeutic reaction seems to be the application of Wurmser's (1990) concept of the splitting of the superego. According to this concept there are various superego introjects making contradictory requests (e.g., one part may propagate autonomy as a high value, while the other part demands dependency); this means a guilt–shame conflict. In a patient with extreme exam problems, a first introject, a "voice in her head" reproaching her with doing nothing, demanded that she should try hard. A second introject was hostile in the sense that it thought she was not capable of being successful, thereby discouraging her. Which of the demands made by the introjects was she to fulfill? Having success was not okay with the second introject, doing nothing meant a hostile first introject. It could be that the negative therapeutic reaction, in its process as proposed by me, constitutes a way to circumvent this conflict: At first, the independence party is calmed by the desire for therapy; then, however, with the dependency party growing, the representation of independence (alternative object, therapy) is made the representation of dependency (and would contribute to it through projective identification). The aggressive disassociation now possible in the form of the negative therapeutic reaction is permitted by both introjects; the dependency representation can be sure that the subject will return to it, and the independency party is content with the disassociation from a new object.

In my opinion, the concept of the negative therapeutic reaction remains justified if used, as stated above, in connection with other apparently paradoxical phenomena, such as examination anxiety, hypochondria, and relationship disorders (ambivalent fear of intimacy) (Hirsch, 2003). Olinick (1964) has presented a limited definition of the negative therapeutic reaction in the sense of a patient's paradoxical reaction to a basically beneficial intervention by the analyst, thus giving it some justification as a clinical phenomenon.

My contribution to the extensive discussion of the negative therapeutic reaction aims at explaining the mostly abrupt change in the transference relationship from a positive to a negative one. As I see it, the therapeutic object seems to become a hostile object through negative transference and projective identification because the demand for separation from the destructive internalized object is too much. The patient turns the alternative object into a new edition of the old one, which he secretly returns to by loudly disassociating from the new one. Freud (1923) saw the negative therapeutic reaction mainly as the expression of a feeling of guilt, caused by a superegolike introject (as we would say today), whose power, he estimated, was rather high when compared to the power of analysis. The view prevailing in the literature emphasizes the autonomy, the individual's ego strength, which defends itself against a negative object in the transference, an optimistic view in comparison to Freud's. There seems to be a dialectic combination: Staying in analysis would mean to have success, to separate from the mother imago. On the other side, breaking off therapy would (also) mean to be able to leave aggressively (the negative mother imago in the transference), but at the same time to give up being successful, and thereby to return to the mother imago! My view is that the negative therapeutic reaction does not mean autonomy but its refusal returns to Freud's pessimism. However, it perhaps helps not to assume the hostile attitude caused by the projective identification, an attitude seen by the patient as the coming true of her projections in reality and as justification for her inability to grasp the opportunity for separation offered by analysis.

References

Asch, S. S. (1976). Varieties of negative therapeutic reaction and problems of technique. *Journal of the American Psychoanalytic Association, 24*, 383–407.

Fairbairn, W. R. D. (1952). *Psychoanalytic studies of the personality.* London: Routledge & Kegan Paul.

Freud, A. (1952). A connection between the states of negativism and of emotional surrender. *International Journal of Psychoanalysis, 33*, 265.

Freud, S. (1916). Some character types met with in psychoanalytic work. In J. Strachey (Ed. & Trans.), *The standard edition of the complete psychological works of Sigmund Freud* (Vol. 14, pp. 309–333). London: Hogarth Press.

Freud, S. (1918). From the history of an infantile neurosis. In J. Strachey (Ed. & Trans.), *The standard edition of the complete psychological works of Sigmund Freud* (Vol. 17, pp. 3–123). London: Hogarth Press.

Freud, S. (1923). The ego and the id. In J. Strachey (Ed. & Trans.), *The standard edition of the complete psychological works of Sigmund Freud* (Vol. 19, pp. 3–66). London: Hogarth Press.

Freud, S. (1924). The economic problem of masochism. In J. Strachey (Ed. & Trans.), *The standard edition of the complete psychological works of Sigmund Freud* (Vol. 19, pp. 157–170). London: Hogarth Press.

Freud, S. (1926). Inhibitions, symptoms, and anxiety. In J. Strachey (Ed. & Trans.), *The standard edition of the complete psychological works of Sigmund Freud* (Vol. 20, pp. 77–175). London: Hogarth Press.

Grunert, U. (1979). Die negative therapeutische Reaktion als Ausdruck einer Stoerung im Losloesungs- und Individuationsprozess [The negative therapeutic reaction as a sign of disturbance in the separation-individuation process]. *Psyche, 33*, 1–28.

Hirsch, M. (1995). Fremdkoerper im Selbst: Introjektion von Verlust und traumatischer Gewalt [A foreign body in the self: Introjection of loss and traumatic violence]. *Jahrbuch Psychoanalyse* [Yearbook of psychoanalysis], *35*, 123–151.

Hirsch, M. (1997). *Schuld und Schuldgefühl: Zur Psychoanalyse von Trauma und Introjekt* [Guilt and feeling of guilt: The psychoanalysis of trauma and introject]. Goettingen, Germany: Vandenhoeck & Ruprecht.

Hirsch, M. (2003). Das hypochondrische Prinzip: zur Psychodynamik der Hypochondrie und verwandter Erscheinungen [The hypochondriac principle in the psychodynamics of hypochondriasis and related phenomena]. In B. Nissen (Ed.), *Hypochondrie: Eine psychoanalytische Bestandsaufnahme* [Hypochondria: A psychoanalytic inventory] (pp. 71–104). Giessen, Germany: Psychosozial-Verlag.

Hirsch, M. (2006). *Das Haus: Symbol für Leben und Tod, Freiheit und Abhängigkeit* [The house: A symbol for love and death, freedom and dependence]. Giessen, Germany: Psychosozial-Verlag.

Kernberg, O. F. (1971). Prognostic considerations regarding borderline personality organization. *Journal of the American Psychoanalytic Association, 19*, 595–635.

Kittler, E. (1991). Gedanken zum Werke von André Green [Thoughts on the works of André Green]. *Jahrbuch Psychoanalyse* [Yearbook of psychoanalysis], *28*, 109–147.

Modell, A. H. (1965). On having the right to a life: An aspect of the superego's development. *International Journal of Psychoanalysis, 46*, 323–331.

Mueller-Pozzi, H. (1985). Identifikation und Konflikt: Die Angst vor Liebesverlust und der Verzicht auf Identifikation [Identification and Conflict: The fear of losing love and the lack of identification]. *Psyche, 39*, 877–904.

Novick, J., & Novick, K. K. (1991). Some comments on masochism and the delusion of omnipotence from a developmental perspective. *Journal of the American Psychoanalytic Association, 39*, 307–331.

Olinick, S. L. (1964). The negative therapeutic reaction. *International Journal of Psychoanalysis, 45*, 540–548.

Pontalis, J. B. (1980): Die negative therapeutische Reaktion: Definitionsversuch [The negative therapeutic reaction: Trial of definition]. *European Psychoanalyical Federation Bulletin, 15*, 23–26.

Rosenfeld, H. (1987). *Impasse and interpretation: Therapeutic and anti-therapeutic factors in the psychoanalytical treatment of psychotic, borderline, and neurotic patients*. London: Tavistock.

Schubart, W. (1989). Bemerkungen zum Konzept der sogenannten negativen therapeutischen Reaktion [Comments on the concept of the so-called negative therapeutic reaction]. *Psyche, 43*, 1071–1093.

Spitz, R. (1957). *No and yes: On the genesis of human communication*. New York: International Universities Press.

Valenstein, A. F. (1973). On attachment to painful feelings and the negative therapeutic reaction. *Psychoanalytic Study of the Child*, *28*, 365–392.

Wurmser, L. (1990). Ueber-Ich- und Abwehranalyse einer masochistischen Perversion [Superego and a masochistic perversion defense analysis]. *Jahrbuch Psychoanalyse* [Yearbook of psychoanalysis], *26*, 135–214.

5

"I HAVE TO DESTROY EVERYTHING I LOVE"

Totalitarian Conscience—Acted Out and Understood[1]

Heidrun Jarass

When we discussed my contribution to this book, I immediately thought of a patient—I will call him Peter—who has been in psychotherapy with me for 12 years. He had developed quite well during treatment, and I imagined that it would not be too hard to present the therapeutic process. How naïve I was! Only when I started trying to tease out a single strand, a coherent "red thread" in the write-up, did I perceive the challenge. As I reviewed the treatment process through my notes, I saw myself time and again confronted with separate pieces that by themselves looked valuable and meaningful. However, when I wanted to join them into a consistent description of process everything crumbled again into separate, disjointed pieces. Thus the case description became, like the treatment itself, a hard piece of mental work where I had to wrestle continuously to integrate the material.

At first, I ascribed this difficulty to the severity of the patient's disturbance, but by and by I recognized, during my own struggle with the treatment process, how much this also touched on my own inner conflicts about our German Nazi past. Thus my head, or rather my capacity to think, had not only to survive all the renewed assaults by my patient, so to speak, but I saw myself confronted, time and again, with my own inner wall of silence surrounding my postwar childhood. Just recently I participated in a conference about the history of psychoanalysis in Germany. Again I saw myself facing the damage caused to psychoanalysis by our Nazi past. Once more it became very clear to me how much we needed and still need ambassadors from abroad who, in the encounter and the collaboration with us, bring us something back of what had been lost because of those events. In my work with Peter, too, the view from the outside was necessary time and again, and I am very grateful to Léon Wurmser for our fruitful exchange: Now to my patient.

At the suggestion of his uncle, Peter came to me in the winter of 1999. He was still hospitalized at a psychiatric facility. While there, he had received medication that had no positive effect upon his symptoms, but rather caused a life-threatening hepatic coma.

During our first interview, Peter appeared as if he were, due to the drug effect, rigid in his motor functions and affectively muted. He told me at once that he was suffering from a "schizoaffective disorder," and by a skillful deployment of psychiatric vocabulary, he engaged in a diagnostic categorization of his disease as if it did not have anything to do with him, but with a third person in the room. Asked how he himself interpreted his problems, he replied that he felt cursed and condemned by God and he mentioned a few things about his father. For me the most important sentences in this first encounter were: "What was missing at home was emotional warmth. This is my main problem: that I am so fish-blooded. The psychiatrists speak of flattened affect."

I experienced him, in contrast to his self-perception, as warm, eager for contact, rather extroverted, and "sensual," in the meaning of "using his five senses." He seemed to me to be intelligent and differentiated, but clearly suffering from his inner isolation. Nevertheless he succeeded in reaching me nonverbally. At first glance, his appearance was that of an attractive, tall, strong, and well-dressed man. Only when looking more closely did I notice that his pants had a glossy shine in some spots and were already threadbare in others, and that he had trampled down his slippers because they were too small for his feet. Later I learned that they belonged to his father.

In a later session, Peter spoke about disquieting and tormenting obsessive thoughts: "Everything that I love I have to destroy." Specifically, he thought he would have to cut off the heads of women he felt attracted to, and he was also afraid that he might be gay, passive, and womanish. Moreover, he was haunted by strongly disgusting images, obsessions that he should ingest semen from father figures in order to find a stable male identity (he actually did try to carry them out): "As in a fairy tale, I probably have to go out and learn how to be scared." At the same time, he was terrified that I would send him away because of the content of his fantasies. These somewhat disconnected thoughts may reflect his fragmented identity and his focus on having something to *do*.

Before I go on, I have to insert some biographical details as they were presented to me at that time. Peter is the second of two children of his married parents, and he grew up on a large former farm in rural Bavaria. His father is said to be a gifted physicist and chair of a department in a university. His mother, 16 years her husband's junior, had met him when she became his assistant. Peter experienced his father as completely unreachable; he spoke little about his mother. From the first few utterances about her, the image arose in me of an unempathic, malicious, and cold woman. He mentioned his brother, 3 years his senior, as someone he wanted to be like, and he described the relationship with father and brother as idyllic.

In particular, his brother had been very important for him because, in contrast to Peter, he was rather extroverted and had many friends. Peter saw himself as his brother's appendage. When the brother left high school after graduation, Peter withdrew completely, believing that without him he could not play any role anymore with his peers. He also was envious of his brother's professional success as an engineer.

Yet, his brother also seemed to suffer from extremely severe conflicts. He rode his motorcycle so aggressively that he had a catastrophic accident, sustaining massive bone fractures and ultimately, because of persistent and uncontrollable infections, losing one leg to amputation. When he confronted this handicap, in an attempt at suicide he threw himself out of a high window at the clinic and was now paraplegic. However, it is necessary to insert here that at a later stage of treatment, it emerged that his brother's handicap appeared less and less dramatically prominent, whether because of intensive rehabilitative efforts or because of Peter's altered perceptions.

About his parents Peter said that their attitude was that children should never be aware of their elders' feelings. He had never heard a loud or emotional word from them. When the father got angry he disappeared into the basement, where they could hear his rumbling; they guessed he might be chopping wood. The children sat anxiously in their room feeling guilty because they assumed they had once again done something wrong. Eventually, the father reemerged from the cellar red in the face from rage, heated and panting, and hid behind the newspaper until all traces of the rage had vanished.

Peter also could not detect any educational ideology in his parents. There were no limits; the children could do and not do whatever they wanted.

In contrast to how he felt inside the parental home, Peter always felt very well playing outside. There he could forget everything and fully immerse himself in his fantasy world.

Although judged by his teachers as intelligent and gifted, Peter's grades were mediocre. He often sat in class looking out the window: "I watched huge steam shovels as they excavated a gravel pit. The rhythmical swinging of the giant shovels, the deep roaring of the motors—those things fascinated me."

From his 16th year on, he frequently suffered from severe depression and dysmorphophobia. He called it his "cheek disease" and believed that his cheeks were strongly swollen and his face distorted, so that he could not speak anymore. At that time, he often withdrew into bed, preferably his father's bed, where he then remained in a fetal position: "There I could bear it best," he said, imagining: "My bed is my grave. I only have to nail it shut. Simply to go on lying there. Not to get up anymore. To soil the bed. To wait until I die, until somebody would redeem me. What holds me back from doing something to myself, is the idea that I would be reborn as a worm or a cockroach."

After graduating from high school, Peter apprenticed as a carpenter, and at 26 he met his first steady girlfriend. She moved to an Austrian city for her medical studies, and, after a few months, he followed her. There he found work in a carpenter's workshop, but he argued frequently with his superior: "He put himself up as the boss without creditably filling that role." Peter was fired.

In his family, he had often heard that he was too bright to work as an artisan, and thus, after the loss of his job, he started looking for an alternative and hit upon psychology. In his relationship with his girlfriend, he felt very inferior and withdrew more and more from her and from his other contacts. Finally they separated, which hit him very hard. He could not understand what was happening within himself and had many pressing questions, but no answers about his inner state. He looked for them by reading psychological text books. More and more his suspicion intensified that he might be homosexual. He drifted ever more deeply into those fantasies, described above, about having to imbibe semen.

Peter gave up studying and worked as a bicycle courier. Apart from this he had no contacts. He developed sleeping disorders and often had states "where I was fantasizing and at the same time dreaming." Eventually he turned to a clinic for help; they gave him antidepressants and later admitted him.

After discharge, Peter was expected to continue the psychotherapy that he had started as an inpatient, but had to change therapists because the physician who had treated him in the clinic and whom he had trusted was not covered by his insurance. Not long after that, Peter broke off the ambulatory psychotherapy because he experienced the new "unloved" therapist as unreachable just like his father, and he felt overwhelmed and terrified by his aggressive, "crazy" feelings toward him. He was counseled to return to his hometown because of the better opportunities for rehabilitation, yet he had to stay in psychiatric inpatient treatment for another 9 months before contacting me.

At first we agreed upon probationary treatment. I wanted to get a sense of whether he was interested in therapeutic work of some duration or if his engagement would tip over into passivity at the first sign of frustration. He had already broken off two therapies, with the explanation that he had become "psychotic" and had developed thought disorders.

After his probationary treatment had been approved by insurance, Peter fell into a hypomanic state. I suggested to him that this confirmed what we already knew: It was difficult for him to tolerate ambivalent feelings. His previous therapist had already labeled him "psychotic," which served to protect him against the relationship. He responded: "When you are understood you become an entirely normal mammal."

During his probationary therapy, some things started sorting themselves out, but this state seemed to Peter unstable and precarious. He met his eventual wife, and she was soon pregnant with their first child. After his son's birth, Peter wanted to start studying some technical field that was close to the area of his father's competence. While his wife worked to support the family he took over the care of the baby. He found it very hard to differentiate his own needs from those of his wife and child.

On the other hand, he frequently used his paternal duties as an excuse to avoid, on the surface, the demands and challenges of his studies, and more deeply to evade separation and individuation from his father. Although he studied for three semesters conscientiously and with inner engagement, he eventually failed an exam that was central to his course of studies. The material corresponded to the scientific area his father had taught at the university and on which he had published a prominent professional work. Peter's professors tried to build him "golden bridges." In spite of that, he concluded from his failure that he should break off his studies and keep himself afloat through temporary work and a monthly allowance from his father. Once more his life appeared to have reached point zero.

Peter experienced me as a good object whose presence made it possible for him to venture upon a closer examination of his relationship with his father. In his experiences dealing with his own son now, he realized the role his father still played in his inner conflicts. The family relationships looked *functionalized*, the roles between Peter and his father fixed and frozen: Peter the confused, sick, and incapacitated son, the father his competent and rational rescuer. It seemed as if his father had projected onto his son his own unsolved conflicts and his unlived and unloved sides in order to manage and fight them there, without any comprehension or appreciation. Peter gained access to forgotten and now reemerging details of his childhood. We established a connection between his "cheek disease" and the *speechlessness* between father and son. The swelling stood for all that had remained unsaid between them. While he began gaining insight into his father's "night side," his memories of his paternal grandfather became more alive. He had been a general in the German army during World War II. There was silence about much of his past; instead, there were glorifying, idealizing, and unrealistic images. It became evident that between grandfather and father, too, a great deal had remained untold, unnamed, and not worked through. Peter recognized how his own disease stood in connection with a *speechlessness between the generations* and that his disorder was "not only my problem."

In the transference relationship, he liked the smell in the treatment room and the sound of my voice: "My mother always yelled and screamed and nagged." I became the good object, and he addressed to me what he wished from his parents. One day he wanted to say: "I kept looking there for solace and counsel," but he misspoke and said instead: "wire and rust-red" (*Immer wieder suche ich dort Rat und Trost*, but says: *Immer wieder suche ich dort Draht und Rost-Rot*).

When I heard this, I had immediate associations to the wire mothers of Harlow's experiments. Harlow's fur-wire-mother experiment shows that monkey babies reared on fur or wire mothers preferred the fur mothers even if it was the wire mother that offered nourishment. Although the monkey drinks from the wire mother, he stays in touching contact with the fur mother. These results contradict the behaviorists' claims that providing nourishment is the most important factor in the development of attachment.

I reflected that Peter could not sufficiently use his primary relations to symbolize and understand his inner world. Instead of gaining insight to his own inner world, his primary relations suggested to Peter rejection, concretism, and incomprehension.

At this time he took many weekend trips and had the urgent wish to describe all his external experiences to me in great detail. Compulsively and meticulously, he was careful to take up the narrative thread in the following session just where he had stopped in the previous one. I understood that he frantically tried "*to make continuity*" because he could not feel it within. With that he became increasingly desolate because his outer life was speeding on while we were falling ever farther behind in his narrative about those events: "The distance between the events and the opportunity to talk about them here keeps getting greater and greater." In this way, perhaps his early experiences of relationships were actualized. Increasingly, outer reality drifted apart from inner experience, without his being able to give that outer reality mental significance because the meaning-giving intimate relationship with his mother was lacking.

Peter had rented land where he spent summer afternoons and evenings with his girlfriend, listening to the twittering of the birds and the rippling of a little brook. From his joy about his "sensual garden" he came to speak about his mother "in whose family the women have to belittle the men." I heard this also as an allusion to his conflict in the transference relationship. This idyll hid his fear that if he gave in to his wishes for a relationship and shared his perverse relationship fantasies, he would be belittled and shamed.

At the end of the probationary period he stated: "There is an abyss in me. My life continues to drive toward failure in order to change me into an unfeeling, cold zombie."

Now I would like to select some facets from the treatment that seemed to me particularly relevant for Peter's development. I will start with some notes from an hour that took place after 4 years of treatment. He was late because he wanted to bring me some sections of his childhood scrapbook, containing everything that he had written down between the ages of 11 and 19, all very neatly organized: He said, "I could not decide what to bring and got caught up in reading. I looked at construction plans that I had drawn when I was about 14. In truth, one should read this from beginning to end. At the start, there are nature pictures from calendars—some bird, or a deer in the forest. And then come the construction machines." He describes them: the deep sound of the motors, their rhythmical, slow, and continuous motions, the vibrations, the expulsion of black soot from the exhaust after the start-up of the engines.

Here he communicated to me his deep longing for a father he could sensually experience, communicating this by means of the sensuality of the rhythm, of the regular swinging motions of the steam shovel, and the sound of the motors, and, behind this, even more strongly fought off, his yearning for a mother who would, in her reverie, address the sensual needs of her baby and so be in contact with him and anchor him in reality. I thought he would most like to return to the mother's body: to start all over again, to come once more from the inanimate to sensual experiences, and to the creation of meaning. These regressive wishes were projected onto his father's body and bodily sensuality.

He went on talking about how during class he observed the machines of the gravel pit lifting the gravel from the pond, then sorting the stones on huge conveyor belts and cleanly separating them with the help of a complicated system. At the end of this process, the gravel was put on one side, the earth materials, like clay and sand, on the other. Then he imagined what would happen to him if he were to leap into the funnel: "Just like [classic tricksters] Max and Moritz in the corn mill. Could the machine then also classify me according to 'mineral resources,' granularity, and valuable rubble? Then I imagine how I would ride up and down on the conveyor belt, like on a roller coaster."

I said: At that time, you had so many questions, and you wished for a father machine that would have sorted your inner life.

He: Yes, but then nobody spoke with me. No one said anything to me although I had behaved at times in such a crazy way. If my son behaved that way, all the alarms would go off. I would try by all means to approach him and not be like my parents, so disinterested and appeasing: "Do not imagine things!" ("Bilde dir doch nichts ein!") Such a thing would have to torment parents when their own child, first thing in the morning, goes to the bathroom to paint, with a mixture of face cream and charcoal, black shadows around his eyes and on his cheeks and constantly tells the neighbors that he was going to die soon because he was incurably sick."

I: You had given such crass signals because your distress was so huge, and you did not get any response.

He: It went so far that I wanted to end it all. I wanted to make it "dead certain," not something like: "Help! Look at me! I need help!" I wanted to make it certainly, irrecoverably, the end.

He decided upon strangulation on top of a high voltage tower, "a sure method that would only cause very brief pain." He could not now remember the hours when he sat on top of the mast, a noose around his neck. At dawn he then felt such an urgent, intensive, and irresistible wish for a glass of orange juice that he eventually climbed down and went home. Asked by his father how he had gotten such a stupid idea, he tried to explain it but was met, as he felt, by cold incomprehension and rude dismissal. Now he himself lost access to his pain: "At that point I became just a case (*Fall*) … I am somebody who has fallen (*gefallen*), fallen out of the relationship for good. That is when I became just a case to myself, too. The next day, I sat on my bicycle and rode to the psychiatric clinic for admission. But they did not want me. It was not so simple, they said. Before anything else, I needed a referral. So I took care of that, too. I went to some psychiatrist: 'Doctor, I am suicidal, yesterday more than today'…."

In my countertransference I was shocked by the extent of the soul blindness of his parents and how strongly he himself identified with this objectification and dehumanization of his person and his inner world. At the same time, I was also glad that he was able to talk with me about all this; and my feelings entered into our encounter.

Returning now to the point in his treatment (2005) when he was telling me these things from the past: He explained that his girlfriend wanted to marry him now and wanted to have a second child. Yet he was deeply worried about giving a wife and children his own name. He would harm them with it: "I am treated with contempt by the entire country."

Step by step and with many breakdowns that brought him and his family to the edge of their ability to survive physically, he learned to ask for compensation for his carpentry work and to have it more adequately paid. He allowed himself to let some aggressions in sublimated form enter into his relationships in order to advance himself in the struggle for survival.

At that point, his father became severely depressed and had to be hospitalized. Confronted with his father's helplessness, Peter talked for the first time somewhat more about his mother, and it became evident how deeply disturbed that relationship was. We were able to work on this in the transference and his transference fantasies.

In our first session after the summer break in 2005, he admitted that he had noticed how much he had missed me. He was "afraid of the fire within, which could burn everything up." It did not suffice anymore to spend the vacation the same way he presumed me to be doing. He assumed I went with my family on trips, and therefore he did the same with his family, fantasizing that we were together all the time. He could no longer deny the separation from me by identifying with me. Now he felt terribly empty without our sessions. This also indicated more access to his inner space.

Again and again he put his relationship with his wife massively into question and talked about his wishes to separate from her. He reacted to her wishes for a second child by impotence, feeling functionalized by her as somebody who should fill women with good feelings and fulfill them. In the relationship with me he felt he should serve as "a good patient" in the interest of my professional success and my narcissistic gratification. It is worth noting the marked contrast to his vision for himself, in which, because of the therapeutic process, he had become so painfully in touch with his own inner emptiness.

For the first time, he spoke with me about the aggressive nature of his sexual fantasies about his wife. When she separated from him in a satisfied and relaxed state after the orgasmic merger, he wanted to choke her and force her eyes wide open with match sticks so that she could not turn her gaze away from him. I interpreted to him that he was doing this because he could not believe, perhaps, that when his wife or I turned away from him and toward something else of our own, he would retain a place in our inner world. For him, "being recognized by the other" must be established violently and concretely; it must be "made." In this fashion, he tried to gain control over feeling excluded from the inner life of the other, over his envy of the richness of experience (*Erlebnisfähigkeit*) and the inner wealth of the other person (*das Gegenüber*), and over his terrible feelings of impotence.

We were now also able to see how for these reasons he had to block our work from becoming fruitful within therapy and translating to success outside therapy. He recognized how peculiar his triumph was in setting himself up for failure: "It is my father's fault if my hands freeze," the sado-masochistic entanglement.

His fear of his and my subjectivity entered into our relationship. We were now able to talk about his idea that we could only be successful if we climbed over others. He also thought that he could not conquer a woman if he was in touch with his helpless side. We understood more and more why on his personal journey he had to keep failing: He could not and was not allowed to resort to his subjectivity: "Only on his deathbed could I confront my father with my own perspective because then I would not kill him anymore with it."

His longing for meaning-giving contact and exchange were in conflict with his anxiety that everything would be destroyed if these wishes were fulfilled: "There seem to be more and more things that cannot be talked about, and it feels like a great danger: that everything would burn up if they were revealed. All my hopes would be destroyed. For that reason, I have to keep them all very secret and bottled up within myself."

At that time, insurance gave permission for a final 50 therapy hours, and we had to discuss if and how we could continue our treatment. He was now working regularly and hoped he could pay for treatment in the future himself: "It is as if I were a fisherman on a boat in the middle of the ocean. With great effort, I have succeeded in lifting a big treasure from the depths with a net. I can already see it glittering under the surface. If the treatment hours were to cease now, it would be as if I gave up the treasure and let it sink back under the waves."

His professional and personal development filled both of us with great hope. A start-up company promised him employment if he proved himself during a trial period. His wife was now pregnant with twins. I have to add that when he transmitted those glad tidings to his mother she responded by asking whether they did not want to abort the babies. Peter reacted to this with massive feelings of guilt and identified with his mother's implied condemnation: "He is able to screw but not to feed his family." In this context he also spoke about euthanasia in the Third Reich.

Suddenly, and for us incomprehensibly, it turned out that he was not going to be employed by the company. This let all the gains collapse like a house of cards, and also put into question the financing of his continued treatment.

In order to gain time we had to reduce our hours. We met now once a week on a "maintenance dosage" and could not really deal with many things in depth. It did indeed seem as if what we had achieved was in danger of sinking back into the depths. I was desperate, and for long stretches of the permitted period I did not know how I could continue giving to him what he so urgently and immediately needed.

In his external reality as well, Peter found himself under tremendous pressure. In short order he had to find a job to feed his growing family; to deal with the loss of his large apartment because the landlords needed it themselves; and with extremely tight finances look for a new abode for his family, with the birth of the twins imminent.

In our sessions he often complained about keeping inside and outside (i.e., therapy and reality) strictly apart and being unable to connect them. This struggle was mirrored in my own experience of an intervision session with colleagues. With my colleagues, I tried to talk about my own distress in the treatment, especially in regard to the great difficulty I had with translating what I experienced as "the inner reality of the hour" into "the outer reality" of the group of colleagues. I felt isolated and alone in my distress, unable to make the others understand it precisely, let alone feel and experience it. What was missing was the dimension of the "Between" (in Buber's sense); I felt caged in with Peter in isolation.

Probably, in the intervision, Peter's problem became "actualized" (i.e., his issue of not being seen and recognized and thus of not filling his inner life with meaning and understanding was reenacted). Because it could not be shared, his inner life remained for him—and now for me—strange and chopped up into meaningless pieces.

Peter had succeeded in communicating to me, through the countertransference, the extent of his own powerlessness to understand how he related to himself and to others, and also not to feel held in a caring relationship. After the intervision, a part of me felt terribly guilty and ashamed, as if I had done something wrong that I could never repair: "I've been whizzing around in analytic spheres without noticing that my patient was dying." Perhaps I was here concordantly identified with Peter's shameful fantasies about his inability to connect inside and outside and his terror of further self-revelation and exposure.

After the birth of his twin girls, Peter became more and more sleepless. He worried that he could not console his little daughters and at night became terrified by aggressive fantasies about them. He also complained that he was losing his emotional tie to his son who was, he feared, doing worse and worse and becoming more and more conspicuous. Before, when learning to read, he had been a smart student, but now the boy became sicker, acting out in ever more bizarre ways. Peter feared that his son was following in his own footsteps. Nevertheless, in his descriptions he did not show any understanding at all for the boy's "crazy" behavior. For a number of months, he dwelled on these concerns about his son, and in my countertransference I struggled not to become infected by Peter's conviction that his child was crazy.

At this time, Peter complained that nothing was reaching and touching him anymore. He was in deep despair about the treatment, "because I have *destroyed everything good that we have achieved together.*"

I was profoundly worried about him and suggested that he should come more frequently because I wanted to hear more about his anxieties and fantasies. Yet at the same time, I was desperately uncertain how I could establish a framework for more therapy sessions to work through this charged material. For weeks I was tormented by fears that Peter could, in an enlarged suicide, exterminate his entire family. During our Christmas separation in 2007, he felt so miserable that he went to a psychiatric hospital. The treating physician, alarmed by his condition, shared my concerns and wanted to admit him. Peter, however, did not under any circumstances want to leave his wife and three children alone at home. We finally succeeded in overcoming this acute crisis on an outpatient basis, with close exchanges between the hospital and me. Subsequently, the hospital psychiatrist and I secured insurance approval for a new number of sessions for continued psychoanalytic treatment (2008).

In addition to his psychotherapy, Peter was being treated in social psychiatry for medication management and reintegration into the labor market. He only slowly put into words how much he felt tormented by loyalty conflicts in this "triangle." In a strongly paranoid way, he was terrified that the full extent of his inability to care for himself, his wife, and his children could become public and lead to the removal of his children by the authorities.

Gradually treatment helped Peter decipher his son's behavior by shedding light on the boy's inner conflicts as well as, on a deeper level, his own. Central to such an understanding was the issue of *jealousy*, both Peter's son's current feelings of jealousy, and Peter's own jealousy of his brother in the past.

Parallel to this, Peter became increasingly able to recognize his fears of persecution as projections of his inner "night side": "I have tendencies to *disappoint* without being able to answer why. I also have impulses to smash everything and run away as a martyr. When I think such things I feel that I am evil. But I have to be good. Doubts also belong to evil. When there is a conflict in me then the world stands still, and everything is forever. Then there exists only silence" (see also chapters 1, 2, and 4 of this book). At this point, something other than just Peter's personal psychopathology seemed to loom: the collective dimension. Because of the archaic structure of his superego, there were only the absolute judgments of either-or; there was no "as well as." This seemed to be a hint at our shared experience of the collective lack of grief- and guilt-work in postwar Germany.

He dreamed: "I am put up against the wall and shot. Then there were many father figures, masters, who were sitting in court over me." This dream brought him to the insight: "I am like a child that is useless for anything; and this goes on in this way in my dreams: the feeling of being worth nothing, of being unable to do anything, of being the worst of all, the lowest worm. When this [feeling] is so strong, then go ahead and add to it: I have to offer myself, my behind, as a sexual object; perhaps I could be useful at least for that. *If I do not function I am put against the wall and shot.*"

It became evident how the little son had to be "exterminated," as the Nazis might have said, as a proxy for little Peter. This made it increasingly possible for Peter to acknowledge "the foreign little Peter" (i.e., the split-off part of his self) in his son, and he learned to understand both better. It meant that gradually he could take back his projective identifications and thus establish some boundaries between himself and his child.

At that point, new central details of Peter's early childhood emerged: He remembered that as a little boy he had remained with his mother while his father went diving with his brother and other men. For the first time, I saw a very different picture of his relationship to his mother. No longer did she appear so demonized, but more reachable and human. Because he did not share his father's passion for diving he had felt rejected and left out by him as weak and womanish, while his brother was a "man." Never had there been an attempt to understand why he did not want to dive: Either he did what a "man" does or he had to remain with mother.

When he was dealing with these moments from childhood he also recalled that his father often made movies of his children. In order to gain more access to the "little Peter" he looked for himself in those movies. To his great disappointment, he only found images of his brother.

This discovery offered a glimpse into the psychodynamic origins of Peter's crucial problem with jealousy: He, his father, and his brother always formed a triangle where Peter was the excluded third. As we now saw, the brother was clearly favored by the father.

Something else emerged that I thought might be a screen memory: He remembered that as a child he loved the color lilac and felt deeply rejected when his father declared lilac to be the color of gays. In a *pars pro toto* equation Peter felt dismissed in his male identity and in his love for his father.

His father had been educated in a Napola school ("National Political Academy" for the children of the Nazi elite). He had been sent there at the tender age of 11. We can surmise that, as a consequence of this indoctrination in Nazi ideology, the father himself had wiped out and split off important parts of his inner life, everything that was tender and soft, and now had, against this traumatic background, to misinterpret and combat them as his own "foreignness in the other" (*das Fremde im Anderen*) in the child. Peter's "cheek swelling" referred symbolically to all the ideas and feelings that are expressed by words, but remained unspoken—the wall of silence.

Thus it became clear how Peter had not only concretely, but also metaphorically entered into the shoes and footsteps of the father and now was on his way to transmitting his transgenerational traumatization to his son.

In regard to outer reality, he was preoccupied by his grandfather who during World War II was a general in the Wehrmacht, and after the collapse of the Third Reich became a prisoner of war in a special camp. In family mythology, this grandfather was greatly idealized: He was a "good general," and his role during the Nazi period was never questioned—yet another idyll. Peter recalled that his father's family lived in a large, confiscated villa, and it is still not clear to us who the previous owners had been (Jewish property?). Even now his parents are proud of family photos where the father as a child shakes Hitler's hand. The fact that the father attended the Napola school became an issue now, too.

When Peter talked about having to leave his rented house because of financial distress, latently it was connected with issues from the Nazi past: "I cannot get rooted; I am not permitted to claim any space." I understood this as alternation between identifying with the persecuted Jews and the Nazi identification of the generation of his parents and grandparents, and also as an expression of the resulting severe feelings of guilt. And later: "I would like to give up, to destroy everything. I have massive difficulties in the world. I am ashamed to say that I am something better (an Aryan), and I am ashamed for the fact that this is not visible (that up to now nobody in the family was openly ashamed about the past). I am ashamed that this was imposed on me by the environment of my childhood." This refers to the lack of mourning work in the family and of acknowledgment of their own real guilt. Another time, after experiencing another dismal failure, he spoke ambiguously about "the Jewish swine that needs to be exterminated." When I heard this I was stunned, and I found it very hard to remain in emotional contact with him. He seemed to sense this shift in my countertransference and appeared shaken by his own coldness and heartlessness. But he immediately switched to fantasies of extinguishing his entire family, annihilating his little twin girls: "Sticking my finger in their genitals—I would annihilate them. How can I hug them during the day and then have such thoughts?" We pondered together in the session this split of emotionality in many Nazi perpetrators.

Subsequently, he sank for almost 2 years into a mute, almost entirely speechless depression. For months he came to the hours, stared ahead, and hardly said a word. Often during that time, eye contact was the only bridge between us. That time and the few words he said were for him and me both extremely tormenting. (See above: "When there is conflict in me then the world stands still, and everything is forever. Then there is only silence"; see also chapters 1, 2 and 4 in this book.) In my countertransference I was often so desperate and quite without hope that I was tempted to give up on him.

After the 2009 summer break, Peter wanted to reduce therapy to one hour a week, rationalizing that otherwise his contingent of hours would be used up too quickly. Eventually we understood that he feared I might lose hope and give up on him; he would have experienced that as a death sentence. He tried to regain control over the situation through action, turning passive into active. Later on we could also talk about his deep fear of his feelings of love for me: "Everything that I love I have to destroy."

A great turn occurred after a severe suicidal crisis during my summer vacation in 2010. Once more Peter had failed in an expectation put upon him, and in a mixture of despair and boundless rage, he used a chainsaw to cut his whole project into pieces. His colleagues at work were alarmed and worried about him. When they tried to stop his actions he ran away intending to throw himself from an Autobahn bridge. In contrast to the suicide attempt in his youth, however, his colleagues brought him back and home; his wife set a date with me, and we could constructively work through this crisis.

In the time that followed, it appeared that Peter had again found access to a split-off part of his inner world and that he had regained his place in time. He was glad to have found a way out of a frozenness (*Starre*, "rigor") that had lasted for almost 2 years, and he found a new well of initiative and joy for life. Because of the precarious living situation of the family, he and his wife now wanted to buy their own house. She wanted a row house near her parents, but he preferred one in the countryside with garden and barn which he could renovate himself and where he could install a carpentry workshop. His wife feared that under the stress of buying a house he might become sick again. Peter was convinced that he would never relapse "in this way" because he felt he was different now from the way he'd been before. It had a lot to do with his changed self-esteem, he added. He believed he would never again lose speech as had just recently happened in his long crisis.

In this connection he mentioned recent nightmares: "They were psychotic dreams. In the dream it was just as I had felt all those long years during the day, too. Everything is dark, and nothing fits together anymore. Everything is in pieces. Speech does not reach anybody. There is no understanding, there are no people, only dark figures, no meaning…. When I wake up I am now so glad that it only was a dream, that everything has become so different in my life."

He rejoiced that he had found *his* language and speech again. It recalled the moment from the beginning of his therapy when he was incapable of naming inner states in any other way than by the skilled deployment of psychiatric vocabulary. Apparently, he had succeeded during our long time together in finding a pathway to his own "personal" language and speech and, in connection with it, new access to hitherto nonmentalized and split-off areas of his self. This was especially true for the transgenerationally transmitted unresolved conflicts around shame and guilt about the Nazi past of the parental and grandparental generations. Indeed, Germany's collective political and historical traumas helped shape Peter's life and treatment, contributing to his lifelong difficulties connecting inner experiences to outer reality, helping shape an ongoing fear of speechlessness and public exposure, and contributing to my own difficulty in constructing a coherent narrative.

Working through these connections made it possible for Peter to gain access to his most intimate experience (*sein ureigenes Erleben*). The treatment is still far from being concluded. In the future, we will certainly deal in depth with his conflicts around envy and jealousy; but we can hope that this will occur within the grounding of a "true, authentic self." In these comments I have tried to show how this had been lost to Peter at a very young age.

Another Glimpse behind the "Wall of Silence": Some Comments by Léon Wurmser

About a dozen years ago, Heidrun mentioned to me, in the course of our regular telephone exchanges about difficult clinical issues, that she had been contacted by a supposedly schizophrenic young man who had almost died from the psychopharmacological treatment he was undergoing. Very soon we both had profound questions both about the diagnosis and the treatment "inflicted," we might say, upon him, and we both felt that it was well worth entering upon deep psychoanalytic work.

Since that discussion, I have more or less constantly accompanied her on a journey whose dangers had at times almost mythical proportions. Thus we took the patient's obsessive ideas about taking an ax and cutting off the heads of women to whom he felt attracted so seriously that Heidrun for a while arranged for precautionary measures during her sessions. Many were the times when we both despaired and doubted all our assumptions. These ups and downs are by no means over. Still, there has been a remarkable change.

One fundamental problem we continue to face is that our familiarity with psychoanalytic technique and theory repeatedly falls short of what we are both confronting. The psychodynamic understanding was and is enormously helpful, but there seemed so much more to what we encountered. The analytic precepts of abstinence are of cardinal importance, especially with patients who are so prone to extreme forms of acting out, and yet there were several times where the "frame" had to be resolutely broken. The best example lies in the temporary participation of the older child and of the wife in a number of sessions. Such introduction of a kind of family therapy, in addition to the traditional intensive and nonintensive individual psychotherapy, proved during certain periods more than useful; it might even have been life-saving.

In fact, it was in our many conversations about this and several other especially difficult and frustrating cases of each of us, which enormously tried our patience and tolerance that we increasingly became convinced that we had to reflect about our experiences in two distinctly different dimensions. One was the orientation toward *theoretical explanation*, one that aspired to achieve some measure of objectivity about what was happening within our patients and in our relationships with them (and their families!), ultimately an explanation that revolves around inner conflicts, especially in their unconscious forms. The other was an attempt to understand the real relationship between patient and therapist, the dialogue. It led both of us, about 4 years ago, to take up once again, together, the study of Martin Buber's work and personality. What we looked at in our work seemed more meaningful when we could see it as a back and forth between living in the I-It (*Ich-Es*) dimension of Being and in the I-You (*Ich-Du*) dimension.[2] Several contributors to this book have made this same point (indirectly Evelyn Schwaber, J.-B. Pontalis, and Anna Ornstein, and very explicitly Mel Bornstein).

In line with this deepened and ultimately philosophical understanding, Heidrun and I wrote a paper on "Buber and Psychoanalysis—Contemporary

Psychoanalysis and Buber," that we presented (in German) in the Buberhaus in Heppenheim, Germany, September 1, 2011.

Heidrun's presentation is a wonderful example of this duality, with particular emphasis, I believe, on the second dimension, "I–You": the very deep experience of the relationship and its curative effects. I would like to expand upon a few aspects of this duality but add some that are more in line with the traditional psychoanalytic understanding of inner conflict (i.e., more the intrapsychic dimension). Yet it is, for both of us, as already stressed in the Introduction and in Mel Bornstein's chapter, an issue of complementarity, not of an either-or.

Another consequence of this duality is that the depth and intensity of dialogue is not restricted to the patient/therapist couple, but also to the couple comprised of therapist/supervisor or, rather, the close analytic friend with whom the case is discussed. It has been postulated rightly, as I have repeatedly heard, that one should not be alone with such difficult and trying cases but rather seek an ongoing dialogue where one can share everything, without fear, shame, and reservation. In contrast to supervision in the usual sense, in this dialogue, the mutuality and symmetry appear to us essential.

In our dialogue I often used the term *chaver ne'eman*, the trusted friend. The term, as I think it, is derived from a Chassidic precept, out of the "little note" (Zettel Katan) of Elimelech from Lyzensk (died 1786): The Chassid

> should each time tell all the base thoughts and obsessions to his teacher in God's way and also to his faithful friend, the *chaver ne'eman*, thoughts that are directed against the Holy Torah which the Evil Drive (*yetzer hara*) lets rise to his brain and his heart, be that at the time of Torah learning or of prayer, be that when he lies down on his bed or in the middle of the day, and he should not hide anything out of shame. And it happens by his telling all those things which he brings forth out of his energy towards action, that this breaks the power of the Evil Drive, so that another time, when he is away from the good counsel that he could get from his friend, it cannot overwhelm him that much. This counsel however is the path to God and something wonderful.

In that sense, what Heidrun has described was a long journey undertaken by her with her patient and an invisible companion following them over stretches of the rocky path, most like a kindly spirit.

Yet, as hinted, I would like now to add my thoughts about the psychodynamics as I understand them. We became more and more convinced that we were observing a particularly virulent form of negative therapeutic reaction. Trying to summarize the psychodynamic structure, we arrive at a circular schema. It is not certain if we can detect a uniform starting point; but I suspect that the trigger is mostly a convergence of separation or rejection, of shame, and of jealousy. Since for this man closeness usually also paradoxically involves distance, being together always ends in being excluded again. For that we have prominently clear predecessors in childhood: certainly in the crucially relevant triangle father, brother, and him, but perhaps also with mother and father. We also know from other experiences that, quite generally, issues of dependency and separation hide jealousy conflicts ("the excluded third wants to be the excluding first"). What appears dyadic is very often a defense against triadic conflicts (see Wurmser & Jarass, 2007). The detailed study of many sessions reveals many such circles of rejection, shame, jealousy, and then vindictive, even murderous rage and renewed exclusion.

Besides this crucial constellation of rejection, shame, and jealousy, there is the paramount force of the inner judge, the absoluteness of the inner and probably also external judgmentalness, in other words, the intensity of the archaic superego that are described by Heidrun vividly and in many variants.

Behind these two large dynamic areas of jealousy and of the archaic superego there rises, as a third area, the monumental wall of silence that has to shield the generations from the memories of the perpetration of colossal historical horrors and cruelties that were at least participated in.

I would like now to present how I visualize the sequence of inner processes:

1. There is above all the severe, cumulative, many-layered relational traumatization. It is mostly in the form of a pervasive soul blindness or a profound lack of empathy and dehumanization present in almost everything that Peter communicates to us from his own inner life and that of his family.
2. As a consequence of these traumata (a kind of "precipitate"), we hear hour after hour how massively his archaic superego condemns and punishes. We see it in the form of implacability, cruelty, and absoluteness of judgment, in the constant threat of suicide and as dehumanization of others in all those perverse fantasies and impulses; we see it in the imagery of "digestion" by those huge machines. Parallel to this, there are severe superego sanctions directed against those repressed affects of jealousy and envy, especially toward his brother, who was clearly favored by his father, but who himself undertook a very serious suicide attempt that left him at least for some time nearly fully paralyzed.
3. These superego aggressions are turned against the outside in all his intimate relationships, particularly in the ones with the analyst/therapist and with his wife and children, something that was often

too superficially "explained" by outsiders in supervision and intervision as manipulation and sadism.

4. These superego aggressions also reflect a very strong fixation to early anal fantasies that keep circling around digestion and evacuation: since early childhood, fascination with loud machines and cyclical processes in excavators, images of violent expulsion and dismemberment, smearing and generally destroying of any kind. We also have to think in this connection of the direct family tradition of the Nazi world and Auschwitz as *anus mundi* ("the anus of the world").
5. The denied and repressed family guilt and family secrets have to be hidden behind that monumental wall of silence, secrets in regard to possibly stolen Jewish property, the participation in war crimes by the grandfather, and the continued identification with parts of the Nazi ideology, resonating and confirmed in the pervasive feelings of personal shame and guilt, in the commandments of silence in family and transference, and in the compulsion to disappoint and to fail (like the case in chapter 1).
6. Reality thus keeps being denied, but repeated in the compulsion to destroy, and is so confirmed.

Of particular importance for the therapist is her weaving together of this vicious circle in the patient with her own suffering under the Nazi past.

Another aspect of countertransference that proved especially helpful is the insight it allowed into the metaphor of digestion, which shows its Janus face throughout: both as an oft-used current image for mentalization on one hand, and on the other as a reflection of archaic fantasies of a mostly anal nature, of dismemberment and chopping to pieces, as in the image of jumping into the funnel and emerging as ground-up pieces like Max and Moritz. This is also reflected in the deep sense of fragmentation of the material in the memory of both analyst and patient, a pervasive sense of discontinuity. This doubleness of the metaphor could perhaps be seen as another example of Freud's (1910) "antithetical meaning of primal words," here not of the words themselves, but of basic images used by the metaphorical process.

One more thought about this image of fragmentation as an expression of the relational traumata: Whoever is not remembered and perceived as a continuous self forgets himself and thus his inner continuity—in a poignant image drawn by Sheldon Bach (2001):

> A person's specific memories and experiences are like individual beads that can achieve continuity and gestalt form only when they are strung together to become a necklace. The string on which they are assembled is the child's continuous existence in the mind

of the parent, which provides the continuity on which the beads of experiences are strung together and become the necklace of a connected life. (p. 748)

And with that of an identity.

The same metaphor was used by another patient of Heidrun's in connection with her emotional distance from her lover. She relayed how she succeeded for the first time, while reaching a climax, in staying in her sensations both with him and with herself: "You have to imagine it that way, as if the feelings corresponded to pearls, and they had been lying scattered on the table, each one wonderfully beautiful in itself, but unconnected, and it was as if in this experience they were strung on a thread: Suddenly they were joined together."

It struck both of us that during the writing of this report and even more so during the translations and corrections, that the discontinuity of meaning was so jarring that there arose again and again the temptation to fill in the gaps and make the text smoother and let the patient appear less sick, much more structured than he really was.

Experiences of meaning and of time grow out of a sense of connectedness of experience, and this in turn develops with remembrance by and of the other in one's own inner life. Central to this sense of identity and inner continuity as well as to their absence are feelings of shame. Heidrun describes to us in the most sensitive and painful way the slow growth of such continuity in her work with Peter and in her own understanding of his and her own history, as the integration of severe trauma into the self. How? By being seen and heard in love.

I will end with a little passage from the Talmud Tractate Megilla (24b)[3] that reflects metaphorically on the life-sustaining power of being seen:

> Rabbi Yose said, All my days I was troubled over the meaning of this verse [Deut. 28.29]: *And you will grope at noonday as the blind man gropes in darkness.* Now, I wondered, what difference is there between darkness and light to a blind man? [Why does he grope more in darkness, as Scripture implies, than in daylight?] Until I witnessed the following incident [which illuminated the verse for me]: One time I was walking in the darkness of nighttime, and I saw a blind person who was walking on the road, and he had a torch in his hand. I said to him: "My son, why do you need this torch?" He answered me: "As long as a torch is in my hand, people see me and save me from harming myself in ditches, thorns, and briers." (quoted from the Schottenstein edition, ArtScrollSeries)

Being seen by the other gives protection and meaning to life; this is the real meaning of the light. It protects against those abysses confronted in this entire volume, and particularly poignantly, in Heidrun Jarass's presentation.

Notes

1. We are very grateful to Dr. Nina Sonenberg for her great help in editing this chapter.
2. I (LW) prefer this translation over the stilted and nowadays utterly far and foreign "Thou," the very opposite of what Buber intended.
3. I (LW) am grateful to Mr. Ron Mitnick, the leader of the Talmud class I am privileged to attend.

References

Bach, S. (2001). On being forgotten and forgetting one's self. *Psychoanalytic Quarterly, 70,* 739–756.

Freud, S. (1910). The antithetical meaning of primal words. In J. Strachey (Ed. & Trans.), *The standard edition of the complete psychological works of Sigmund Freud* (Vol. 11, pp. 153–161). London: Hogarth Press

Wurmser, L., & Jarass, H. (2007). *Jealousy and envy: New views about two powerful feelings.* New York: Analytic Press.

Wurmser, L., & Jarass, H. (2011, September 1). *Buber und die Psychoanalyse: Die heutige Psychoanalyse und Buber* [Buber and psychoanalysis: Psychoanalysis today and Buber]. Lecture presented at the Buberhaus, Heppenheim, Germany.

6

"OMNIPRESENCE," A MASKED CAUSE OF NEGATIVE THERAPEUTIC REACTION

Considerations of the Long Shadow of Totalitarian Repression[1]

Jörg Frommer

Understood in a wider sense, negative therapeutic reaction (NTR) does not refer to a purely psychological or intrapersonal, but to a communicative or interpersonal phenomenon. Affected by it are the patient and his or her counterpart, the analyst or therapist whose actions are thus part of the phenomenon. Moreover, the use of this negatively judgmental term points toward a particular world order or worldview, a particular conception of therapeutic success, to a normative order that determines what is positive or negative. This also accounts for the explosive nature of this topic: Focus on negative reactions not only throws light on the patient's development, but also on the analyst's interventions and judgments. This occurs most notably when analysts, effectively dazzled by their own authority and power of interpretation, quite simply misunderstand the patients, who for their part desire something completely different from what analysts assume, suspect, interpret, or consider to be a demonstration of therapeutic progress.

Viewed in a narrow sense, Freud (1923) considered the chief cause of NTR as a reaction to mutually acquired progress during treatment to be "a *moral* factor" (p. 166), a feeling of guilt, or a predominating need for illness that was opposing the will to recovery, understood as an expression of destructive and self-destructive forces in the patient's superego. A comparison of the narrower and the broader definition of NTR leads to the consideration that particularly serious analysis-threatening NTRs very possibly do not distinguish themselves by a persistent and clearly recognizable "attitude of defiance towards the physician" (p. 166), but by the patient's unconscious success in incorporating the analyst into destructive acting out. The analyst is unwittingly and unintentionally maneuvered into the position of an accomplice. Patient and analyst then jointly block and destroy progress without being consciously aware of what they are doing. This type of fatal development is especially to be feared when the patient brings transgenerationally charged destructive forces into analysis, when an archaic need for punishment is inflamed by an unconscious, "*borrowed*" (p. 166) feeling of guilt taken over from a near relative deeply mired in injustice and inhumanity.

Here I would like to formulate a number of considerations on the psychoanalytic theory of resistance, based on my own involvement with the legacy of nearly 60 years of totalitarian rule in East Germany until 1989. These efforts can be understood as a supplement to current and growing scientific interest in the generation of Germans who survived the end of Second World War and experienced totalitarianism and Nazi dictatorship in childhood or infancy (Lamparter, Thiessen, Wierling, Wiegande-Grefe, & Möller, 2010). Common to both areas of research is the basic premise that the "legacy" of this experience continues to have an effect today and will continue to do so in coming generations (Bar-On, 1998; Bergmann & Jucovy, 1982; Kogan, 2007; Krystal, 1968; Oliner, 2011).

In concrete terms, I will attempt to describe a form of defense, which I believe can be justifiably called "omnipresence." This particular form of defense will need to be defined and set in relationship to other forms of psychopathological reaction to chronic societal repression. For a better understanding of its psychodynamics, this defense form will also be investigated in relation to neighboring forms of defense. Aspects of the anal development stage as well as phobic aspects will be delimited from preanal narcissistic aspects and their relationship to paranoid and manic dynamics. I then propose to illuminate a further psychodynamic aspect of omnipresence: the return of repressed elements and failure to succeed. I will then discuss treatment aspects, in other words, how omnipresent resistance translates into masked NTR during treatment. I will close with the somewhat provocative question of whether omnipresence is specific to posttotalitarian personalities, or whether it is actually an ubiquitous phenomenon of postmodern societal development, basically nourished by decreasing immediate "natural" sensual experience, which in these societies tends to be replaced by media-mediated "artificial" types of experience.

Psychic Defense between Drive Repression and the Social *Mise-en-Scène*

To this day, defense mechanism theory is numbered among the core areas of psychoanalytic theory. Various neuroses, types of personality and personality disorders, and levels of maturity in personality development are characterized by specific defense mechanisms and processes. In the early stages of psychoanalytic theory, the notion of defense mechanisms served to conceptualize how, guided by culturally predefined values and norms represented in the superego, the ego represses aggressive and sexual drive impulses and how this repression causes neurotic symptoms, which symbolically represent compromises between value orientation on the one hand and drive needs on the other (Freud, 1894). In later phases of theory development, ego psychology understood defense mechanisms as instruments of the ego in its struggle for a compromise (A. Freud, 1937; S. Freud, 1923).

Among Freud's successors, object relations and interpersonal approaches emerged. Their conceptualization of defense mechanisms was linked with the juxtaposition of so-called language related *mature* intrapsychic defense mechanisms typical for neurotic processes and so-called *primitive* defense mechanisms. Defense function that is dependent on inclusion and involvement of additional persons through preverbally transmitted scenic interaction proved specific to the latter form. Seen in this light, the degree of integration of heterogeneous aspects of the ego, which simultaneously shows the degree of integration of the body-ego and of the safety of the delineation between ego and nonego, lends each defensive process a characteristic color. Structural levels of personality are thus clinically recognizable (Kernberg, 1993). This implies that a certain maturity of psychic functions is a prerequisite for the ability to experience one's counterpart as "Thou," that is as an alter ego. Contrarily, on lower levels of personality integration, the other person is not fully recognized as a person, but disintegrates into partial objects lacking in personal character. Within the subjective experience, these partial objects occupy a transitional status between mere nonpersonal objects or "things" and significant others or persons.

The Loss of "Thou" in the Significant Other as a Result of Political Repression

A further, less discussed facet will now be added to this rough sketch of the history of the theory of defense mechanisms. This facet deals with the correlation between defense and societal structure seen in relation to the fact that each epoch, each cultural and political system imprints human existence with an individual stamp. Traces of this impregnation can be found in patterns of experience and action of each member of that particular societal system.

This thesis is based on the correlation between individual biographical development and defense mechanisms. This correlation was first systematically and psychoanalytically illuminated in Freud's *Three Essays on the Theory of Sexuality* (1905). In the brief essay "Character and Anal Erotism" (1908), Freud further observed that during analysis, the "anal character" (p. 174), characterized by extreme neatness, stinginess, and stubbornness, consistently exhibits an early penchant for libidinous preoccupation with his own excrement. "In the course of development and in accordance with the education demanded by our present civilization" (p. 171), this preoccupation later falls prey to defense. Conspicuous in this statement is that Freud relates this observation without questioning what purpose could be served by conforming to "our present civilization" or what dangers might be contained therein. Those interested in this particular aspect may consult Freud's later writings on cultural and religious psychology. In *The Future of an Illusion* (1927), for example, Freud clearly and unambiguously defines the *conditio humana* as an unrelenting, terrible, and brutal struggle between unconditional drive claims and "restrictions of civilization" (p. 15). This struggle is not only staged between individuals, but also manifests itself in the inner conflicts of each person between drive desires and culturally preformed superego commands.

Freud does not discuss a specific societal and cultural situation in which internalized drive repression is systematically strengthened and abused by a ruling elite, whose unrestrained aspirations to power and prestige don't fight shy of destroying all in their path. On the eve of the social catastrophe that overran Germany, and from there large areas of the world, it was left to the next generation of socially engaged psychoanalysts, led by Erich Fromm (1932), to show that defense can generate not only individual, but also collective pathology. It was proved that especially hidden irrationality and satisfaction of destructive drives, which culminated in a tidy ordering of dehumanized products, could lead to the selection of humans to be transported to the gas chambers. The Frankfurt Institute for Social Research has conducted theoretically, and due to a combination of quantitative and qualitative method, methodologically groundbreaking investigations showing the ways in which character structures are imprinted by authoritarian societies. The investigations also point out the barbarities of which individuals are capable who are socialized in this manner and unable to tolerate ambiguities (Adorno, Frenkel-Brunswik, Levinson, & Sanford, 1950; Fahrenberg & Steiner, 2004).

Since Hannah Arendt's (1963/2006) writings on Adolf Eichmann and the ensuing demystification of national socialist perpetration, Freud's findings from 1905 have been confirmed in a most barbaric manner. In pregenital stages of libido development, only partial objects and thus no integrated self and no object in the sense of another complete and significant human being, no person, no real "Thou," can be an object of the libido. Evil becomes banal. The injured fellow man is not understood or experienced as an alter ego, but is experienced and treated as a thing, somewhere between human and inanimate object. This occurs both transitively ("the other individual is less worthy, not really a person") and intransitively ("I am not being treated like a person, but like a thing, a piece of dirt"). The underlying philosophical consideration provides the foundation for current empirical research on the capability of mentalization (Fonagy, Gergely, Jurist, & Target, 2002) without this political dimension finding sufficient resonance in current dialogue.

The last aspect in particular, the experience of being treated in a dehumanizing manner from early childhood on, cannot remain without consequences for self- and world experience. We know from psychoanalytic trauma research that psychic survival from this sort of trauma brings forth, at the very least, a partial identification with the perpetrator, which in the form of "totalitarian" inner objects (Šebek, 1992, 1996, 1998) brutalize the conscious and, even more, unconscious psychic life of the traumatized person. Accompanying factors are massive problems in the areas of guilt and shame as well as consistent destructive and autodestructive behavior. In a strongly autobiographical essay about life in totalitarian societies, the Magdeburg psychoanalyst Ludwig Drees (2011) wrote: "the prevailing affect within these societal formations is fear, a monstrous fear of being eliminated from the community, of dropping out; the awakening of ancient fears of annihilation ..." (translation by Liz Franzen). According to Drees, this fear leads to collective processes of psychic regression accompanied by massive denial of reality and the readiness to assume seemingly paranoid ideologies. During national socialist rule, a slight deviation from social norms or membership in certain social groups was enough to put one in actual danger of death, and the GDR, supported by an omnipresent system of spying and surveillance, developed effective methods of threatening an individual's social existence, and used psychic pressure in forcing him or her to conform. Spontaneous human reactions were impossible in public, and might even prove to be dangerous within the family or in private social circles.

In summary, I would like to refer to Karl Löwith's (1928) phenomenological anthropology and to Martin Buber's (1951) dialogic philosophy in suggesting the terminology: the *loss of the "Thou" in the other*, at least in part, for the processes of interpersonal coexistence mentioned above. By this, I mean a lifelong and fearful certainty grounded in a specific traumatogenic mentalization deficiency that a particular assumption will surely be shattered: the assumption that others will perceive one as an alter ego and that one will be able to perceive others as an alter ego in an empathic sense. This enormous fear, portrayed by Drees as the central phenomenon of totalitarian repression, may thus not only be accounted for by the constant, latent threat to one's self, a threat characteristic of life under such conditions, but furthermore by the loss of security due to the collapse of basic assumptions of reciprocity in human relationships, which are necessary conditions for the constitution of our social world.

Under such living conditions, alternatives to ideologically distorted identification with the totalitarian regime such as flight, escape, and possibilities of withdrawal become central themes in fantasies of preservation and rescue that enable survival. It is important to distinguish between inner escapism and real flight. The former concerns withdrawal from individual social fulfillment into an "inner emigration." This refers to outwardly superficial submissiveness and the appearance of functioning combined with an inner, detached, and apparently free world of fantasy. Real flight is taken into fitting societal niches or into a different country. Flight into inner worlds is consistently accompanied by the loss of real social chances. Thus it acts as a source of envy and hate of those who truly experience social fulfillment. Real flight, in contrast, carries the price of danger, which can lead to actual physical annihilation.

Mixed "Account Balances" (*Bilanzen*) and "Embitterment" as Results of Internalization of Problems Caused by German Reunification

"Account balances" (*Bilanzen*) are always mixed when a totalitarian system collapses. Despite sweeping improvements in living conditions, in the erection of democratic structures in state and society, in the restoration of a public civil sphere, and in areas of personal lifestyle, infrastructure, morbidity and mortality, the reunification has also produced losers. A particular example of this can be found in the employment market. In order to understand the inner "balancing of accounts" by individuals negatively affected by reunification, it is important that the same negative postreunification event can be attributed by different persons to varying causes. A radio and television technician, who has become unemployed as a result of the political turnaround that rolled through East Germany after reunification in 1989, can ascribe the loss of his job to the fact that up until the reunification, his competence only extended to the repair of hopelessly antiquated appliances. Thus, after reunification, he was not qualified to meet new requirements and performance levels. He attributes this break to the fact that the GDR economy had lost connection with technical progress in the rest of the world. Or he may attribute his unemployment to reunification's introduction of a capitalistic economic system, a system only interested in maximum exploitation, which dismissed him because of his inability to make a sufficient contribution to profit maximization.

In Germany, postreunification discussions between East and West over the past 20 years have frequently been characterized by disputes over the "correct" attribution of guilt for the negative consequences of reunification. Adherence to fantasies about the "good," or at least "not so bad," GDR (Berth, Förster, Bräler, Balck, & Stöbel-Richter, 2009; Leuenberger, 2006) points out the complexity of postreunification development and the challenges this poses to those affected. In writing about this subject a decade ago, I discussed psychological processing of the posttotalitarian situation following the collapse of the GDR and postulated that coming to terms with everyday Western culture would be made in a stepwise process. This process could be called an *internalization or intimization of problems caused by German reunification*. During the first stage of this process, immediately after reunification, personal characteristics, values, and habits identified with a Western lifestyle were felt by many East Germans to be characteristics of a completely foreign group (i.e., West Germans) within the population. Later, during the second stage, these qualities were considered to be characteristics of other individuals (e.g., their own children) within the same social environment. At the end of the developmental process, during the third stage, these characteristics were seen to be more or less assimilated and integrated parts or aspects of their own personality (Frommer, 2000). The central task of this process became the overcoming of obsessive-compulsive defense maneuvers, and thus of functionalizing and feeling functionalized on a partial-object relationship level. This favored the reestablishment of *real* alter ego relationships within the public area of a civil state experienced as safe, protected, and calculable.

Today, more than 20 years after the political reunification of Germany, this surely lifelong virulent process of development has reached a stage characterized for many people by increasingly successful integration of old and new experiences and features of identity. This is especially true of those persons fortunate enough to have lived through the totalitarian period within families, social milieus, or niches in which sufficient space for real human relationships, trust, and reliability was available to enable survival of the dehumanizing processes in public life. Experience gained within these "islands" of humanity could then be tapped into when totalitarianism ended. What, however, is the case with persons who are unable to fully or partially experience these sorts of experiences? For these individuals, it is to be feared that the posttotalitarian processes of development, assimilation, and integration described above were hindered or made impossible. For those people, time has stood more or less still.

One of the resulting psychopathological problems has been categorized diagnostically as posttraumatic embitterment disorder. Against this background of historic upheaval, it is hardly coincidental that this specific form of adjustment disorder was introduced as recently as 10 years ago by a group of psychiatrists whose clinical experience was primarily based on work with patients in a large psychiatric rehab hospital in Berlin on the Brandenburg border. Michael Linden and colleagues define the core criterion of this disorder to be a grave, negative life event, followed by a condition of suffering interpreted by the affected as resulting from the incident. According to operational criteria, the incident is experienced by the affected person to be unfair or unjust. When spoken to about the incident, those affected react with bitterness and emotional agitation. In addition, the disorder is characterized by intrusive memories of the incident, as well as by further obligatory and facultative criteria less relevant here. Employment loss and conflicts at the workplace stand at the top of the list of triggers (Linden, Rotter, Baumann, & Lieberei, 2007).

Discussed within a critical perspective it must appear to be problematic that the authors remain within a tradition of purely static–descriptive psychiatric diagnostic classification and in so doing, awaken the impression of operationalizing a "disorder" taken out of social context. The impression can be gained that societal, cultural, and historical conditions at the start of the disorder as well as a psychodynamic and historical understanding of the condition of suffering are being ignored.

In this context, an attempt is made to understand the embitterment syndrome as an expression of excessive demands made on one by post-totalitarian personal development requirements. The reunification, that is, the sudden availability of previously denied chances to achieve personal growth and development, becomes a trauma for individuals only able to perceive these phenomena in others with feelings of envy and angry disappointment. They are so bound and set in compulsive patterns of experience and behavior that they are unable to implement newly won increments of freedom. They continue to function according to a sort of inner totalitarian corset. Freedom is not experienced as freedom, but as the expulsion from external structures of supply. The individuals' personal inability to make decisions and take action make them dependent on these external structures, without which they freeze into a state of helpless passivity.

A Case Study[2]

Through observations both within clinical settings and of daily life in Eastern Germany, I have become convinced that since the collapse of the totalitarian GDR regime, one can observe the development of a pathological coping mechanism in a significant number of individuals, particularly those with talent and an interest in furthering their own personal development. I now propose to describe this development in a case vignette, which will portray the nature of the extreme position called *omnipresence* in ideal-typical form. In some respects, this position can be viewed as an opposing pole to embitterment as a pathological form of coping. This point of view may serve a more multidimensional form of understanding. In reality, one can reckon with less clearly marked expressions of omnipresence, transitional phenomena pointing on the one side toward embitterment, on the other toward more mature and successful forms of coping.

I propose to explain this point by means of a brief case study. Mr. R was a large and vigorous man in his early 50s. During our first meeting, I was struck by his calm and superior smile. It was difficult for me to empathize with his reports of daily headaches. These were not constant; however, they started up immediately when Mr. R felt he was being put under pressure. He brooded frequently and was hugely dissatisfied with himself and with the world. He felt tired and worn out and had difficulty concentrating. His thoughts kept him awake at night. He felt blocked and had to force himself to perform necessary tasks. He withdrew from others and felt that life was slipping away from him. He was no longer able to make plans. He downright fled from people and tasks, at the same time suffering from a fear of failure. He was unable to cope with pressure. Shortly after the beginning of our first conversation, I was overcome by extreme tiredness and feelings of heaviness that almost completely hindered me from listening attentively. A dark vortex appeared to grasp at me and pull me down. I was filled with displeasure, and without consciously meaning to, I thought about how to escape, how to get rid of him. These countertransference feelings were accompanied by massive physical unrest, which manifests itself in my changing my seating position.

In relating his biography since reunification, the patient stated that he left his actual academic profession at that time. In the GDR, political factors prevented him from advancing in his career. In the years following reunification, he pursued an extraordinarily successful career as a real estate broker. After a short time, he was numbered among the 10 best brokers in the new federal states. In 1994, the company he worked for rewarded him for his work with a trip to Mauritius where he met his second wife. In Leipzig, she also worked in real estate: they had "almost identical histories."

Both their previous marriages broke up as a result of this new "overnight" relationship. The first wife fought for him. He, however, moved out on Christmas Eve of the same year. The jointly built house, a "giant villa," was completed only shortly before the separation. He left this house "without personal belongings, without memories," as he put it. As I listened to him, I noticed the brief appearance of an abyssal sadness at this point. This affect faded almost immediately, however, against the drama and velocity of the following narrative.

The separation brought about a veritable campaign of revenge on the part of the first wife. She brought charges against him, among them theft and document falsification. Mr. R claimed that there was nothing to these allegations and related that four complaints had been dropped. His car tires were slit repeatedly and the paint of his car was scratched. Two years after the separation and shortly after the divorce, he became the victim of an attempted "assault": At 1:30 a.m. a block of stone weighing several kilograms was suddenly thrown from the neighboring house through the window of his new flat in Leipzig. The stone landed next to the bed breaking the window. Fortunately, he and his new partner were not injured. At the same time, Mr. R was denounced to the tax authorities regarding the sum of DM180,000 in undeclared income. The former wife accused herself at the same time. The ensuing tax investigations stretched over a period of 6 years, ending in Mr. R's conviction. He was now faced with a debt of €520,000. Interest on the original amount ran his total debt up to over €1 million. He attempted to apply for personal bankruptcy. There was no room for briefly emerging countertransferences of fear, uncanniness, and consternation. Confused, I listened to what happened next.

Immediately after the divorce, Mr. R married his new partner. Shortly thereafter, a son was born. During this period, he flew to Thailand alone for the first time. His wife encouraged him, thinking that this would help lift his depressive mood. Since then, he had been there three times a year, returning to Germany in a worsened condition each time. In the meantime, the tax authorities have also latched on to his second wife. During Mr. R's visits overseas, he has kept up intimate and unprotected contact with numerous women, among them prostitutes, although he is well aware of the high HIV infection rate in Thailand. He has purchased a house in Thailand from a fellow European emigrant. Prior to bankruptcy, he had taken out a mortgage for this house. No one in Germany, not even his wife, knew about any of this. He has gone on high-speed motorcycle tours in areas known to be very dangerous for tourists. Once, a nonswimmer, he rented a tiny rowboat and took it far out on the ocean. He fought with currents for 4 hours, surviving only because of a chance rescue. By the end of the narrative I felt exhausted and tormented. Feelings of hopelessness remained.

The term *omnipresence* refers to the compulsive attempt, as this example shows, to eliminate all boundaries of development within a social area and render them inoperative. This includes lifting all physical borders. No vacation spot is too far away. Every attempt is made to get from one place to another as quickly as possible with no regard for possible danger. No price is too high, no attachment provides stability. Each possibility for professional self-realization is utilized with the utmost effort and at breathtaking speed. Family ties are made and broken. No taboo stands in the way of satisfying sexual and erotic desires. The physical body appears to be indestructible and ageless, infinitely malleable and resilient. Every possibility is tried. Every thrill is followed by the search for the next one.

What kind of biographical background can result in phenomena of this kind? Mr. R was born in a village only a few kilometers east of the border that for decades bore the name *iron curtain*. His father was a hard man, who showed no emotions. He ruled over the family like a dictator. He drank and beat his wife and son frequently and brutally. He was a convinced socialist and allowed no doubts regarding the government. His mother was from a displaced family. She submitted to her husband, remaining a pale figure. Her father, a large-scale farmer and convinced national socialist, was shot by Russian soldiers on his farm in 1945 in front of her. Mr. R's adolescence and early adult life were marked by attempts at rebellion, which led to expulsion from the socialist "Free German Youth" and from his studies. This was accompanied by countless summonses to appear before state security forces. Mr. R's personal biography, together with its transgenerational links to parents and grandparents, is an ideal-typical example of injustice and oppression.

On the Psychodynamics of "Omnipresence"

Psychodynamically speaking, the urge toward omnipresent self-fulfillment can first be understood as a sort of "genie in the bottle" phenomenon, as rebellion and defense against compulsive restriction. From the point of view of developmental psychology, during the anal development phase, primitive, narcissistic, "oceanlike" feelings of spreading out and merging the self with the world make a first connection with cognitive processes. This results in fantasies that can be thought out and remembered and revolve around the theme of "omnipotence of thoughts" (Freud, 1909, p. 234). At the same time, these narcissistic experiences and thoughts with their ego nuclei become connected with interpersonal conflict dynamics, which are concerned with motor movement in space and the "fate" of anal products or excretions. The resulting concept, that there is or might be a powerful single being who rules the whole world without limits, later becomes, in a more or less sublimated form, both the foundation of a spiritual and religious intellectual edifice (Freud, 1912–1213) and a possible model for societal and political organization.

The terminology used here has its roots in and is borrowed from dogmatic theology. *Omnipotence*, *omnipresence*, and *omniscience* are the three central attributes of God, who himself is not only almighty and all-knowing, but also ever-present in an immeasurable way in all objects and spaces: "Deus totus oculus est, quia omnia videt; totus manus est, quia omnia operatur; totus pes est, quia ubique est" ["God is all eyes because he sees all things; he is all hands, because he does all things; he is all feet, because he is everywhere"] (Augustine, quoted by Ritter, 1971, p. 162; translated by Jörg Frommer and Liz Franzen). In addition to thoughts about omnipotence, fantasies of omnipresence also include magical thinking as found in small children. Thanks to their structure forming power, fantasies give a feeling of control over, and safety against, sudden outbreaks of ungoverned, aggressive, and libidinous drive forces, and thus contribute to intrapsychic balance. It can be assumed, especially when massive repression occurs during very early upbringing, that conscious and unconscious derivatives of omnipotence problems remain highly relevant into old age. This applies both to the introjected form, the desire to be almighty, and to the projected form, being completely at the mercy of an almighty power, which controls all things and prohibits all forms of freedom.

While the embittered individual views himself as being still at the mercy of others and damned to inactivity even after his external fetters have fallen away, the omnipresent individual tries with all his might in a constant state of high alertness to withdraw himself from the grasp of powerful objects, to elude these and escape to another place. His intent is the attempt to complete personal projects of self-fulfillment at a racing speed before being overtaken again. This specific omnipresent form of avoidance is that much more regressive or based on earlier processes in child development compared with anal regression, as anal access is linked to space and time, whereas omnipresence fantasy assumes the enforcement of personal will "everywhere," outside fixed time or space. It concerns a kind of "submergence," a disappearance into an intangible area, into the world of a philobatic "structureless primitive state, where there are as yet no, or only very few and unimportant unpredictable objects" (Balint, 1959, p. 84). For this reason, omnipresence phenomena sometimes bear uncanny features (Freud, 1919).

I am indebted to Léon Wurmser for pointing out references to phobic defense mechanisms relevant to the concept of omnipresence, above and beyond the aspects already mentioned. From his point of view, fears of being locked in, captured, or restrained refer back to superego structures about which one is highly ambivalent. The relevant superego parts stem from socialization experiences in a constrictive environment, resulting in unbearable agonies and superego anxiety brought about by interpersonal closeness and restrictions caused by responsibilities; for example, in personal life. Wurmser views such anxiety as leading to aggressive attempts at breaking free. These attempts, instead of reducing superego problems, strengthen them by provoking inner accusations, guilt charges, and impulses toward punishment. Wurmser describes superego splits to be one of the results of this constellation. Within such a split, a partial superego, characterized by fantasies of protection and rescue, functions in a completely nonintegrated manner adjacent to yet another partial superego representing restrictive directions and prohibitions on free development (Wurmser, 2000). The struggle against real (external) repression has thus become an unbearable inner conflict, in which the projection of totalitarian superego parts into the outside world makes a nearly indispensable contribution toward the preservation of psychic equilibrium. This is especially the case when actual repression has ceased.

The characterization of this defense form as an early childhood disturbance is made clear by two additional psychodynamic connections. The case study shows the great role played by mistrust, by betraying and being betrayed, and by paranoid aspects. With Freud (1911), these phenomena may be understood psychodynamically as claims of omnipotence, omnipresence, and omniscience that are projected onto other individuals. Even after the end of real spying, surveillance, control, and restrictive measures, the world appears to be divided into like-minded people and opponents. Radical spatial, social, and cultural shifts, typical for omnipresence, serve the purpose of being with the right people, with good people, and of escaping one's pursuers. Feelings of being pursued or restrained can be projective fantasies without any correlates in reality. However, paranoid dramatization and mise-en-scène play an additional role, in which the affected person unconsciously stages entanglements, which actually threaten his physical, socioeconomic, and moral existence, sometimes even ending in self-destruction. The other individual is forced into the role of pursuer. Each frustration, no matter how minimal, is interpreted as proof of hostility and evil purpose.

The paranoid aspect behind omnipresence's constant anxiety, tension, and readiness for flight can appear to be a continual, shadowing mistrust, poisonously invading all relationships. In the light of this mistrust, the entire world appears threatening. This aspect can also erupt in the form of a crisis. During noncrisis periods, a worldview can be upheld, which allows for the existence or at the very least the suggestion of positive and trustworthy aspects. These periods are interrupted by sudden threats to their world picture. Causes for the eruption of crises are sometimes recognized only after long psychoanalyses. Occasionally, the paranoid aspect appears in delegated form: A near relative or other close reference person is described as talking nonstop about mistrust, interference, and persecution.

At least since Alexander and Margarete Mitscherlich (1975), we have become aware that the inability to mourn is one of the difficult inheritances of totalitarian rule. Under authoritarianism, not only are the ability to feel empathy, stand ambiguity, and take different roles and perspectives destroyed for good. Resistance to feelings of guilt and shame built up by suppression and denial of one's own emotional attachments and by identification with partial aspects of the totalitarian system block genuine personality transformation after the end of totalitarian rule. This is combined with conscious and unconscious desires for a return of the past. In its omnipresent form, resistance to grieving appears characteristically in an almost hypomanic busyness over longer periods of time. In the face of the real misery of one's life, inadequate, euphoric mood states alternate with the paranoid episodes described above. The halo of the omnipresent individual with its inherent fantasies of greatness, invulnerability, and invincibility are an expression of an imagined triumphal victory over the aggressor. The personal, imagined ability to constantly escape one's aggressor and to further one's development in all areas is set against the aggressor's all-encompassing power and ubiquity. Although the omnipresent individual, like the manic individual, demonstrates his "liberation from the object which was the cause of his suffering" (Freud, 1917, p. 255), omnipresent defense cannot completely be explained as manic defense, because the relationship between omnipresence and defense against grief is only one of many aspects contributing to psychodynamic understanding of this phenomenon.

Since Freud's brief footnote in *The Ego and the Id* (1923), we know that unconscious feelings of guilt and shame, the latter added by Léon Wurmser (1997, 2011), are those that most stubbornly resist further development of personality and psychic structures. As Freud already knew, these feelings are not infrequently "borrowed": the result of identification with a near person, often a parent or grandparent, ensnared or suspected of being ensnared in guilt. Thanks primarily to the work of Friedrich-Wilhelm Eickhoff (1986, 1989; see also Frommer, 2007), we are now able to make these judgments when referring to political aspects of German identity problems. Behind over 40 years of repression in East Germany, we find the preceding period of national socialism, a weighty inheritance for Germans in both East and West. These persons are entangled in guilt, which carries long-term transgenerational consequences up until the present. From the phenomenon of the so-called *Wirtschaftswunder* (economic miracle) in West Germany during the 1950s and 1960s to the still constant migration of young people from the new federal states, quite a number of social phenomena can be linked to the concept of omnipresence and other forms of coping and defense against guilt feelings and shame.

Omnipresent Defense as Masked Negative Therapeutic Reaction (NTR)

Unconscious and unconsciously borrowed guilt feelings number among the main roots of defense through omnipresent acting out as well as of NTRs. Thus, it is not astonishing that this special form of psychic defense predestines standstills and setbacks that are both difficult to understand and to analyze during psychotherapeutic and psychoanalytic treatment. Through the use of restrained and sparing interventions, the analyst can accidentally stumble into the transference role of a heartless, unempathetic, and cold observer, who watches, spies on, and listens in on the analysand like a *Stasi* (state secret police) employee. One of my analysands, for example, told me toward the end of a high-frequency analysis over a period of many years, that he had been convinced for at least the first 100 sessions that a hidden cassette recorder was activated somewhere in the room. In a worst case scenario, occurring most notably when he too consistently interprets the patient's omnipresent actions, the analyst becomes a malignant pursuer, stalking and preying on the analysand, ferreting him out, and threatening him in such a fashion that he tries to escape in increasingly life-threatening ways. These attempts at flight may be "camouflaged" as a harmless holiday trip. Only after close enquiry does it become clear in what great danger the analysand finds himself. After several preliminary sessions in which positive contact appeared to have been made, a homosexual patient who had suffered severe political persecution suddenly insisted on undertaking a long-distance journey to a far-Asian country shortly before the start of actual treatment. It later emerged that he had also had unprotected sexual intercourse with a number of different acquaintances in an area known for its high rate of HIV infections.

In early phases of treatment, one of the most notable countertransference phenomena is the extraordinary contrast between dramatic events in the patient's real life and the substantial absence of drama in the analyst's countertransference feelings. The loss of "Thou" in the other person manifests itself as "empty" countertransference. As a consequence of the feeling of having no "other," no partner, patients produce "an experience in the countertransference of helplessness, pointlessness, and emptiness" (Rose, 2001, p. 1). Robbed of his most important aide to orientation, the analyst experiences a fundamental feeling of being lost. This increases the chances of his being seduced by masked proposals to enter into destructive acting out. In my experience, feelings of guilt and insufficiency in the analyst's countertransference can become nearly unbearable when, for example in the case described above, the patient presents his path to social self-destruction and flirts with physical self-destruction. At the same time, the analyst lacks concern, sympathy, or interest, thinking instead about his grocery list. Other countertransference reactions can be a torturous feeling of boredom, sudden physical unrest, and the impulse to movement, as well as feelings of uncanniness, falling into deep chasms, or a vital loss of support.

Against this backdrop, the analysand's projects of self-fulfillment in the external world, often introduced with a high level of dynamism as well as an element of surprise, are often misunderstood. These projects are rapid and highly complex. Cognitive understanding requires great concentration, which in turn draws attention away from dealing with the patient's inner world. The more activity there is on the external stage, the less obvious the emptiness of the internal world. The form of NTR specific to these patients is marked by a number of factors: A highly dynamic succession of events suggesting mobility, fulfillment, and success over a longer period of time is misidentified as progress. At the same time both parties, analysand and analyst, due to mutual involvement in the phenomena deny that analysis has come to a standstill. These phases alternate with catastrophes, during which everything built at that point collapses like a house of cards in an existentially threatening manner. This is accompanied by helplessness and the shattering of a feeling of "we" between analyst and analysand. Agonizing silence indicates that the actual problem is the lack of a partner, a nonverbal feeling of early abandonment similar to Enid Balint's (1963) description of her patient, Sarah, and to what Green (1999), in referring to Sartre, called "psychic holes."

In later stages of analyses, the analysand's deep despair is felt in countertransference, even before becoming a theme in dialogue. Paradoxically, the appearance of a difficult, almost unbearable "countertransference depression" (Rose, 2001, p. 4) is not a sign of regress, but of progress. This points out the danger of false interpretation, should the analyst allow himself to stimulate the cascade of "self-fulfillment" projects of the patient's *false self* (Winnicott, 1965), instead of bearing with the patient's developing ability to mourn and exploring with him his gloomy, dreamlike inner world filled with "virtual objects" (Rose, 2001, p.6). An examination of this special form of defense, here called omnipresence, in its relation to NTR is fruitful, as it points out that NTR does not always appear in easily recognizable form. Apparent progress can signal deeper blockades, apparent regress can be a sign of successful analysis.

Omnipresence and Postmodern Acceleration: Closing Considerations on the Question of Specificity

Omnipresence as a special defense can only be roughly outlined here. Numerous questions thus remain temporarily unanswered. In conclusion, however, we should touch on the essential question of the specificity to posttotalitarian personal development. Numerous sociological diagnosticians currently discuss the fact that technology and media are no longer a means to an end, a separate entity from the individual, but have increasingly become an end in themselves, fused with the individual (Latour, 2005). As Freud (1930) recognized early on, this fusion of the individual with media transforms him into a kind of "prosthetic god." In our terminology, he becomes a technically upgraded being, constantly in danger of forgetting his actual limits, his finality, and his marginality in favor of a medially staged appearance of almightiness, all-knowingness, and ever-presence. Currently, this is joined by a constantly increasing acceleration of all processes in all areas of life (Rosa, 2005). If one confines oneself to the phenomenological surface, one could conclude that omnipresence is an unspecific phenomenon constantly affecting individuals in advanced modern society and in no way typical only of the consequences of repression.

This assumption overlooks an important point, however: The form of omnipresence discussed here, and shown in the case study, always implies a large measure of destructiveness and self-destruction. The destructive side of omnipresence is fed by various sources, among which archaic frustration-aggression plays just as decisive a role as the need for punishment of a pathological partial superego, which is identified with the cruel agents at whose hands repression was suffered. The latter explains the high measure of self-destruction in omnipresent defense. The deeper and more unconscious the identification with one's tormentors, the more unpredictable are the resulting self-destructive actions. Destructiveness is proportional to the strivings toward omnipresence. The bigger and more energy-consuming these aspirations for self-expansion are, the worse is the failure. The unconsciously triggered failure to succeed is thus one of the most important characteristics of omnipresent defense against irritation, obstruction, punishment, and humiliation experienced during repression. Repressed trauma urges toward reenactment. Escape from this pattern of behavior is difficult.

Although this chapter clearly pleads for a separation in terminology between omnipresence strivings and ubiquitous postmodern, media-supported acceleration of development, it is conceivable that one might consider their culture-critical implications. At the beginning of this chapter, it was pointed out that each historic epoch imprints the defense forms of its inhabitants with a personal stamp. It may thus be asked, what consequences certain factors carry for a particular generation. These factors include: An increasing decline in the number of concrete physical bodily spaces in which experience can be had; the resulting physical inactivity and lack of sufficient sensual experience; simultaneous overflooding by media-produced experience; and a continual growth in the number of options available in symbolic space. In debating this question, it is not only important to discuss the increase in depressive psychopathologies (Ehrenberg, 2010). The question of the reactive nature of symbolic and medial development "at any price" should also be more sharply examined. Against the backdrop of the destructive and self-destructive implications of behavioral traits, which at first appear to be free development, one must pose the paradoxical question of whether forced self-realization in all areas does not in fact point to an area of loss or may even be understood as an unsuccessful reaction to traumatization caused by repression and by a lack of fulfillment of basic needs. This proves especially bitter for those who, having finally escaped repressive traumatizing by GDR state terror set their entire hopes in the seemingly infinite possibilities of development in a reunited Germany. These individuals must learn through painful experience that not all is gold that glitters.

Notes

1. English translation by Liz Franzen.
2. Personal information about the patient has been changed in order to preserve anonymity.

References

Adorno, T. W., Frenkel-Brunswik, E., Levinson, D. J. & Sanford, R. N. (1950). *The authoritarian personality.* New York: Harper & Row.

Arendt, H. (2006). *Eichmann in Jerusalem: A report on the banality of the evil.* New York: Penguin Books. (Original work published 1963)

Balint, E. (1963). On being empty of oneself. *International Journal of Psychoanalysis, 44,* 470–480.

Balint, M. (1959). *Thrills and regressions.* New York: International Universities Press.

Bar-On, D. (1998). *Fear and hope: Three generations of the Holocaust.* Cambridge, MA: Harvard University Press.

Bergman, M. S., & Jucovy, M. E. (Eds.). (1982). *Generations of the Holocaust.* New York: Basic Books.

Berth, H., Förster, P., Brähler, E., Balck, F. & Stöbel-Richter, Y. (2009). "Vorwärts und nicht vergessen": Wie bewerten junge Ostdeutsche 20 Jahre nach dem Mauerfall die DDR [Forward and do not forget how young East Germans 20 years after the fall of the GDR see the East]. *Psychosozial* [Psychosocial], *117*(2), 37–46.

Buber, M. (1951). Distance and relation (R. G. Smith, Trans.). *The Hibbert Journal, 49*, 105–113.

Drees, L. (2011). "Ich bin nicht besser als meine Väter…" Regression und Gegenübertragung des Analytikers nach zwei totalitären Systemen—Spurensuche ["I am not better than my fathers…": The analyst's regression and countertransference after two totalitarian systems—Clues]. In P. Diederichs, J. Frommer, & F. Wellendorf (Eds.), *Äußere und Innere Realität* [Exterior and interior reality] (pp. 295–315). Stuttgart, Germany: Klett-Cotta.

Ehrenberg, A. (2010). *The weariness of the self: Diagnosing the history of depression in the contemporary age.* Montreal, Canada: McGill Queens University Press.

Eickhoff, F.-W. (1986). Identification and its vicissitudes in the context of the Nazi phenomenon. *International Journal of Psychoanalysis, 67*, 33–44.

Eickhoff, F.-W. (1989). On the "borrowed unconscious sense of guilt" and the palimpsest character of a symptom: Afterthoughts on the Hamburg Congress of the IPA. *International Review of Psychoanalysis, 16*, 323–329.

Fahrenberg, J., & Steiner, J. M. (2004). Adorno und die autoritäre Persönlichkeit [Adorno and the authoritarian personality]. *Kölner Zeitschrift für Soziologie und Sozialpsychologie* [Cologne journal of sociology and social psychology], *56*, 1–31.

Fonagy, P., Gergely, G., Jurist, E., & Target, M. (2002). *Affect regulation, mentalization and the development of self.* New York: Other Press.

Freud, A. (1937). *The ego and the mechanisms of defense.* London: Hogarth Press.

Freud, S. (1894). The neuro-psychoses of defense. In J. Strachey (Ed. & Trans.), *The standard edition of the complete psychological works of Sigmund Freud* (Vol. 3, pp. 41–70). London: Hogarth Press.

Freud, S. (1905). Three essays on the theory of sexuality. In J. Strachey (Ed. & Trans.), *The standard edition of the complete psychological works of Sigmund Freud* (Vol. 7, pp. 123–242). London: Hogarth Press.

Freud, S. (1908). Character and anal erotism. In J. Strachey (Ed. & Trans.), *The standard edition of the complete psychological works of Sigmund Freud* (Vol. 9, pp. 167–176). London: Hogarth Press.

Freud, S. (1909). Remarks upon a case of compulsion neurosis. In J. Strachey (Ed. & Trans.), *The standard edition of the complete psychological works of Sigmund Freud* (Vol. 10, pp. 151–318). London: Hogarth Press.

Freud, S. (1911). Psychoanalytic notes on an autobiographical account of a case of paranoia (dementia paranoides). In J. Strachey (Ed. & Trans.), *The standard edition of the complete psychological works of Sigmund Freud* (Vol. 12, pp. 1–84). London: Hogarth Press.

Freud, S. (1912–1913). Totem and taboo. In J. Strachey (Ed. & Trans.), *The standard edition of the complete psychological works of Sigmund Freud* (Vol. 13, pp. 1–163). London: Hogarth Press.

Freud, S. (1917). Mourning and melancholia. In J. Strachey (Ed. & Trans.), *The standard edition of the complete psychological works of Sigmund Freud* (Vol. 14, pp. 237–260). London: Hogarth Press.

Freud, S. (1919). The uncanny. In J. Strachey (Ed. & Trans.), *The standard edition of the complete psychological works of Sigmund Freud* (Vol. 17, pp. 217–256). London: Hogarth Press.
Freud, S. (1923). The ego and the id. In J. Strachey (Ed. & Trans.), *The standard edition of the complete psychological works of Sigmund Freud* (Vol. 19, pp. 1–66). London: Hogarth Press.
Freud, S. (1927). The future of an illusion. In J. Strachey (Ed. & Trans.), *The standard edition of the complete psychological works of Sigmund Freud* (Vol. 21, pp. 1–56). London: Hogarth Press.
Freud, S. (1930). Civilization and its discontents. In J. Strachey (Ed. & Trans.), *The standard edition of the complete psychological works of Sigmund Freud* (Vol. 27, pp. 57–146). London: Hogarth Press.
Fromm, E. (1932). Die psychoanalytische Charakterologie und ihre Bedeutung für die Sozialpsychologie [Psychoanalytic characteristics and their significance for social psychology]. *Zeitschrift für Sozialforschung* [Journal of social research], *1*, 253–277.
Frommer, J. (2000). Psychoanalytische und soziologische Aspekte personalen Identitätswandels im vereinten Deutschland [Psychoanalytic and sociological aspects of personal identity change in a united Germany]. *Zeitschrift für Qualitative Bildungs-, Beratungs- und Sozialforschung* [Journal of qualitative education, counseling and social research], *1*(2), 365–383.
Frommer, J. (2007). Unbewusst entlehntes Schuldgefühl und traumatische Identitätsbildung—Ein Beitrag zu den Generationen übergreifenden Spätfolgen von Täterverstrickungen der Psychiatrie im nationalsozialistischen Deutschland [Unconsciously borrowed sense of guilt and traumatic identity formation—A contribution to the intergenerational sequelae of perpetrator involvement of psychiatry in Nazi Germany]. *Psychoanalyse-Texte zur Sozialforschung* [Psychoanalytic texts for social research], *11*, 64–80.
Green, A. (1999). *The dead mother: The work of André Green*. London: Routledge.
Kernberg, O. (1993). *Severe personality disorders: Psychotherapeutic strategies*. New Haven, CT: Yale University Press.
Kogan, I. (2007). *The struggle against mourning*. New York: Jason Aronson.
Krystal, H. (1968). *Massive psychic trauma*. New York: International Universities Press.
Lamparter, Holstein C., Thießen, M., Wierling, D., Wiegand-Grefe, S. & Möller, B. (2010). 65 Jahre spatter: Zeitzeugen des "Hamburger Feuersturms" (1943) im lebensgeschichtlichen Interview [65 years later: Witnesses of the "Hamburg firestorm" (1943) in the oral history interview]. *Forum der Psychoanalyse* [Forum for psychoanalysis], *26*, 365–387.
Latour, B. (2005). *Reassembling the social: Introduction to actor-network-theory*. Oxford, England: Oxford University Press.
Leuenberger, C. (2006). Constructions of the Berlin wall: How material culture is used in psychological theory. *Social Problems*, *53*, 18–37.
Linden, M., Rotter, M., Baumann, K. & Lieberei, B. (2007). *The posttraumatic embitterment disorder*. Toronto, Canada: Hogrefe & Huber.
Löwith, K. (1928). *Das Individuum in der Rolle des Mitmenschen* [The individual in the role of the other]. Munich, Germany: Drei Masken Verlag.
Mitscherlich, A., & Mitscherlich, M. (1975). *The inability to mourn: Principles of collective behavior*. New York: Grove Press.

Oliner, M. (2011). Drehen Sie sich nicht um, Frau Lot [Do not turn around Mrs. Lot]. In P. Diederichs, J. Frommer, & F. Wellendorf (Eds.), *Äußere und innere Realität* [External and internal reality] (pp. 261–275). Stuttgart, Germany: Klett-Cotta.

Ritter, J. (Ed.) (1971). *Historisches Wörterbuch der Philosophie: Band 1* [Historical dictionary of philosophy (Vol. 1)]. Darmstadt, Germany: Wissenschaftliche Buchgesellschaft.

Rosa, H. (2005). *Beschleunigung: Die Veränderung der Zeitstrukturen in der Moderne* [Acceleration: The change of time structures in the modern]. Frankfurt/Main, Germany: Suhrkamp.

Rose, J. (2001). The presence of absence in the transference: Some clinical, countertransference and meta-psychological implications. *Bulletin of the British Psychoanalytical Society, 37*(6), 1–13.

Šebek, M. (1992). Anality in the totalitarian system and psychology of post-totalitarian objects. *Mind and Human Interaction, 4*, 52–59.

Šebek, M. (1996). Fates of totalitarian objects. *International Forum of Psychoanalysis, 5*, 289–294.

Šebek, M. (1998). Post-totalitarian personality: Old internal objects in a new situation. *Journal of the American Academy of Psychoanalysis, 26*, 295–309.

Winnicott, D. W. (1965). Ego distortion on terms of true and false self. In *The maturational processes and the facilitating environment* (pp. 140–152). London: Hogarth Press.

Wurmser, L. (1997). *The mask of shame.* Baltimore, MD: John Hopkins University Press.

Wurmser, L. (2000). *Flucht vor dem Gewissen* [Flight from conscience]. Göttingen, Germany: Vandenhoeck & Ruprecht.

Wurmser, L. (2011). *Scham und böser Blick: Verstehen der negativen therapeutischen Reaktion* [Shame and the evil eye: Understanding the negative therapeutic reaction]. Stuttgart, Germany: Kohlhammer.

7

ANXIETY IN THE NEGATIVE THERAPEUTIC REACTION

Cordelia Schmidt-Hellerau

Freud introduced the negative therapeutic reaction as a clinical concept. But, as always, he also reflected on it on a metapsychological level. At the end of his 32nd lecture, in which he considers the relation between "Anxiety and Instinctual Life" (1933), he reveals how he came to develop his second drive theory: It was the negative therapeutic reaction that gave him pause. Hence, Freud's conception of the negative therapeutic reaction is the clinical root of his second drive theory and his introduction of the death drive. It follows that in order to fully appreciate and explore its meaning and value in contemporary psychoanalysis, it seems sensible to consider this particular connection from the perspective of a contemporary drive theory (Schmidt-Hellerau, 2002, 2005, 2006). It is my contention that we can still gain new territory from making use of a revised drive theory for which I will provide a brief introductory sketch before tackling the question of anxiety and the negative therapeutic reaction.

Freud's Basic Assumptions

Freud's theory of psychic functioning, his metapsychological model of the mind, is based on the two axiomatic concepts, *drive* and *structure.* The *drive* (*instinct* in Strachey's misleading translation) can be defined as a one-directional movement, emanating from a bodily stimulus that affects the mind (Freud, 1915, p. 121) in stirring a need or desire that propels the subject toward the object of satisfaction; it is an energizing force driving virtually endlessly until it reaches the object. Thus it not only links the body to the mind but also the subject to the object and the world. The structure, on the other hand, is what the mind has stored and retained but also constructed and developed in the course and consequence of its interactions with the objects and the world. The structures are basically the memory of the system, containing on various levels of complexity and maturity of conscious and unconscious representations of self and object, traces of experiences, wishes and fantasies, up to the major structural

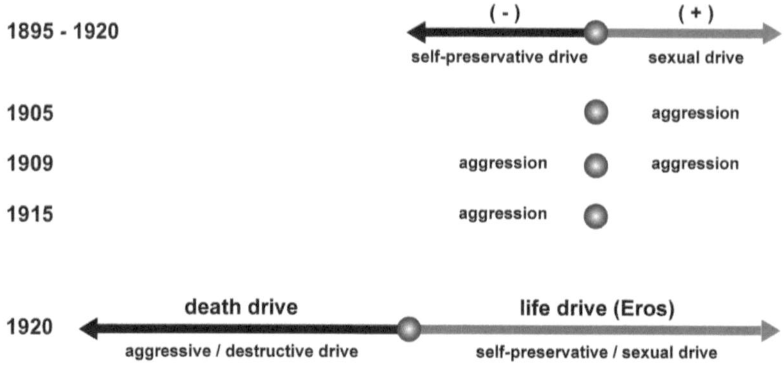

Figure 7.1 Development of Freud's drive theory. The antagonism of self-preservative and sexual drives are indicated with the opposite directions of the arrows and the (+) and (-) signs. Aggression held various places in Freud's drive theory before 1920 when it became the representative of the death drive.

configurations of id, ego, and superego. While the drives are the same for every human being, it is the structures that make an individual unique and different from any other. The interaction between drive and structure consists in the drives providing the energy and activating the structures, and the structures directing, distributing, and balancing these energies within homeostatic levels (pleasure principle) while giving them meaning. In short: Without the drives we wouldn't need or wish anything, and without the structures we wouldn't know what we need or wish.

Freud started out by postulating two primal drives, the self-preservative and the sexual drive (see Figure 7.1). Even though the sexual drives were his main interest, he always emphasized the necessity of retaining the concept of the self-preservative drives. With these two primal drives he creatively developed his psychoanalytic theory and clinical practice until 1920. Aggression held various positions throughout these years, but always merely as a component of the two primal drives. In 1920 Freud fundamentally revised his drive theory, now suggesting a life drive (Eros) and a death drive (aggression or destruction) as primal antagonists. The change was complex, involving a new general definition of drives, a new understanding of aggression, masochism, the repetition compulsion, and the negative therapeutic reaction. At once it opened up a number of puzzling questions that psychoanalysis has grappled with ever since. Intrigued by Freud's cranky transition from his first to his second drive theory, I eventually embarked on a long journey through the intricate landscape of metapsychology that led me to a different solution to what presented itself to Freud as the dilemma of 1920 (Schmidt-Hellerau, 1997, 2001, 2006).

When Freud introduced his new pair of life and death drives, he saw no problems with making his former sexual drive a representative and part of a life drive/Eros. However, the self-preservative drive seemed to flatly contradict and strongly oppose any subordination under a death drive. Thus Freud dissolved his first drive antagonism in order to unite self-preservation with sexuality, both now considered as libidinal and placed under the umbrella of his life-drive/Eros. Then (for lack of something better, as he admitted) he declared aggression to be the representative or synonym of the death drive, thus elevating it for the first time to the status of a primal drive.[1] From that time on, we have considered sexuality and aggression as the two primal drives in psychoanalysis.

Is this set in stone, untouchable, and beyond doubt? Freud didn't think so. In 1924 (!) he admitted in a footnote added to his *Three Essays on Sexuality*: "The theory of drives is the most important but at the same time the least complete portion of psychoanalytic theory" (1905, p. 168), and his awareness of this invites us to continue to work on this particular portion of his theory, and here is the result of my working through of Freud's drive theory.

How to Relate the Preservative and Death Drives?

Let us depart from Freud's second drive theory, the antagonism of life and death drives. Let us not be distracted by what "life" and "death" might mean, but rather focus on their antagonism, symbolized in Figure 7.2 below by a (+) and a (-) sign; this conceptually emphasizes the drives as one-directional forces, exemplified by virtually endless striving in opposite directions. For the newborn then everything is a matter of life and death. Hunger signals a dangerous surge toward death, which can only be stopped by the intervention of the nursing object. The repeated interaction with the nursing object will be stored in memory traces (representations) that will increasingly halt and contain consecutive drive excitations

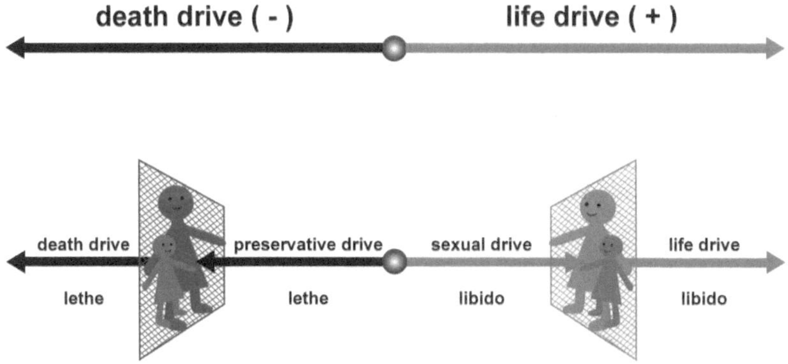

Figure 7.2 On the basis of Freud's second drive theory (1920) it can be postulated that it is the structuring intervention of the caring/soothing and loving/exciting object that introduce the preservative and the sexual drives into the more general strivings of the death and the life drives with their energies (lethe for the death and preservative drive, libido for the sexual and life drive).

emanating from the same source, and define what self-preservation is (hunger in this case and the need to be nurtured). It follows that it is the object that "cuts" as it were the death drive into half and calls into being what can only then be defined as the self-preservative drive. Hence, self-preservation is an area of drive-activity wrested away from the pursuits of the death drive. To put it differently: Self-preservation and sexuality as distinct drive activities are only introduced by the structuring intervention of the caring and loving object (Green, 1993, p. 117). Drive activities however, that go beyond the structures of healthy self-preservation reach into the dimensions of the death drives.

These ideas entail a number of further changes:

1. Self-preservation is no longer considered as part of the life drive (Eros) but as part of the death drive. This conceptualization maintains the original antagonism between the sexual and the self-preservative drives, now integrating them as partial drives into the life and death drives.
2. Freud never elaborated much on his concept of a self-preservative drive, and Laplanche (1997, p. 153) has argued that self-preservation is a biological instinct not a psychological drive, explicitly excluding it from psychoanalytic consideration. I contend that this generally shared omission and rejection caused a blind spot in our thinking, a blank that was filled with other concepts, namely aggression and narcissism, which can be part of self-preservation but are essentially different from it.
3. The notion "self-preservation" is misleading; it indicates that this drive only cathects the self. However, since every drive can cathect various objects (Freud, 1915), the self as one of them (e.g., the libidinal cathexis of the self in narcissism), it would be more appropriate to speak of a preservative drive the goals of which can be self- as well as object-preservative.
4. Preservative drive activities are not limited to the preoedipal phase; they are important strivings throughout life, continuously requiring challenging psychic work. Thus the emphasis on this forgotten concept does not aim at advocating preoedipal issues or diminishing our interest in the sexual drives. On the contrary, to differentiate between the concepts of sexual and preservative strivings allows us to more clearly recognize when there is a lack or a diminution of libidinal drive activities in favor of self- and object-preservative ones; in other words, to better distinguish between caring for and loving an object. Or, to put it still differently: While both drives are experienced as urges, the sexual drives elicit desires, preservative drives express needs.
5. Since Freud never came up with a convincing energy notion for his self-preservative or his death drive, I suggested the notion of *lethe*

(Greek: the river of forgetting flowing into the realm of death); this allows us to speak of lethic cathexis and lethic objects in the same way as we talk about libidinal cathexis and libidinal objects.

Aggression is no longer viewed as a primal drive with its only goal as destruction. Instead I suggest picking up Freud's (1909) conception following which both drives have the capacity to become aggressive in order to reach their goals, and define aggression as the intensification of either one, the sexual or the preservative drive when the psychogeometrical distance to the object of satisfaction requires such an energetic increase (see Schmidt-Hellerau, 2002).

From here we can take a further step (Figure 7.3). If we agree that it is the structures that halt and organize or bind the unbound, unruly urges of bare drive activity, thus giving them meaning, we can also see that we will need not only the structures of healthy self- and object preservation. Our experience (memory traces) will also establish structures representing malady and sorrow, the many kinds of physical and psychic hurts. Intensified strivings of the preservative drives will reach beyond the representations of sound self- and object preservation and activate the representations of self and object in the state of disease, suffering, and the fear of approaching death. It is necessary that we can represent ourselves and our objects as sick or sad, because this will lead us to initiate what can be healing and help recapture sanity. However, these representations can also be neurotically emphasized (as in hypochondria), creating a heightened concern and fear of being sick or an overprotective attitude toward the object. Finally, beyond these structures of malady and sorrow representations of death (e.g., infantile beliefs, religious faith) will be established (at the left end of Figure 7.3)—residues of dead and forgotten ideas that once had been vital, dead and lost objects, as well as the shadows of a dead or deadened, traumatized self or object. Again, these representations of death are important in order to halt and thus somehow familiarize oneself with the

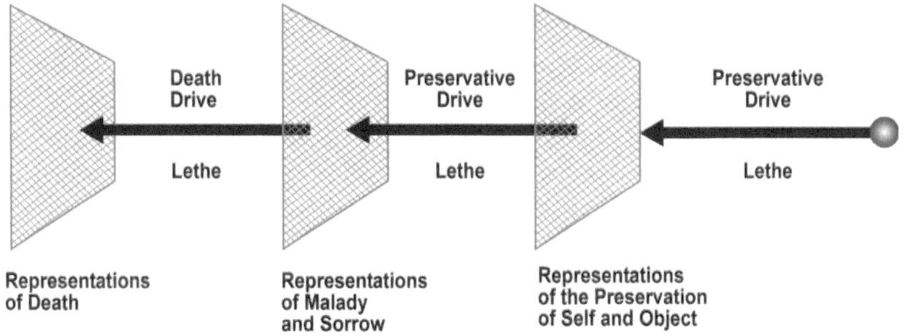

Figure 7.3 Organization of the structures that carry the representations of healthy (normal) self- and object-preservation (on the right side), the representations of malady and sorrow (in the middle) and the representations of death (on the left side).

otherwise endless and uncannily frightening lethic strivings toward something beyond words, images and meaning—something we call death.

In short I suggest that:

1. The spectrum of self- and object preservation is the most densely structured area of the death drive.
2. Between the representations of healthy self- and object preservation and the representations of death there is an equally important structural area organizing the representations of disease and survival threats with related anxieties and concerns, with fear of helplessness and the ensuing rescue fantasies. Whether these threats to one's safety and survival are real or imagined, it is the intensified activity of the preservative drives that will cathect these representations, resulting in the subject's inner reality of being endangered in his survival. Or, viewed from a structural perspective: If there is a lack of solidly established preservative structures (the mother's *no*—or shall we call it "the law of the mother"?), the excitations of the self-preservative drive (e.g., the urges of hunger) will not be contained and limited, thus allowing for a lethic surge into the area of disease (e.g., eating disorder) and potentially death.
3. Finally I would hold that even death, as vague and unknown as it will always remain, needs to be and will be represented, consciously or unconsciously, in order to shield us against this uncanny surge of the potentially endless strivings of the death drive.

My revision of drive theory retains the essence of Freud's thinking while reorganizing and integrating the death drive, aggression, and most importantly the preservative drives. As I put it previously:

> I think that one important explanation for the widespread dissatisfaction with drive theory among analysts in the United States is that it is part of the (indirect) response to Freud's unfortunate decision to drop his notion of the self-preservative drive by merging it with Eros when he introduced aggression as a new primal drive in 1920. To construe all the infant's and adult's daily activities and interactions as the expression of an aggressive or sexual drive or their conflicts felt artificial, odd, or unconvincing. I wonder how psychoanalysis would have developed if Freud had stayed with and explored his first self-preservative drive? (Schmidt-Hellerau, 2005, p. 1020)

Anxiety Turns the Page

How do these reflections relate to anxiety? Freud conceptualized anxiety always in quantitative terms. What elicits anxiety is a certain amount of drive energy (in response to an external stimulus or an inner need/desire) that exceeds the apparatus's capacities for containment (binding) and thus not only interferes with its working properly and effectively, but also threatens to damage or even destroy psychic structures. It is the idea that a surge of drive energy, an overwhelming excitation, causes trauma from within (be it by the effects of *Nachträglichkeit*). The second theory of anxiety also relates to the quantitative, now refined to a signal, a tiny portion of drive energy that allows the ego to probe *en miniature* (by investing a fantasy in the unconscious) the possible consequences of a full-fledged enactment of the unconsciously aroused need or desire. The possibility of using only a small amount of drive energy in order to raise signal anxiety that activates protective defenses is a sophisticated, ingenious, and economical way for the psychic apparatus to preempt damage, initially not available but eventually achieved in the course of the structural development of the ego.

In his 32nd lecture Freud emphasizes that starting from birth, anxiety is a response to danger. The danger can be real (toxic, external) leading to "realistic anxiety." If there is no real danger and anxiety comes up all the same we call it neurotic. In struggling to find a theoretical explanation for the latter anxiety Freud (1933) suggests: "What he (*the neurotic, CSH*) is afraid of is evidently his own libido. The difference between this situation and that of realistic anxiety lies in two points: that the danger is an internal instead of an external one and that it is not consciously recognized" (p. 84). Freud, using libido as a synonym for drive energy (excitation), here captures the idea that neurotic anxiety is stirred by an unconscious (but also at times preconscious or even conscious) fantasy of danger (e.g., separation from the caretaking object, castration). This fantasy is entirely psychic; it is the expression of a specific drive activity, because "every drive tries to make itself effective by activating ideas that are in keeping with its aims" (1910, p. 213). And since Freud acknowledges: "anxiety serves the purposes of self-preservation" (1933, p. 84), we might very well conclude that anxiety is the expression of the self-preservative drives in response to a realistic or imagined danger for the subject's (or the object's) wellbeing and survival—hence the release of quantitatively increased lethic energies reaching into the area of disease—or even death, because "what is feared, what is the object of the anxiety, is invariably the emergence of a traumatic moment, which cannot be dealt with by the normal rules of the pleasure principle" (p. 94).

Freud joins his concepts of anxiety and drives in order to summarize for his imaginary audience the most important of his theoretical developments since his first lecture series in winter of 1916/1917. He ends his reflections by declaring that the starting-point for his introduction of the death drive was the negative therapeutic reaction, a resistance to getting better because of an unconscious sense of guilt, a powerful masochistic "need for punishment" that is "satisfied by the suffering which is linked to the neurosis, and for that reason holds fast to being ill" (Freud, 1933, p. 108). Freud presents the example of a woman who he had freed from the symptoms of a long tormented existence; however, while she was eagerly plunging into the activities of her life she started to produce a series of accidents (hurting her ankle, knee, and hand) and then illnesses (catarrhs, sore throats, influenza, and rheumatic swellings) "which put her out of action for a time and caused her suffering" (p. 109). Freud explains this chain of new physical sufferings as caused by an "unconscious sense of guilt," a superego aggression turned against the ego, hence a need for punishment—in short, a negative therapeutic reaction.

Let us remember Freud's finding: "What is feared, what is the object of the anxiety, is invariably the emergence of a traumatic moment." As I have developed previously (see Figure 7.4, from right to left), "trauma breaks through the protective shields of the preservative screens and jams the representation of self and/or object into the backyard of death" (Schmidt-Hellerau, 2007, p. 1066).

As we know, anxiety seeks to protect against the damages of trauma. Not all threats would end up causing trauma. Not all anxiety patients show the negative therapeutic reaction, but those who do can be considered as traumatized. They require long lasting analytic work and only slowly show signs of progress. And when these traumatized patients only briefly step out of the backyard of death and for a moment reenliven those parts of their self-representations that had been deadened by trauma—they often develop physical symptoms or depression, withdraw fearing breakdown and disease, or don't show up for a while in order to get back to where they had been before. At a later state when their capacity for verbalization in this area has considerably increased they might say: "If I'd get better, I'd surely be diagnosed with cancer!" Or they may be convinced that any bit of further progress will end in disaster. All these occurrences seem to be the signs that Freud emphasized, signs of the patient's wish to not get better: the negative therapeutic reaction.

However, looking at the organization of representations on the continuum of lethic drive activities in Figure 7.3, we can come to a different

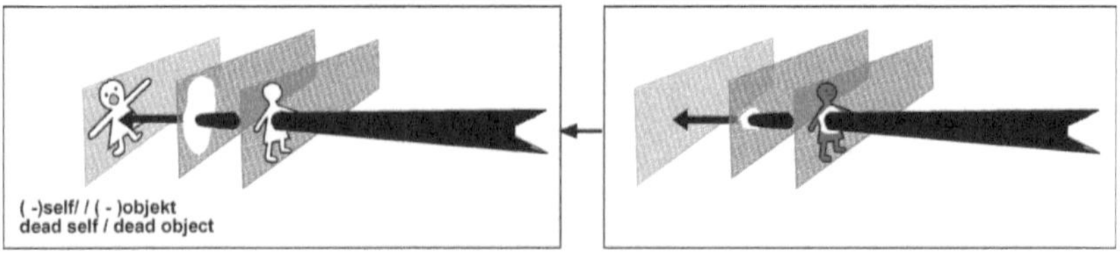

Figure 7.4 A traumatic assault on the representation of a healthy self or object (on the right side) will lead to a break or rupture of the preservative structures, as a result of which self and object will be represented as dead/deadened (on the left side).

interpretation. A traumatized patient with (parts of) his self represented in the area of death doesn't show much concern for his survival. It is only when he gets better in his analysis, when he has built up structures beyond the quiet area of his deadened self that all of a sudden he becomes capable of fearing for his life. It is only then that he is cathecting self-representations in the anxiety-laden area of disease and sufferance, which makes him feel worse. It is precisely through these newly developed (often physical) symptoms that he can express his heightened concerns for his self-preservation. These anxieties signal a surge of lethic cathexis, comparable to the one summoned up in a normal person during illness. I suggest that the anxiety to fall ill as well as intermediate illnesses are an unavoidable and necessary transitional phase on the reconstructive way from a traumatized, deadened self-state to a safely established representation of a well-preserved self and object. What Freud called the negative therapeutic reaction is therefore not a resistance against getting better, but a sign of getting better and should be interpreted as such. Borrowing from Quinodoz (1999), I would hold that these worries and affections are symptoms "that turn over a page" and that they should be interpreted progressively as a newly achieved capacity to elicit the analyst's object preservative, as well as the patient's own self-preservative concerns. That is to say: Instead of interpreting them as a resistance against getting better, as a regressive move, and as an expression of aggression turned inwards, we interpret to our patients that these symptoms can be understood in the context of their progression and be worked through like any other neurotic symptoms.

This does not mean that Freud was wrong in finding an unconscious sense of guilt (often borrowed from an early love-object) underneath the negative therapeutic reaction. However, in the light of the above this unconscious guilt reveals its defensive function; it can be understood as a grandiose denial of the helplessness experienced in the traumatic assault. I am guilty says "it was my doing; I was in charge"—while the trauma had overwhelmed the individual's capacity to manage and protect himself from the devastating blow of the onslaught (be it from within or from outside).[2] Thus, at the bottom of the negative therapeutic reaction is helplessness so dramatically increased in the moment of trauma that from then on survival will forever require and deny the object's preservative assistance. The negative therapeutic reaction not only shies back from the frightening acknowledgment of being vulnerable (in not cathecting the representations of malady and sorrow), it simultaneously wants to make sure that the patient doesn't get better and remains in the analyst's care—thus clinging to the analyst while foreclosing his or her helpfulness. The difficulty of working through this unconscious guilt as a denial of helplessness has to do with the patient's unconscious anxiety over an overwhelming rage in response to the trauma that would come up, a rage that always looms large and threatens to destroy not only the caretaking object (analyst) outside, but also the fragile self-preservative structures inside the traumatized psyche. This anxiety to lose or fight off the object one feels totally dependent upon envisions a repetition of the old trauma and leads the patient to continue to suffer what he is used to and can manage on his own than risk any step forward. Thus the anxiety in the negative therapeutic reaction is that of an overwhelming helplessness and rage, it is the patient's aggressively intensified self-preservative response to his or her trauma that needs to be analyzed as such in order to structure and limit the patient's lethic energies according to the requirements of normal healthy self- and object preservation.

Notes

1. Primal means that a drive seeks satisfaction for its own sake. For instance, the sexual drive pushes the individual to have sex; the self-preservative drive of hunger pushes him or her to eat. Hence an aggressive drive, conceptualized as primal, would make the individual attack and destroy. The difference between the former two and the latter is that in evolutionary or biological terms, to have sex (procreation) or to eat (self-preservation) follows a vital purpose. However, to destroy only in order to destroy doesn't seem to be an evolutionarily stable or sustainable function or strategy.
2. The same accounts for the borrowed guilt that is a grandiose denial of *not* being able to lift up or repair the object's failure.

References

Freud, S. (1905). *Three essays on sexuality*. In J. Strachey (Ed. & Trans.), *The standard edition of the complete psychological works of Sigmund Freud* (Vol. 7, pp. 123–242). London: Hogarth Press.

Freud, S. (1910). The psycho-analytic view of psychogenic disturbance of vision. In J. Strachey (Ed. & Trans.), *The standard edition of the complete psychological works of Sigmund Freud* (Vol. 11, pp. 209–218). London: Hogarth Press.

Freud, S. (1915). Instincts and their vicissitudes. In J. Strachey (Ed. & Trans.), *The standard edition of the complete psychological works of Sigmund Freud* (Vol. 14, pp. 109–140). London: Hogarth Press.

Freud, S. (1933). New introductory lectures on psycho-analysis. In J. Strachey (Ed. & Trans.), *The standard edition of the complete psychological works of Sigmund Freud* (Vol. 22, pp. 1–182). London: Hogarth Press.

Green, A. (1993). *Le travail du negative* [The work of the negative]. Paris: Éditions De Minuit.

Laplanche, J. (1997). Une métapsychologie à l'épreuve de l'angoisse [Metapsychology as a test of anxiety]. In *Le primat de l'aure* [The predominance of the aura] (pp. 143–158). Paris: Champs/Flammarion.

Quinodoz, J.-M. (1999). "Dreams that turn over a page": Integration dreams with paradoxical regressive content. *International Journal of Psychoanalysis, 80*, 225–238.

Schmidt-Hellerau, C. (1997). Libido and Lethe: Fundamentals of a formalized conception of metapsychology. *International Journal of Psychoanalysis, 78*, 683–697.

Schmidt-Hellerau, C. (2001). *Life drive and death drive, libido and Lethe: A formalized consistent model of psychoanalytic drive and structure theory*. New York: Other Press.
Schmidt-Hellerau, C. (2002). Why aggression? Metapsychological, clinical and technical considerations. *International Journal of Psychoanalysis*, *83*, 1269–1289.
Schmidt-Hellerau, C. (2005). We are driven. *Psychoanalytic Quarterly*, *74*, 989–1028.
Schmidt-Hellerau, C. (2006). Surviving in absence: On the preservative and death drive and their clinical utility. *Psychoanalytic Quarterly*, *75*, 1057–1095.

8

THE NEGATIVE THERAPEUTIC REACTION REVISITED[1]

Anna Ornstein

One of the many questions posed in this book is whether or not the concept of the negative therapeutic reaction has lost its usefulness in the pluralism of contemporary psychoanalytic theories. In this chapter, I shall address this question and summarize 2 weeks of analytic material to indicate the way I think about this clinical phenomenon.

The Concept of the Negative Therapeutic Reaction in Contemporary Psychoanalysis

Our view of the analytic process has changed a great deal from the one in which the concept of the negative therapeutic reaction was born. To view patients and their particular psychopathology alone as the sources of negative therapeutic reactions would take us back to a time when psychoanalysis was practiced as a one-person psychology and the correctness of the analyst's interpretations could not be questioned. Such an orientation prescribed a technique in which analysts offered interpretations in keeping with their particular theory of psychopathology and theory of development. When patients rejected such theory-based interventions, this was interpreted as their resistance. Focus on patients and their psychopathology *alone* would disregard what becomes activated in the transference–countertransference interaction in a particular analyst–patient dyad. Analysts' verbal and nonverbal communications, their style, and the unique qualities of their personalities can no longer be taken out of the analytic equation. Among traditional analysts, Jacobs (1996) has been writing most convincingly about the bidirectional nature of the analytic process.

Progress in psychoanalysis requires periodic reexamination of all concepts of traditional psychoanalysis; this includes the concept of the negative therapeutic reaction. Such reexamination has been occurring ever since this clinical phenomenon was first observed in the analysis of the Wolf Man when Freud (1918) described the exacerbation of the patient's difficulties each time he succeeded in clearing up a symptom.[2] Eventually, Freud (1924) tied his observations to unconscious guilt, the need for punishment, and the death instinct; explanations that, with some variations on the theme, were accepted by most authors who observed and wrote about this clinical phenomenon (Abraham, 1919; Asch, 1976; Loewald, 1972; Olinick, 1964, 1970; Riviere, 1936). However, there were a few exceptions in which the narcissistic elements, specifically, unmet developmental needs or outright traumatic experiences in childhood, were considered to be responsible for a negative therapeutic reaction (Balint, 1932; Brandchaft, 1991, 2007). It was of interest to me in this respect that although Abraham (1919) accepted Freud's view on the matter, he also described patients who are easily disappointed, and quickly react with a "withdrawal of libido." "If signs of transference do appear," he wrote,

> the wishes directed onto the physician will be of a particularly exacting nature; thus they will be very easily disappointed precisely in those wishes, and they will then quickly react with a complete withdrawal of libido. They are constantly on the lookout for signs of personal interest on the part of the physician, and want to feel that he is treating them with affection. Since the physician cannot satisfy the claims of their narcissistic need for love, a true positive transference does not take place. (p. 306)

Long before Kohut (1971) described the specific narcissistic transferences (which he later called selfobject transferences), Michael Balint (1932) described patients who, in the termination phase of their analyses, expressed long-forgotten infantile wishes and demanded "gratification from their environment." He concluded that the imperative nature of these transference demands were related to "object failures" in the patient's childhood and that these patients *utilized their* analyses to make a "new beginning" possible. Balint also described the development of pathological (defensive) psychic structures by which a child accommodates to the reality of his failing objects. Brandchaft (2007) referred to these defensive psychic structures as "pathological accommodations" and cited clinical examples to indicate that when analysts insist on the correctness of their well-intentioned interpretations, they inadvertently repeat the patient's original traumatic experiences and thereby are most likely to facilitate the appearance of a negative therapeutic reaction.

In his plenary presentation in 2006, Harry Smith presented several clinical situations in which he illustrated that "patients use the words, setting, and activity of analysis to *gratify* [emphasis added] the very wishes they are analyzing, and so disavow the work of analysis" (p. 713). In his view, the disavowal represented an effort on the patient's part to defeat the aim of the analysis; it was a persistent resistance, the expression of a negative therapeutic reaction. Referring to "Remembering, Repeating and Working Through," Smith reminded us that Freud (1914) considered thought and action as being mutually exclusive. The aim of analysis was to verbalize the patient's experiences so that with increasing insight, enactments and repetitions would be discouraged. But, what to do when no sooner does the analyst put the observed behavior into words, than this is repeatedly disavowed and patients continue to enact their hidden wishes?

I am suggesting that patients' *use* of their analysts' words, the tone of their voice, the setting as well as their personalities, ought not to be viewed as unwelcome byproducts of psychoanalysis but the very essence of the transference. I am here speaking of transferences that help us recognize and appreciate the efforts patients make to *extract experiences* from the analytic situation that would compensate them for legitimate but frustrated developmental needs. Freud separated words and actions because only words (interpretations) could make the unconscious conscious. However, as far as patients are concerned, the analyst's verbal and nonverbal communications cannot be separated; the implicit and the explicit aspects of communication flow in parallel, they are intertwined. So far as patients are concerned, the analyst's words may be experienced as demeaning, an assault, and critical, or caring and soothing, and may have little to do with the *meaning* the analyst had intended. Patients give meaning to experiences in the analytic situation in keeping with their existing psychological structures and in keeping with their newly activated needs and desires. In other words, our focus has to shift from *what* we intend to say to *how* our words and actions (implicit and explicit aspects of our communications) are being experienced by our patients.

As we have indicated elsewhere (Ornstein & Ornstein, 1996), any concept within a particular psychoanalytic theory is embedded in the total context in which it had originally developed and attained its particular meaning and function. Changes in some of the significant concepts, or changes in the fundamental assumptions of the theory, make it necessary to reformulate the concept in order to fit them into the new context—or, it may be necessary to abandon the concept altogether. In psychoanalysis, the process of reformulation and the acceptance of new paradigms take several decades. We have now been at this juncture for some time and such reformulations have been taking place continuously in the various contemporary psychoanalytic theories.

One of the most important changes that have affected the concept of the negative therapeutic reaction is the increased appreciation of the dyadic nature of the psychoanalytic process. Interpretations are no longer thought of as reflecting the analyst's unassailable "knowledge" of the patient's unconscious, which, when handed over to the patient in a neat package in the form of interpretations, ought to be accepted by them. Today, we speak of the interpretive process (Ornstein & Ornstein, 1975,

1996; P. Ornstein, 2004) that requires an ongoing dialogue between patient and analyst. This is a process of negotiation in which patients actively participate, one in which analyst and patient are *jointly* engaged in the exploration and ever better understanding of the patient's inner world. Once we recognize that psychoanalysis is a joint undertaking, we can no longer maintain that there are such things as "proper technique" and well-timed, "correct interpretations." This fundamental change in psychoanalysis makes the idea of a negative therapeutic reaction obsolete.

The Role of the Patient's Psychopathology: A Clinical Example

The nature of psychopathology—as Abraham already indicated—plays a part in what has been called a negative therapeutic reaction. Patients with relatively severe forms of self-pathology may get worse and may drop out of analysis because of the intensity of their transference experiences and because they tend to provoke some of the most hard-to-manage counter-transference responses. These are patients who suffer from a narcissistic personality disorder or are diagnosed either as "borderline" or having a sadomasochistic personality organization. While listening and responding from the patient's perspective facilitates a sense of safety and the establishment of one of the selfobject transferences, the analyst's increasing importance also increases the patient's narcissistic vulnerability. It is under these circumstances that patients are likely to respond with intense rage to relatively insignificant appearing slights and misattunements.

As an example, I shall summarize 2 weeks of analytic material from the complicated web of the working-through process. The case will demonstrate the way in which the combination of the nature of the patient's illness, my attitude, and misattuned interpretive comments have created repeated disruptions in the transference, followed by the patient returning to her symptomatic behavior at the time when her progress outside of the analysis became most visible. What I am describing here are not negative therapeutic reactions because, in this self-psychologically informed theoretical perspective, disruptions in the transference are expected in the course of the working-through process. These are times when the patient's psychopathology is fully engaged, when the reactivation of childhood longings in the transference are most likely to create the feeling of frustration and suffering; it is then that profound disappointments shatter fantasized expectations that the analyst will make up for past hurts and unmet developmental needs. These are the times in the analysis when fantasies that had been sequestrated (disavowed) from consciousness are likely to become exposed, creating secondary conflicts and increased shame, and triggering in patients a need to return to habitual ways of behaving. In our view, the reinstitution of old defenses and behavior patterns are expectable responses to actual or imagined threats of retraumatization.

For psychoanalysts, the challenge is to facilitate the modification of these maladaptive psychological structures which, on the one hand, are protecting a vulnerable self, and on the other hand, create the greatest obstacles to change.

The patient was a 45-year-old married woman with two children. She was chronically anxious, rarely finished a task she began, and she felt insecure in all her relationships except her marriage; her husband was the only one who tolerated her occasional outbursts of rage. She was not on speaking terms with her sisters and she hated her mother. Each angry outburst would be followed by feeling "shitty" about herself, undeserving of her husband's love, and at such times, she could become suicidal. I understood this clinical picture to be related to chronic narcissistic rage, namely, that disavowed rage had become the source of her irritability, her "chip on the shoulder" attitude, and her tendency to collect injustices. The patient, the oldest of three girls, did poorly in school and was not an attractive child; she was tall and overweight, while her mother and sisters were attractive women who could dress stylishly and took great pride in their looks. My patient grew up feeling that her mother preferred her two more attractive and brighter sisters; "I was not the child my mother wanted," she would say. The only person she experienced as being "on her side" was her father who died when she was 11 years old. Mother became depressed after father's death and was even less available to the children than before.

The series of disruptions reported here occurred in the fifth year of a 9-year analysis. Monday, she came into the office extremely angry for having missed the previous Thursday hour, which I had to cancel. She complained that she was not given sufficient time to prepare for the cancelation: "I don't give a shit what you have to do … this is unfair." With resignation and sarcasm in her voice, she said, "I better get used to this…. Here you do this and you probably enjoy your day off. If I really let go, you will be sorry. Your calmness only makes me more furious. Do you feel anything? My husband tries to tell me that I already had three hours last week—but when you cancel one, none of them counts." As she spoke, I was feeling a mixture of rage and guilt and made every effort to sound natural which made me sound stilted. I said that in the past we had discussed the meaning that these changes in the schedule had for her, that they seem to signify her insignificance to me. Not having given more time for the cancelation, made her feel that I had forgotten how these changes made her feel. I then added that when she feels so hurt it is hard for her to reflect on the source of her feelings.

The patient heard my reference to earlier discussions of similar incidents as a reprimand—which, in a way, it was. The meaning of my communication was something like this: "Now that you know the meaning that changes in the schedule have for you, it is time you use this insight and stop simply reacting." At the end I softened my reprimand by saying when feelings are strong it is hard to reflect on them.

This interaction was representative of my feelings toward this patient. I might say "the right things" but, as in this instance, the patient could perceive my disappointment with her inability to use insights that she had gained so far in the analysis. My critical attitude toward her was particularly significant because to be criticized, to be found wanting, was a repetition of her childhood experiences, this was the area of her greatest vulnerability. The patient left the hour less agitated and she obviously reflected on the hour because the next day, Tuesday, she came in saying, "I scream because I don't want to do what I have to do. Beating on you keeps me from feeling my total dependence on you."

I was pleased because she now said what I liked to hear. I became more relaxed and told her that the intensity of her anger made me realize how important it was for her not to take it sitting down this time. By now, I had time to reflect on the fact that her outburst at me indicated that she had achieved a sufficient level of safety in our relationship to express her rage without being concerned about losing her attachment to me. I also thought that having the rage in the transference can only make our work easier in relation to the character pathology that kept her chronically anxious and suicide-prone. My patient, whose tension regulatory capacity was minimal, reacted to frustrations or to the sudden emergence of archaic needs either with fragmentation, disorganizing rage reactions, or an increase in her need to protect herself by withdrawing from relationships where this could occur. Considering her rage at me as progress in the analysis rather than that her refusal to use insight was a resistance, affected my attitude: I became more accepting and less defensive. When I then said that as a child, she had to accept passively her mother's attitude and behavior toward her, but that she now felt safe to express her anger, the patient agreed but then asked, "But how much can you take? I have to push you as far as I have to go … but I am afraid I might find your limits.… I feel terribly exposed, so vulnerable. I know I am not here to please you but how can you accept all this horrible shit?" I said, "You are concerned that when I see your rage, I won't see anything else. This has been an important question for you all along: what I think of you, whether or not I value you." She replied, "All very true, *I do want love, not analysis.* The rage disorganizes me … the intensity is unbearable."

By Wednesday, she felt much better. But there was a new hurt: I failed to appreciate her insight that what she wanted was love and not analysis. By sharing this wish, she felt further exposed. Did I know that? Did I know how hard it was to share that wish with me? I said that I understood her increasing ability to express her rage and her wish for my love as indicating her feeling safe with me but she now needs to know more urgently how I feel and think about her.

Thursday, she said she felt better than ever in her life: "I have a strong sense of myself as if something has been released. This is a different kind of power; it comes from feeling good, not from anger." With connection reestablished between us, this disruption appeared to have been repaired only to be followed by a new cycle.

The next week, the patient came to the Monday session so enraged she could barely breathe. She saw me talking to someone in the hallway just before entering my office. "Everybody is more important than I am," she says. I found myself reacting to her anger similarly to previous reactions: My throat became tight and dry and I knew I had to calm myself before I opened my mouth. When I spoke, I found myself reaching for a genetic interpretation because I was eager to avoid an affect storm directed at me. I referred to her feelings toward her sisters who, she felt, were favored by their mother. She then said what she knew I wanted to hear: "When I rant and rave, it is to check out whether these feelings are really okay." With her anger subsiding, she added with a sense of resignation: "My jealousies will kill me one of these days." Tuesday, she was very much afraid of a new storm. She hated these experiences but feared that there was no way of avoiding them. She spoke of feeling better with her coworkers but rather than this making her happy, she felt a strange sense of discontent.

I was not sure how this related to what was going on between the two of us but considered the possibility that feeling better would mean the loss of me and said something to this effect. "The fact remains," the patient said, "that I will have to remain tied to you." She remembered a dream in which she was expected to drive a truck: "I was expected to know how to do that just because I know how to drive a car. Do I have to accept your going away just because I can understand my reaction to it? You never really pushed me. Why am I so afraid?" I said, "Every move ahead seems to be filled with anxiety that there is no return." I then said something about children having to learn gradually how to cross a street. There was a long silence which the patient broke by saying, "Love is something we never expressed in my family. I think of my mother, all I remember is her getting ready to go out in the evening … the red velvet dress she wore. I still love to fondle velvet. She always looked forward to going out." She started the Thursday hour, the end of the second week, by saying that my "crime" had to match her rage. "If I am not angry, who am I? It is my major contact with you." She spoke of her possessiveness of me. With some self-mocking in her voice she said, "You should sit in that chair 24 hours a day, wait for me, and think of me. The rage is that I can't have what I want, when I want it. When I leave, time is altered, I become disoriented. Every time I leave this office I become temporarily disoriented. I don't miss people, I just fall apart." Statements such as these indicated the intensity of the selfobject transference. Her fear of premature termination was also indicated by a dream in which her 10-year-old son was a grown man with hair on his chest. I commented on her continued fear that I will dismiss her before she is ready to leave and that right now she feels that time will never come. "Yes," the patient said, "I am growing up too fast; I can't stand the sense of needing you!" But there was something that helped. When she did something well, she imagined that I was watching her and was proud of her. These thoughts calmed her and she did not feel the tug-of-war between feeling better and the fear of losing me.

At the time of termination, I learned to respect and admire the patient for her determination to complete the analysis that severely taxed both of our resources. She had become relatively free of rage outbursts and revenge fantasies and was better able to experience her husband's love and to feel deserving of it. Not being burdened by the symptomatic consequences of her chronic narcissistic rage and being better able to regulate her tension states, she was able to create situations in which she was free to receive and to give love in and outside of her family. Kohut (1977) suggested that the goal of psychoanalysis was reached when patients achieved "functional rehabilitation" and were able to secure needed selfobject responses from their emotional environment and from their creative activities.

Comments on the Clinical Example

This brief segment of a lengthy analysis was to indicate that patients' psychopathology may contribute to frequent disruptions which, when viewed from a traditional theoretical perspective could be considered to represent negative therapeutic reactions. I had chosen this clinical example to indicate that patients who suffer from a relatively severe form of self pathology develop intense selfobject transferences and, with the deepening of the transference, they become increasingly more vulnerable to the analyst's absences and empathic failures. From a self psychological perspective, such cycles of disruptions and repairs are part and parcel of the working-through process of transferences that have become established in relation to legitimate but frustrated childhood developmental needs. If patients are able to experience their analysts as making an effort to understand and validate their subjective experiences, these new experiences destabilize the pathological psychic structures that have maintained their self-system. When, at these crucial times in the analysis, there is any indication of the analyst's emotional absence, patients become enraged and demanding. Such reactions indicate that modifications in the defensive structures are taking place; the safety in the analysis permits the expression of disavowed narcissistic rage. It will depend on the analyst's responses to these disruptions whether or not the rupture will be repaired or it will lead to the patient withdrawing into an angry silence. Any indication of defensive or retaliatory behavior on the part of the analyst at this time can create a stalemate as patients retreat to their habitual ways of protecting themselves from potentially disorganizing affects. Rather than considering that patients get worse in spite of their analysts best efforts, such an outcome is more likely related to experiencing their analysts' responses as repetitions that had proven to be traumatic to them in the past. Once we consider psychoanalysis as a process that involves both participants, we can no longer speak about "proper technique" and "correct interpretations," and without these conditions being met, the concept of negative therapeutic reaction loses its usefulness.

Notes

1. This chapter is based on a contribution to a panel on "The Negative Therapeutic Reaction," American Psychoanalytic Association Winter Meeting, January 20, 2007.
2. The Wolf man produced "*transitory* negative reactions," rather than an immutable bedrock as this phenomenon was later described in the literature. There were many ups and downs in the analysis of the Wolf Man but his attachment to and need for Freud could never be questioned. From my perspective, important in this analysis was the fact that the Wolf man experienced himself as valued and important and also actively participating in his analysis: "I felt myself less a patient than as a co-worker, the younger comrade of an experienced explorer setting out to study a new, recently discovered land" (cited by Gardiner, 1971, p. 140).

References

Abraham, K. (1919). A particular form of neurotic resistance against the psychoanalytic method. In *Selected papers of Karl Abraham* (pp. 303–317). New York: Basic Books.

Asch, S. S. (1976). Varieties of negative therapeutic reaction and problems of technique. *Journal of the American Psychoanalytic Association, 24*, 383–407.

Balint, M. (1932). Character analysis and new beginning. In *Primary love and psychoanalytic technique* (pp. 159–173). London: Tavistock.

Brandchaft, B. (1991). Countertransference in the analytic process. *Progress in Self Psychology, 7*, 99–105.

Brandchaft, B. (2007). Systems of pathological accommodation and change in analysis. *Psychoanalytic Psychology, 24*, 667–687.

Freud, S. (1918). From the history of an infantile neurosis. In J. Strachey (Ed. & Trans.), *The standard edition of the complete psychological works of Sigmund Freud* (Vol. 17, pp. 1–121). London: Hogarth Press.

Freud, S. (1924). The economic problem of masochism. In J. Strachey (Ed. & Trans.), *The standard edition of the complete psychological works of Sigmund Freud* (Vol. 19, pp. 157–171). London: Hogarth Press.

Gardiner, M. (1971). *The Wolf Man by the Wolf Man*. New York: Basic Books.

Jacobs, T. (1996). Analysis, mutual analysis and self-analysis: On the interplay of minds in the analytic process. *Canadian Journal of Psychoanalysis, 4*, 255–277.

Kohut, H. (1971). *The analysis of the self.* New York: International Universities Press.

Kohut, H. (1977). *The restoration of the self.* New York: International Universities Press.

Loewald, H. W. (1972). Freud's conception of the negative therapeutic reaction with comments on instinct theory. *Journal of the American Psychoanalytic Association, 20,* 235–245.
Olinick, S. (1964). The negative therapeutic reaction. *International Journal of Psychoanalysis, 45,* 540–548.
Ornstein, A., & Ornstein, P. (1975). On the interpretive process in psychoanalysis. *International Journal of Psychoanalytic Psychotherapy, 4,* 219–271.
Ornstein, A., & Ornstein, P. (1996). Speaking in the interpretive mode and feeling understood: Critical aspects in the therapeutic action in psychoanalysis. In L. Lifson (Ed.), *Understanding therapeutic action: Psychodynamic concepts of cure* (pp. 87–101). Hillsdale, NJ: Analytic Press.
Ornstein, P. (2004). The elusive concept of the psychoanalytic process. *Journal of the American Psychoanalytic Association, 52,* 15–41.
Rivière, J. (1936). A contribution to the analysis of the negative therapeutic reaction. *International Journal of Psychoanalysis, 17,* 304–320.
Smith, H. F. (2006). Analyzing disavowed action: The fundamental resistance analysis. *Journal of the American Psychoanalytic Association, 54,* 713–737.

9

AN ADDITION TO THE PSYCHOANALYTIC UNDERSTANDING OF THE NEGATIVE THERAPEUTIC REACTION AND CLINICAL SADOMASOCHISM

Melvin Bornstein

Forty-four years ago, as a psychoanalytic candidate, I began my first supervised analytic case. It was before Kernberg (1975) redefined borderline conditions and suggested that they could be understood and treated dynamically. Using our current diagnostic criteria, my patient would be seen as having a borderline personality disorder. He was a 27-year-old man with symptoms of depression and anxiety, socially inhibited, and very bright. Three months after he began his analysis, as he increasingly experienced affects of safety with me because of my ordinary analytic attitude of kindness, consistency, and interest, a dramatic change developed that was unfamiliar and unlike anything that I had experienced in a dynamic psychotherapy. He began ranting and railing at me and telling me about some of his history for the first time. He described masturbatory fantasies where he was having sex with his mother while stabbing his father. He would hit his chest and cut his leg while masturbating. His ranting contained the same content as the criticism that he frequently directed at his parents: I was inept, uncaring, and neglectful. At that time, I did not have a clinical model I could use or adequate clinical support from my supervisor to understand his actions or to respond analytically to him. I had only my intuition to help me make analytic sense out of my experience with him.

I became aware that frequently he appeared comfortable and hopeful. I would intervene, usually making a connection with themes in his associations, but my intervention would be followed by his outburst of emotional chaos that included suicidal thoughts, destructive ideas, and sadistic comments directed at me.

At the end of such a session, I was not only confused, but also emotionally frozen and preoccupied with images and memories of my patient in a sadomasochistic battle with me. He and I were in actuality experiencing something similar. We had started a session with a degree of comfort which he communicated to me, but when I responded with an intervention that I thought would be helpful, "all hell broke loose" and for both of us the turmoil continued long after the end of the session. We were in a situation in which each of us was attempting to establish control of the other. In the back of my mind, I was filled with self-criticism and shame. I knew that I was avoiding something which started with a sense of well-being and feeling like a competent analyst. As I write this, I can see that for many years I have struggled to make sense of this sort of clinical experience, one that has been repeated over and over with this and other patients.

At that time, my patient had told me some of his history. He was chronically traumatized by his mother, who slept with him and fondled his genitals until he was 7 years old. His father was withdrawn and indifferent to the abuse that was taking place. As he grew up, he excelled in school although he was socially backward, extremely dependent on his mother, and ensconced in a sadomasochistic relationship with both parents. Upon entering professional school, he applied to the analytic clinic at my institute for analysis. He was accepted.

The progress I have made in my initially desperate effort to understand what had taken place in my first psychoanalytic encounter with a patient corresponds to the progress in psychoanalysis itself over the subsequent 40 years. The treatment I described lasted for 3 years. My patient improved somewhat and then left treatment. At that time I did not understand why he improved and how I could have helped him more.

I knew that we were immersed in a sadomasochistic and negative therapeutic dead end. The ease for both of us to withdraw into sadomasochism was frequently present. The response of a reversal of therapeutic progress with interventions that should have promoted progress indicated the pervasiveness of the negative therapeutic reactions. Technically much of what I did was in the service of trying to find a way out of this impasse. The sadomasochism and negative therapeutic reactions that permeated our clinical encounter diminished, but did not disappear. The dynamic meaning of sadomasochism and negative therapeutic reaction in this clinical situation (and many other similar clinical situations) has remained the unsolved problem of my clinical life. In the past few years, as current advances in psychoanalytic theory have led me to a deeper understanding of these clinical situations, the clinical conundrum of sadomasochism and the negative therapeutic reactions that shadow it has begun to dissolve.

When I started the analysis I described above, I was imbued with an understanding of conflict theory that rested on the centrality of the instinctual drives as sources of energy and motivation for the multidetermined conflict that comprised sadomasochism. Yet with my patient, I could not explain his conscious fantasies of having sex with his mother, stabbing his father, and inflicting pain on himself. Within the theoretical model I had been taught and was using, I could only find repression and drive derivatives as an explanation, and this explanation didn't make sense to me. I had no understanding of the negative therapeutic reaction other than as a reaction to guilt or to the abstract concept of a death instinct. I just winged it until I discovered Otto Kernberg's (1966) integration of Kleinian psychology, object relations theory, and ego psychology.

With the conceptualization of a person's ability to turn away from a painful and traumatic external world of actual objects into a safer internal world of fantasy, which I learned from Freud (1913) and Fairbairn (1952), I could understand that my patient's vituperative outbursts were his way of expressing that reality was dangerous and that safety was only achieved by a withdrawal into a world of fantasy. He was immersed in aggression, and he expressed his rage to me. In essence, he was internalizing his aggression and using projection and projective identification to communicate it. Being closer to the external world (here, to me) was associated with being too "feeling alive," vital, and whole, and that feeling state was terrifying to him.

As I conveyed these ideas to my patient, he became more organized. There was more of him in the session, but his storms had not died down and he remained in an ongoing angry, demeaning transference in which he was continually sarcastic, trying to injure me by emphasizing all my faults. Experientially, I was not fully getting to the sadomasochism nor to the negative therapeutic reaction which was so much of the clinical material.

With this clinical introduction to the topic of sadomasochism and the negative therapeutic reaction, I will turn to Léon Wurmser's book *Torment Me, But Don't Abandon Me* (2007), a contemporary exploration of masochism. Later I will add my current thinking on the topic. For years, Wurmser has written and taught about masochism. In this book, he presents a comprehensive historical overview and his current thinking on the topic, with extensive clinical material. Many of the steps I have taken in understanding sadomasochism are embedded in the analytic literature through the years and are beautifully described by Wurmser with his special emphasis and perspective.

Beginning with his psychoanalytic roots in classical training, Wurmser understands that conflict and unconscious fantasy are paramount in masochism. My patient's unconscious fantasies were manifestly oedipal, but their content, as it was expressed in the analysis, was also preoedipal, this latter both an expression of the patient's deficiencies and an unconscious strategy to repair them. The intense affects that he expressed were usually related to his mother's seduction of him, and her disregard for him as a separate person. I have come to understand the terror that I experienced as he ranted and raved at me as his desperate attempt to communicate to me the way he experienced his world.

Wurmser's major contribution to our understanding of masochism in his book is his integration of the many models and ideas related to the superego, trauma, and narcissistic injury. He understands that these models complement one another, that masochism is the result of trauma that is internalized and then gives rise to a demonic superego that is created out of vast internalized rage, helplessness, pain, and splitting. The absolute ruthlessness that characterizes this primitive superego is the result of the patient's inability to bring coherence to his trauma so that he can go on living with a sense of well-being, and the patient expresses this lack in a variety of ways because masochistic experience is filled with multiple conflictual components.

The narcissistic injury of the trauma feeds the absoluteness and viciousness of the superego. The patient's need to maintain his self-esteem in the face of trauma becomes part of the resultant conflict. Trauma bridges the internal and external world. Wurmser quotes from Novick and Novick's (1996) work on sadomasochism. They describe both the open and closed systems for maintaining self-esteem that can be observed clinically. The open system is directed at the external world where work, creativity, and relatedness all contribute to maintaining self-esteem, while the closed system operates within the narcissistic defenses of idealization and grandiosity, that are created in the midst of being overwhelmed and shocked, where a person's boundaries are not clear while having to find a way to live within the experience. In the closed masochistic system with its poor boundaries, the primitive superego rages and self-esteem is maintained through grandiosity, attempts to control the other, and poor boundaries.

Withdrawal into this closed system after trauma is a line of defense that helped my patient avoid recognizing his chronic traumatic experiences and responding to them within an open system that could allow them to be integrated into his self and personhood. Wurmser describes the shame dynamics that follow the revelation that one is traumatized and incapable of maintaining oneself by overcoming the shame and humiliation of exposure in an open system. Actually the attractiveness of the closed system is that it is a system of fantasy and unreality. The generation of shame because of exposure rests within the superego. And the analytic situation is a rich opportunity for generating shame because self-exposure is so much a part of the (asymmetrical) clinical relationship.

Returning to my patient, the concepts that I took from ego psychology, Kleinian psychology, and object relations theory enabled me to understand his ranting as an expression of his trauma, helplessness, "done to" feeling, rage, and damaged self-esteem, which he internalized and which contributed to the creation of his relentless superego which he then projected on and into me. As I learned more about self psychology, I included many of the ideas about the integrity and fragmentation of the self into my conceptualizations of what was going on between me and my patient.

Yet after three years, my patient stopped treatment. His emotional state had improved, but I was unsatisfied and believed that within the clinical situation the analysis I had conducted was inadequate, insufficient, and incomplete.

My early analytic understanding and approach to the patient at that time can be found in Wurmser's description of complementarity, that is, in the use of different theoretical perspectives that cannot be integrated at the time but that balance each other. Also, I just did not have any workable idea of how to resolve the sadomasochistic transference, countertransference, and negative therapeutic reactions that limited the progress of the analysis. Wurmser believes that clinical psychoanalysis calls out for a complementarity between our valuable empirical theories with their qualities of objectivity and a philosophy of subjective experience that embraces the humanity of the clinical relationship.

One of the shortcomings in clinical psychoanalysis is the lack of a means to describe and study the qualities of being human in the analytic relationship, a lack that results in a significant deficiency in describing and understanding what takes place in the actual clinical situation. The experience of personhood, the whole person of the patient and the analyst, the identity, vitality, and agency of both participants that actively contribute to the "doings" in each moment of the analysis, is absent in our theory. Here is where the rubber meets the road in clinical psychoanalysis, and we find major gaps in our description of, and theorizing about, personhood.

Freud attempted to make a science out of psychoanalysis based on the positivism of his times, but he never was fully committed to that endeavor because he insisted on including the power of reason that was embedded in the ego and that could transform the forces within the unconscious into humanity. This reflected a dichotomy between science, of how things work, and philosophy, of what it is like to be human, that runs through all of Freud's work and through the development of psychoanalysis to the present day. This dichotomy has been the source of difficulties in clinical psychoanalysis. The personhood of patient and analyst in the clinical situation has been given insufficient attention and been insufficiently theorized. We act as if there are only "dynamics" and relationships in the clinical situation and that these can be reduced to small parts and studied empirically, rather than two whole people who live within the dynamics and the relationship. In other words: How do patients experience and look on their dynamic experience? What are they trying to achieve from session to session? How do they understand what is taking place? These are questions that are not easily addressed and that are, most of the time, omitted in our psychoanalytic lexicon. But these questions are essential to understanding the negative therapeutic reaction. Why does a whole person turn away from the experience of a reality of hope, safety, promise, and pleasure? Before starting his analysis, my patient had lived his life principally alone and into himself. Whatever my deficiencies in understanding his situation in his analysis, I was unequivocally interested in him. I was using all I had and conveying that to him in my interventions. He recognized that, and yet he turned away with great emotional force, withdrawing into his pain, suffering, hopelessness, helplessness. He was entrenched with me without clear boundaries.

Before including personhood within the clinical perspective of masochism and the negative therapeutic reaction, it will be useful to follow Tauber's description from his book *Freud, the Reluctant Philosopher* (2010), a book that is devoted to a history of the tension between empiricism and humanism in Freud's works. Tauber reviews the history of the meaning of reflexivity as a baseline for his thesis, a term that originated in the Enlightenment from the writings of Descartes and Locke. Reflexivity refers to introspection with the goal of discovering the activities that take place in the mind. It ends with the discovery of a self and all the components that comprise the self that can be studied empirically. Yet the meaning of reflexivity evolved with the inclusion of Hegel's addition, that reflexivity was not possible without the presence of the other. Freud's challenge was to find a way to bring Hegel's addition of the other to the biological, empirical model of psychoanalysis that he was creating, which he did by creating an inner voice connected to reason that functioned outside of its biological roots. This capacity was part of the ego and the postulation of this inner voice enabled Freud to describe interpretation as part of lifting this inner voice above its biology. It is the reflexivity that enabled one to think organized thoughts and to understand.

To quote Tauber (2010):

> Freud based his science on a biological conception of human nature, but he characterized the interpretive faculty as humanistic. This basic unresolved tension, truly the paradox of a free-willed reason coupled to deterministic unconscious forces, demands address. Exploring the moral implications of this schema frames chapter 7, where we examine how through various modes, human identification and interpretation, psychoanalysis presents a method by which the analysand attempts to redefine herself in hope of more effectively pursuing satisfying love and work. In this context, "moral" refers to the values that orient individual needs and motivations. Defined by the existential and psychological challenges of the analysand, Freud's criteria reflected underlying currents of Romantic and Enlightenment ideals, which in turn are based on a humanistic vision of human potential. So beyond the character of human nature exposed by Freud's inquiry, the humanistic configuration of psychoanalysis as a therapy for a sick soul tilts his endeavor towards a tempered optimism. (p. 21)

Wurmser (2007) described the dialectic in analytic understanding. He states:

> I present some of the major conclusions for the technique of treating patients with severe neurosis, but also the great importance of seeing the *fundamental dialectic between a technical and theoretical view of psychoanalysis and a philosophy of the basic human relationship* always at work in the intensive encounter that is a prerequisite for good analysis. "Transference-countertransference" and "relationship" are two different ways of looking at what is happening. There is legitimacy to both perspectives; they complement each other. We could also say that there is an analytic-scientific approach to human nature, and there is a dialogic-philosophical one, and both require each other. To use Buber's terms: the former is an I-It relation, the latter is an I-you relation. Using one without the other is like clapping with one hand, the Talmud says. (p. 13)

This dialectic runs through the technical problems of masochism and the negative therapeutic reaction, partially because we have not followed the technical implications of the dialectic far enough in psychoanalysis in general and in sadomasochism and the negative therapeutic reaction in particular. I have written (Bornstein, 2010) that there is a glaring gap in our clinical psychoanalytic model: The whole person is not considered, and that results in the omission of an essential part of what goes on in the analytic situation. There has been an inability to conceptualize the most important aspect of the present moment in the clinical situation, a conceptualization that would contain the intimate humanity of the analyst and the patient in the clinical situation where analyst and patient as whole people are immersed in the task of the analysis and devoted to communicating to each other what each is experiencing, framed by the different roles of patient and analyst. The patient is unable to create her narrative because part of her narrative is unspeakable. She has some deep understanding that this is true and she is motivated to do something about it with her analyst, so to some degree they are partners, two human beings in a dialogic relationship. The whole person is conveyed by the "I." The concept of the whole person is essential if we are to understand the psychoanalytic process, especially our conceptualizations of some of the experiential pillars of clinical psychoanalysis like agency, intimacy, vitality, and closeness.

There is a developmental line in the experience of oneself as whole, an "I," and it includes the vulnerability to trauma (especially in childhood) and the inordinate demand of development to transform the trauma into a narrative and to include it in one's identity. Clinically one can examine this developmental line in the repetitions which contain within them a view of how the patient dealt with her traumas at different stages in her development.

To embellish the clinical theory and technique that is relevant to sadomasochism and the negative therapeutic reaction, I am suggesting that clinically, conflict begins with the desire to be whole, vital, and alive. This desire is the impetus for development (i.e., to grow and become more complex as one integrates as much of the relevant external world as possible). Yet there is a danger that the desire to develop and transform a traumatic state into one's wholeness and one's narrative can result in the exposure of too much affect, knowledge, vitality, and being alive. By withdrawal into the internalizing process of sadomasochism, one is adding to a preexisting narrative of hiding one's traumatic state. This is a source of the negative therapeutic reaction, that is, avoiding feeling alive and taking ownership of one's trauma. Put experientially, this horrible traumatic event happened to me. I am motivated to make it into a narrative and go on living with the trauma as part of my identity, but I am overwhelmed with pain and shame. I must avoid feeling too alive and vital because living with the trauma is too much. I must give up. I can defend against living with the trauma by withdrawing inward into a world of sadomasochism. As I understand it, this is an example of the Novicks' move from an open to a closed system in a sadomasochistic world of fantasy without clear boundaries and with numbness to oneself in the external world.

I will use another example to highlight my contention. I first saw Mrs. A, who was brought to me by her husband, because of her severe depression and suicidal thoughts. She said very little in the first session until I asked her husband to leave so she and I could talk alone. Over the next several weeks her story began to unfold. As the Nazis continued to gain power in Europe when she was a young girl, her parents decided they must leave their home immediately. Plans were made that she would remain with her mother and sister and eventually reunite with her father. During the next 2 years she hid with her mother and sister in the forests and in the homes of people who were willing to hide them. Many days would go by with little food. The war ended and they survived. Upon returning home without her father, her mother became very depressed and abusive to Mrs. A. She would whip her, become frantic if Mrs. A refused to eat, and several times made her eat her vomit when she threw up. By the time she was an adolescent she felt numb, especially with her mother. She began cutting herself and developed anorexia. Shortly after adolescence she met her husband and they immigrated to the United States. Neither could speak about the chronic trauma of the Holocaust.

Shortly after the birth of Mrs. A's second child, her mother became ill. Her mother and sister had moved to the United States with Mrs. A but had settled in a different city. Mrs. A would leave her family for long periods to take care of her mother. The anguish she caused her children by her long absences has been a source of great guilt and depression for Mrs. A.

For the first 3 years of her analysis, Mrs. A actually improved, although the sessions were filled with her complaints, suicidal threats, depression, and hopelessness, and with her desire for punishment. If I said anything that was remotely optimistic, she ignored me and responded with more complaints. If I interpreted an additional meaning to her manifest content, she responded as if I had been critical of her. I felt enraged, helpless, and ignored. I became preoccupied with my anger and hurt; I wanted to argue with and scold her. There was no manifest joy in our work, just a sadomasochistic need for each other which was continually reinforced by states of feeling alive, motivated, and hopeful. Actually, I turned from the experience of being her analyst challenged by the joy of my work into a withdrawn, not terribly alive shadow of myself. My state came forth as if she had control over me; our boundaries were not clear. In other words, I was immersed in a sadomasochistic countertransference that enabled me eventually to understand the part of her narrative that she was playing out with me.

The perspective of Mrs. A and I as whole people—vital, alive, and immersed together in a psychoanalytic situation for the purpose of helping Mrs. A get in touch with her narrative, including her chronic trauma—was essential in understanding the dynamics of her trauma and sadomasochism. To reach this understanding, it was essential that I also get more in touch with my own narrative, including my own traumas that continually slip away into isolated dissociated pieces of sadomasochism. Actually this activity of bringing dissociated parts together, especially those that are fixed in a repetition, occurs because we are whole people who are agencies with reflexivity and who are motivated by powerful inner forces to make narratives out of multidetermined experiences. Traumas are central to the clinical difficulties in creating narratives. In traumatic states it becomes easier to deny our personhood, agency, and reflexivity and to withdraw into sadomasochistic fantasies where, rather than feeling helpless, vulnerable, and out of control, one experiences control in a simple one-dimensional fashion without any agency or reflexivity.

In Mrs. A's repetitive complaints of not getting better, not being able to do anything to improve her situation in life or in her analysis and blaming herself without any reference to what she wanted to do about it, she was denying that she was a whole person with agency, reflexivity, and vitality. In her complaints she did not feel fully alive. My reaction frequently had the quality of helpless rage and not being immersed in the reality of being her analyst in an analytic process. In other words, I was not feeling fully myself or fully alive. We were stuck in sadomasochism. Her unconscious fantasy of being tied and tortured reflected a similar fantasy of mine.

In the context of our being whole people who were devoted in the analysis to creating a narrative out of the sadomasochism and the inhumanity of the Holocaust, the trauma was disguised by the sadomasochism and the negative therapeutic reactions. I understood the sadomasochism as a defense against the trauma. Thus, in the context of the analysis, my patient dealt with the trauma of living through the Holocaust by entering a state where she could avoid experiencing what actually happened to her. She could avoid making the trauma with all its painful affects fully a part of herself while feeling vital and alive and ensconced in the reality of the present moment. In the sadomasochism, she was not fully alive. She was instead numb to the present moment and immersed in a fantasy of controlling idealization where boundaries were porous. Her nagging desire to live was the source of the pain and I was continually emphasizing it by my activity, especially by my interpretations. The negative therapeutic reaction followed. The danger was feeling alive, good, and motivated to make her trauma into her narrative. Her negative therapeutic reaction was in fact the revival of the repetition of the dreaded earlier experience that she had to hide from her full awareness because there was no other to help her to contain and bear it.

Thus my aim in Mrs. A's analysis became to demonstrate to her that in the present moment, it was possible to feel fully alive and to experience the difficulty that must have been present after the trauma. I showed her that now her trauma could be talked about with me, her analyst, and tolerated in the present moment with her present capabilities; in this way, we were making the trauma part of her narrative with her full agency, reflexivity, and ability to know and understand.

The challenge of Mrs. A's analysis was to recognize that the major issue we had to work out was the repetition of the trauma in my consulting room. Because Mrs. A's trauma had not been adequately integrated, Mrs. A was repeating with me her inability to maintain herself as a person with an agency with reflectivity and to take ownership of her overwhelming pain, loss, disappointment, and helplessness. Unable to do this, she gave up and moved away from her motivation to rise above her trauma. She entered a state of withdrawal and sadomasochism, and in this sadomasochistic state, her boundaries were vague; her anger was directed inward into fantasies that were narcissistic, primitive, and rebellious and that were directed against everything that was real and whole.

For the months when Mrs. A was locked in this sadomasochism, I was interpreting many of its components like her rage, hurt, and helplessness; the presence of an unconscious fantasy of being tied and beaten; her inability to deal with the trauma; and the self-punitiveness that protected her against the experience of feeling alive in the present moment. I told her that feeling alive required that she live with the helplessness and finality of the trauma. As long as she repeated the trauma, I continued, she did not have to reach out, talk about it, and find a place for it in her narrative. The transference was present as a midpoint between playing out her trauma with me and making it into a narrative that was part of who she is, her "I," which she could communicate to me.

Yet there appeared to be something more that was needed, for Mrs. A remained distant. I felt frustrated because it appeared that she was ignoring our work together. My reaction was of being hurt and helpless in my ability to reach her. It eventually came to me that she was communicating her own experience as she reached out to her mother for help in bringing a sense of coherence to her traumas. In other words, she had tried to pursue her desire as a whole person to rise above what was happening and find a way to go on living with it, but to no avail. Her hurt and disappointment because of her mother's distance and inability to help her (because of the mother's own trauma) appeared in the treatment as she began to describe feeling better and hopeful. She could rapidly revert to a state of depression, control, and hopelessness. As this sequence repeated itself over and over, it became clearer to me that the state of hopefulness and wholeness became her principal danger and had to be avoided by an experience of hopelessness and defeat which then merged with the sadomasochism in a state of withdrawal. In this state of withdrawal, she immersed herself into fantasies of primitive idealization without clear boundaries. In other words, the powerful desire to continue to develop and live in spite of the trauma was followed by the emergence of her old experience of being ignored and overwhelmed with affect when she became aware of what had taken place in the trauma. She would say that she didn't want to feel hopeful, that hope only brings sadness and terrible pain. It was only when I began including this dynamic into my interventions that Mrs. A. could progress. The additional understanding of the negative therapeutic reaction that I had been searching for was in front of me.

I have given one example out of many that I have had where sadomasochism and the negative therapeutic reaction can be better understood if we include the wholeness of the analytic situation and the humanity of both the patient and the analyst to explore the multidetermined nature of sadomasochism. Invariably, I found sadomasochism always appeared in the service of helping to defend against an experience of being alive with the motivation to find a way to make a narrative of trauma. This powerful desire to continue to develop, to feel more and know more, was itself overwhelming because of its origins in an immature state where there wasn't any emotional help. The patients felt overwhelmed by their desire to develop further with their traumatic experiences. They were too much for themselves, so they gave up and withdrew into the crypt of their sadomasochism and their negative therapeutic reactions. Their psychoanalyses were to help them integrate this aspect of a developmental line.

To conceptualize the dynamic of moving from the danger of wholeness and feeling alive to a withdrawal into sadomasochism and where one feels only partially alive, one must focus on the whole person who feels overwhelmed by being a whole person and alive because of having to live with the trauma. Thus a patient withdraws into a sadomasochistic state for protection, a state where she is numb to being whole and alive and can avoid having to live with the trauma. Thus to understand sadomasochism, we must move from examining the parts of the sadomasochistic state to a focus on the whole person.

I can now extend the Novicks' (1996) conceptualization of the open system by including the dynamics of the danger of being in the open system: feeling too whole and too alive. Knowing too much, being aware of one's vulnerability, going on living with the developmental demand of bringing one's traumatic experiences together and seeking pleasure, creativity, and vitality from life—these experiences and feelings that are activated in the open system can be traumatic in themselves and can be such a great danger that one must retreat from them.

That there are dangers inherent in being too whole, too close, and too alive has important implications for understanding the therapeutic action of analysis. Simply put, analysis demands that the analyst demonstrate to her patient that she can remain whole, close, and alive while being immersed in the patient's difficulties, especially the sadomasochism that protects the patient from feeling alive with the trauma she brings to her analysis. The analyst demonstrates this in the analytic situation by being able to talk about what has been impossible to talk about. Thus, talking within the intimate analytic relationship is a demonstration that safety and vitality can be maintained with another even though in earlier times it was impossible. The analyst is able to do today what could not be done at an earlier time. Pessimism and the internal giving up of the past, former aims of analysis, are no longer relevant. The patient's past doesn't require giving up, but rather being transformed into a narrative while the patient is immersed in the analytic process.

Mrs. A began remembering that prior to the Holocaust she wanted to be a doctor. Even at a young age she was deeply concerned about social injustice, a topic that her parents frequently would talk about. She then spoke about how depressed her husband seemed to be lately. He was only interested in his work. He never speaks about his own experience in the concentration camp where he lost his parents. He really hasn't recovered from it and he doesn't want, or is unable to, talk about what he knows. I said that I think she is speaking about herself and the further work she needs to do, although she has come a very long way. The pain in her husband and in her is great. She responded to me by talking about how she doesn't trust me. I am cold and she doesn't think that I ever cared about her. I said I think that my last comment brought up feelings that I do care which is what frightens her because there is hope in this, that she was feeling more alive with me. Feeling hope and alive in the past only brought her to a keener awareness of who she is and what was taking place. At one time it was too much. She had to protect herself by hiding hope and replacing it with hopelessness.

Wurmser emphasizes the need for more attention to be paid to a philosophical perspective so that we can talk about the humanity of the analytic relationship. This humanity pervades the clinical situation which we analysts are immersed in each day, as we use our conflicts and emotions in exposing ourselves in our communication to our patients. The exposure in dealing with shame and humiliation is ever present. We need a description of the analyst and patient as whole human beings if we are to conceptualize how the analyst and patient handle the humiliation and shame. We analysts cannot be therapeutically effective while hiding to avoid humiliation and shame. We must demonstrate to the patient that it is safe to transform the repetition and play contributed by both participants into a narrative that is created by the patient and analyst as whole people.

Unconscious fantasy, instinctual conflict, and severe trauma comprise the sadomasochism that serves as a defense against feeling alive, vital, and whole. It is only states of aliveness and vitality that promote the experience of great affect and humiliation as one endeavor to bring coherence into one's experience. It is apparent from my argument that I see nothing negative about a negative therapeutic reaction. This constellation of feelings is the expression of the enormously powerful force of development when it is experienced as being too much to handle when the experience of reality contains overwhelming trauma and there is insufficient support from the external world to contain it and to continue one's development. This dynamic is impossible to conceptualize when the predominant force of development throughout life is not included in the experiences and observations one finds in the clinical situation.

The essential dynamic of the analytic relationship involves a combination of objectivity and subjectivity. Psychoanalysis awaits a means to improve the integration of objectivity and subjectivity because there is no other body of knowledge and technique that demands this integration as much. The dynamic begins with the patient's experience of trauma and the desire to organize the trauma through a human interaction which, in the past, could not be done, and so instead the attention of the patient moves from the reality of the trauma in the present moment to a fantasy where narcissistic components are intense and boundaries between patient and analyst are diffuse. A fantasy is used as a replacement of reality. Freud described turning from reality to fantasy as a model for neurosis, but without a description of the I, self, or person with his accompanying reflexivity. Since we are dealing with a repetition, the challenge in clinical analysis is to assist in transforming the repetition and integrating it into the whole person who then can experience more wholeness with an agency as she communicates her narrative rather than retreating by repeating it without this sense of wholeness and agency, a retreat into sadomasochism and the negative therapeutic rests upon this dynamic.

References

Bornstein, M. (2010). Why is it so difficult to describe what actually goes on in the minds of the patient and analyst? *Psychoanalytic Inquiry*, *30*, 347–356.

Fairbairn, W. R. D. (1952). *Psychoanalytic studies of personalities*. New York: Basic Books.

Freud, S. (1913). The disposition to obsessional neurosis: A contribution to the problem of the choice of neurosis. In J. Strachey (Ed. & Trans.), *The standard edition of the complete psychological works of Sigmund Freud* (Vol. 12, pp. 311–326). London: Hogarth Press.

Kernberg, O. (1966). Structural derivatives of object relationships. *International Journal of Psychoanalysis*, *47*, 236–252.

Kernberg, O. (1975). *Borderline condition and pathological narcissism*. Northvale, NJ: Jason Aronson.

Novick, J., & Novick, K. K. (1996). *Fearful symmetry: The development and treatment of sadomasochism*. Northvale, NJ: Jason Aronson.

Tauber, A. (2010). *Freud, the reluctant philosopher*. Princeton, NJ: Princeton University Press.

Wurmser, L. (2007). *Torment me, but don't abandon me: Psychoanalysis of the severe neuroses in a new key*. Lanham, MD: Rowman & Littlefield.

EPILOGUE

Some Thoughts about the Broader Background

Léon Wurmser and Heidrun Jarass

The "Flaming Letters in the Sky"

"[M]ine was a trained Presbyterian conscience and knew but the one duty—to hunt and harry its slave upon all pretexts and on all occasions, particularly when there was no sense nor reason in it," writes Mark Twain in his autobiography (1924, p. 99). Once as a boy he had given a match to a drunkard on the street who had asked him for it. The vagrant was put into jail, set it on fire, and, horribly wailing and pleading, burned to death there. For a long time thereafter, Sam Clemens (i.e., Mark Twain) lay awake during the night tormented by guilt feelings, in the revenant's reproach: "If you had not given me the matches, this would not have happened; you are responsible for my death."

Torn between his wish to help the imprisoned Jim, the runaway slave, and his culturally impressed conviction that "nigger stealing" was evil, as well as feeling bad witnessing the cruel punishment of the fraudulent "King" and "Duke," Huckleberry Finn

> was feeling … kind of ornery, and humble, and to blame somehow—though *I* hadn't done nothing. But that's always the way; it don't make no difference whether you do right or wrong, a person's conscience ain't got no sense, and just goes for him *anyway.* If I had a yaller dog that didn't know no more than a person's conscience does I would pison him. It takes up more room than all the rest of a person's insides, and yet ain't no good, nohow. (1884, p. 253)

Throughout the case presentations and theoretical writings of our now completed book, there is a similarly haunting feeling of such an overmighty, tormenting inner power. Then we are reminded of many sayings of Nietzsche: He speaks, for example, about "the essential fight of motivations—for us something entirely invisible and unconscious" (1886/1976,

p. 113). In *The Gay Science* (1882) he talks about the man who is told to control himself; "he always stands there with a defensive gesture, armed against himself, with a sharp and suspicious eye, the eternal guardian of his castle which he has made himself into" (p. 204).

"There is a *defiance against oneself* manifested in many forms of askesis. Certain people have such a great need to exert their violence and domination that, lacking other objects or because they have otherwise always failed in it, they finally turn to tyrannize certain parts of their own being, as it were segments or steps of their own selves" (1878–1880/1978, p. 123).

Metaphors like these accompany us throughout this book, images for the hidden forces that incessantly say: "Nothing good is allowed to stand. Everything good I must destroy. All that I love is cursed. No joy or pleasure is permitted."

The "unholy trinity" of envy, jealousy, and resentment (see chapter 1) seems embodied in that "harrying" inner figure that mercilessly judges and condemns the self and the other. Yet we are not only struck by the individual suffering expressed by this drivenness to condemn and destroy everything that is good, but by its political, historical, and especially theological analogues. These large scale historical and religious forces seem to emerge out of the cauldron of inner conflicts, as it were in the form of a luminescent writing in the sky, as Ibsen most sharply expresses it in his early dramatic poem, *Brand* (1866/1991). The zealot-pastor Brand's ideology demands that self-sacrifice, readiness for martyrdom, and sacrificing what is dearest in the service of what one sees as God's grim Law, is immutable: "Precisely sacrifice stands in flaming letters as God's demand behind the break of the clouds" (p. 169); he speaks of "the cruel hawk and falcon of the Law" (p. 98). "Know this: Were you to renounce everything but your life, you have not given up anything" (p. 39). Correspondingly, his motto is "Nothing or everything!" and one that is repeated throughout (e.g., pp. 56, 61, 82, 158), in contrast to any compromise: "No cowardly compromise!" (p. 62; similarly pp. 158, 162, 166, 182). The Ibsen quote we put at the beginning of our book, "the greatest victory is defeat" (p. 77) is in accordance with this view, and similarly: "To victory in falling down!" (p. 167). "The main principle is, that *one wants* the death at the cross, to *want to* [step] into the middle of the suffering of the flesh, to *want to* be in the middle of the soul's anxiety" (pp. 64–65).

The history of the last three millennia is replete with testimonies like these for such a grimly and cruelly demanding force projected into metaphysical realms. Thus most chapters of this book interweave psychology, political history, and religion, often in subtle, barely visible threads, sometimes in broad, almost glowing strands (especially in chapters 5, 6, and 9), yet always circling around this figure of the cruel inner judge.

How can we get to a deepened understanding of what this inner force is that shows not only clinically, in the NTR, or more generally in the major forms of masochism and depression, but that we know so well as the background to historical analogues?

In order to do this we need a different vantage point than simply that of the internalization of parental or societal value systems. Repeatedly throughout this book, psychology has called upon political history and theology to add essential dimensions to what we know as NTR.

The Inner Contradictions in "Exclusive Monotheism"

In his important work *The Mosaic Distinction* (2003), the leading German Egyptologist and philosopher of culture and religion, Jan Assmann, starts out with the "psycho-historical aspect," stressed above all by Freud: "The turn to monotheism with its ethical demands, its emphasis on the inner man and its character as the 'father religion' is joined with a new mental attitude and new 'nature of soul' [*Seelentum*], that have decisively shaped the Western view of mankind" (p. 12). Assmann adds:

> I call the crucial point of this turn "The Mosaic Distinction." It is not the distinction between the One God and the many gods that seems to me decisive, but the distinction between true and false in religion, between the true God and the false gods, the true teaching and the erroneous teachings, between knowledge and ignorance, between faith and wrong belief [*Unglaube*]. (p. 12, note)

Specifically this entails, as Freud (1937–1939) had postulated, the following:

> The secondary religious experience coincides with the "invention of inner man." The distinction between truth and lie does not only divide the outer space, but it cuts midway through the human heart which now truly becomes the arena of religious dynamics. The secondary religion is in a new and very emphatic sense "a matter of the heart," as it is so powerfully expressed in the central prayer of Judaism, the "Shma Yisrael," "Hear Israel": to love God with one's whole heart, with one's whole soul, with one's whole power. (p. 156)

We might modify this and add: The discovery of the inner person is also the discovery of inner conflict as something that is deeply constitutive for mental life; dynamics indicate inner conflict. The "mosaic differentiation" is not only an external, but above all also an inner division between antithetical forces standing in incessant conflict with each other. We recognize this division also in sources that are independent of this distinction, but lack this emphatic, central understanding of the soul, of the mind.

Assmann (2006) traces this strand in the idea of God back to the "law of Assyrian kings that demands absolute loyalty from the vassals" (p. 27) and states that the vehement threats in passages of Deuteronomy are literal copies of Assyrian texts, not of a religious, but of a political nature. He significantly adds: "The transposition of Assyrian despotism onto God and the new idea of an exclusive bond with God was an act of liberation making Israel independent from external despots. In this 'rewriting' (*Umbuchung*) a spiritual resistance is articulated that proved extremely successful in the long run" (p. 31).

We have to pose the question: Do the supposed hallmarks of exclusive monotheism of intolerance, violence, and patriarchal rule not themselves stand in sharp, although usually implicit contradiction to its other major commitments?

Concretely that means: Where we find a postulate of exclusiveness with its "language of violence," should we not also expect to find its opposite, perhaps partly hidden, but not altogether forgotten: the inclusiveness? Besides murderous intolerance and self-righteousness, do we find a wiser tolerance, besides the single, also the many and the manifold, besides the imageless and ineffable also a rich, although spiritualized world of imagery, metaphors, and names? Not only do we encounter conflict, but also always again complementarity, the idea of dialectic, Niels Bohr's motto: *contraria sunt complementa* or the "*coincidentia oppositorum*" of Cusanus (Holton, 1973).

Even more seriously we have to pose the question: What are these other central tasks (*Anliegen*) of Mosaic religion? They entail above all what both Freud and Assmann stress as "progress in spirituality" (*Fortschritt in der Geistigkeit*): the increase in symbolization, at the cost of the mythical concreteness, a large scale attack on the religious use of mythology, and even to some considerable extent on what Cassirer analyzed as the rules of mythical thinking. It culminates in the prohibition of tangible, visible images in regard to God.

The second central aim in this monotheistic revolution is the insistent pursuit of *justice*: *Tzedeq tzedeq tirdof*—"justice, justice you should pursue" (Deuteronomy 16:20); it is a task strongly reminiscent of the leading commandment in ancient Egyptian culture to strive after *Ma'at*, justice, truth, reciprocity, and cosmic and societal order, just as are the commandments shared by Israel and Egypt; to protect the weak, the poor, those who are unfairly treated.

What in our view, however, separates some forms of monotheism in their core ideals most stringently from other cultures is the vehement protest against the deification of human beings, animals, things, and in general of what exists in the material world. This sharp separation of God and world, as Assmann describes, would ideally be equated with a resolute renunciation of any form of dehumanization and degradation of human beings.

And yet, it is precisely this dehumanization that recurs in the categorical thinking, the judging, and the killing. It seems to us that a profound cleft opens here, an unsolvable, largely unarticulated inner conflict at the center of exclusive monotheism.

As a counterpoint are two passages from Rashi's (1040–1105CE) Torah comments. In accordance with the second central aim just mentioned, we read in Leviticus 24:22: "You shall have one standard for stranger and citizen alike: for I the Lord am your God." Rashi, the leading medieval commentator: "'I am the Lord your God—*your God*—the God of all of you (*elohé kulchém*).' Just as I attach my name *specially* (*meyachéd*) to you, so do I attach it *specially* to the strangers (*kach ani meyachdó al haggerím*)" (p. 112b). Thus he hints at the chosen nature of each individual and nation, each in its special essence.

Another passage in Rashi testifies to the same idea. He comments on Numbers 27:16 where YHWY is called "source of the breath of all flesh" (*elohé haruchót lekol-bassár*):

> Moses said to God [*hammaqóm*, lit. the Place] ... : "Lord of the Universe! The minds [the understanding] of every single one are revealed before you (*galúy lefanécha da'ató shel kol echád we'echád*), and you know no one is similar to the other. Appoint a leader (*manhíg*) for them who will tolerate each person according to his mind (*sheyehé sovél kol echád we'echád lefí da'ató*)."

Again there is the stress on tolerance for every individual's specialness and own understanding. Doesn't this imply that every single person is a chosen one, wherever he or she stands and with his or her own individual specialness, and that the personhood of God, His oneness and uniqueness, is symbolic for the personal dignity of man in general? That "each person shall camp under his own flag, the signs of his ancestors" (*ish al-digló, be'otót levét avotám*) (Numbers 2:2), as it is symbolically reinterpreted in Midrash Rabba, *Wayiqra* 36.2.

We will mention briefly a fourth central value and aim represented by Jewish monotheism: the dialogue between man and God, parallel to the interpersonal dialogue. Having stated this, in many concrete ways, was one of Buber's great achievements. Man is personally called upon again and again: "Where are you?—*ayéka*?" and he answers: "Here I am—*hinnéni!*" From the therapies sketched out in most of the preceding chapters, we know the healing power of a deep relation of I-You as an antidote to the archaic superego. It might have been that way also in religion, as we will encounter it later in the "tolerance midrash."

There is the complementarity of the "mosaic distinction" in its exclusivity and its tolerance of the stranger. This doubleness is evident furthermore in the continual rich appropriations from the surrounding cultures during the progress of Jewish religion and culture, a dialectic of exclusionary self-delimitation and of broad tolerance and acceptance.

This complementarity, in contrast to a sharp either-or of the "mosaic distinction," of true and false, is also well shown by Assmann in the synthesis of primary and secondary religious experience:

> In a way very different from Freud, we could call those forms of primary religious experience that are melted into the secondary religions as "archaic heritage." Even though not scripted into [the] human psyche, it forms a depth dimension, a "crypta" of religious tradition itself. It carries, just like language, much more of knowledge and memory than those who live in it are usually conscious of. (2003, p. 153)

Already Maimonides (Rabbi Moshe ben Maimon, Rambam, 1135–1204 CE) assumed, "that monotheistic religion contains a deep layer that had become unconscious, a layer into which denied and repressed paganism had been pushed away. Of course, those who practice the law are not conscious any more of the pagan counter-meaning (*Gegensinn*)" (Assmann, 2003, p. 153). Maimonides calls the laws "*divréi kfiláyim*," "double words, words of doubleness": "They have a manifest and a hidden meaning.... Only because of the structure of antagonistic layering or transcription of a previous and rejected tradition, religion becomes two-layered (lit. having two floors: *doppelbödig*)" (p. 154).

And yet, the question imposes itself: May God's so often emphasized jealousy (*El qanna'*) and the violence supposedly connected with it (Assmann claims that this was much more so in writing than in historical fact) not be part of such doubleness—i.e., the return of something repressed, archaic, ultimately rooted in a claim for power that serves anything but "a progress in spirituality"? Are they not themselves indices for an "archaic psychological heritage": the dynamic unconscious of religion?

With this term, *archaic heritage* I refer to Freud's (1937–1939) "assertion that *the archaic heritage of human beings comprises not only dispositions but also subject-matter—memory traces of the experience of earlier generations*" (emphasis added, p. 99).

Moreover, I think that, as Nietzsche and after him Scheler have elaborated, the power of resentment vested in the conscience, in the ethics of the Western world, and with that in the images of God also belongs to this "archaic inheritance" and works in opposition to the "progress in spirituality."

All three, the archaic superego, jealousy, and resentment, live on, even until the present, in all religious fundamentalism, in the intolerantly destructive self-righteousness and absolutism of "holy wars" ("*Gotteskriege*") of any kind.

God as Representation of Moral Systems

For many of us, Assmann's assertion of the "profane origin of justice" is indisputable and self-evident and must lead to the need and task to examine ethics empirically (i.e., at least partly psychologically), in addition to the sociological, cultural, and historical approaches; these four overlap and mutually condition each other. That implies that we have to study thoroughly the genesis of moral systems and their nature and structures, systems moreover that both within the individual and in cultures often stand in sharp contradiction to each other.

The idea of God may be seen as a powerful symbol for the inner judge, for the court within, the commandments and prohibitions within, but also very much for an ideal image of the self and of mankind, i.e., for the complex inner structure comprised, and made into one agency, by Freud with the help of the metaphor of the superego.

All scientific constructions are built upon metaphors. The systematic study of the mind relies in particular upon those metaphors that can best serve the given task. In our clinical work, we use such images for the superego as "inner judge," "inner demon," or "inquisitor," or "guardian," even "inner dictator," and many others. The first of these really goes back to Kant (1797–1798/1983, p. 574).

Almost since the inception of written documents we find hints for what we try to entail with the psychoanalytic superego. In the literature of ancient Egypt, the principle of *Ma'at* (Assmann, 2000), that of "justice, truth, and order" (p. 104), "the ideal of a just order" (p. 182), or in his book *Ma'at*: "world order as justice" (p. 34) is all-encompassing, the foundation of man, state, and cosmos. A similarly fundamental role is played in the Bible by "Tzedaqa" or "Tzedeq" (justice); even God is called upon to respond to its jurisdiction.

For the study of such moral systems, we can use Freud's metaphor of the superego in the broadest sense as an encompassing structure of mental functioning. Its concepts vary somewhat within different psychoanalytic theories. Generally it is understood to be a complex, largely unconscious inner agency of many-layered origin. We can divide it up into different functions with each group entailing its own metaphors.

What are the main functions of the superego? They are:

Various, partly contradictory sets of expectations, on the one side moral commands, like duty and responsibility, on the other the ego ideal (i.e., an ideal image and code of ideal actions, leading values and ideals);

The evaluating and judging self-observation—"the inner eye";

Self-criticism and self-condemnation, if there is a shortfall, compared with these expectations—"the inner judge";

Self-approval, self-care, and self-protection;

The protection of the inner and outer boundaries and barriers, with particular emphasis on the limitations of time;

Stabilization of mood and regulation of affects.

The values and ideals in the sets of expectations can be divided into at least two large groups of particular psychodynamic importance. Thus, shame and guilt form the basis for two value scales, two systems of what is seen as right and wrong, two ranges of judgment which to some extent contradict each other (this was dealt with in some detail in Wurmser, 1999, pp. 317–318). The values consist of pride and honor versus those of consideration for the rights of others and acceptance of the needs of others—the parallel scales of shame and guilt. In the former case, the fear is of weakness and failure; in the other case, the fear is of abusing one's power and hurting the other.

All these moral feelings are intensively shaped by individual history, mostly the interpersonal relationships that are themselves highly complex and many layered. Parts of the superego, its "voices" and "images," are strongly identified with persons, but cannot simply be reduced, for example, to father or mother.

Crucial for our epilogue is the examination of the extent to which the ideas of God are projections of these inner moral systems (i.e., of the superego). What we subsume under the superego functions can be found in the various forms that the idea of God has taken. In the Jewish-Christian conceptualization the emphasis lies very strongly on justice, on sin, on condemnation, forgiveness, and redemption (i.e., what is called in a narrower sense "the conscience part" of the superego). In the Greco-Roman world much more attention is paid to the "ego-ideal part" of the superego, in terms of certain virtues and abilities (*aretái, virtutes*): beauty, pride, nobility, skillfulness and artfulness, cleverness, and power, hence the crucial role played by visibility and success, and their opposites: veiledness and shame. Punishment occurs by metamorphosis or disappearance and petrification. Honor has to be maintained and defended at all costs, above everything else.

The duality and dialectic of the guilt part and the shame part of the superego, their antithesis and complementarity, their back and forth, have for a long time been neglected in psychoanalysis, if not entirely overlooked and reburied. Only in the last 30 years has this started to change somewhat, at least in American psychoanalysis.

It seems essential that the God of "exclusive monotheism," as Assmann has so sharply delineated, only too often represents a superego figure well known from our psychoanalytic experience, namely what we call the "archaic superego."

As already alluded to, conflicts of conscience form an essential part of human nature, and the more intense and extreme they are, the more severe the suffering and the distress, consciously or even more so unconsciously. They must turn unsolvable as soon as they claim exclusivity. The more they incline toward absoluteness, the more widely they are separated and the deeper the gulf between them. But making a value absolute means theologizing it—one value is being transformed into God's cause or elevated to something resembling divinity. Such a deified value may be the state, particularly a dictatorship, or one class or party or one ethnos—or it is religion, the religious tradition which is sanctified, as a condition of salvation, in an absolute form.

One consequence of every absoluteness in whatever form it takes, as already stated, is the dehumanization, the objectification, "the making into a thing": The individual person is subsumed under a category and finally sacrificed for whatever has been set as absolute. But such depersonalization is something utterly dangerous, the greatest danger of all: by this means doors are opened to cruelty and intolerance and finally to genocide.

Dehumanization, depersonalization, when man is degraded to a thing, is intimately connected with disgrace, with humiliation, thus with the affect of shame, and is a cardinal trauma. Dehumanization in the service of holiness or any "sacred cause" is the most dangerous one. Holy war is merciless and implacable, even if it is carried out in the name of the God of love, of pity, of justice, and of peace. And the shame evokes resentment, and very soon violence, terror, and renewed shaming.

Right and morals always run this risk of dehumanization, even in our world today. When technology itself assumes a place close to divine power and salvation it threatens to despise and dismiss the personal essence ("personhood").

There seems to us particular actuality to this theme even today. The self-righteousness in political discourse again and again assumes that air of absoluteness and inherently the threat of violence, be that in the United States or in Europe and the Middle East. Ideology knows no shades of gray; the world is split into black and white. The archaic superego and the claims of omnipotence and omniscience lead to analogues to the NTR: Nothing good is allowed to stand because it does not reach the desired ideological purity. The consequences are denied (e.g., no taxes, but all the wished for services!). There reigns at present an air of gloom and foreboding.

If I understand it properly it is a main intention of Biblical monotheism, perhaps its most essential meaning, to radically reject all godliness of power, to oppose the equation of the worldly power of pharaohs and kings with something divine, at the behest of the sole rule of God in His spirituality, beyond image and spoken name. But in this intention we discover a self-contradiction: On the one side, power arrogated by man over his fellow men and taking possession of them is deemed as evil; but jealousy ascribed to the Deity (*qin'ah*) is itself a masked form of taking possession and a claim for power that is set as absolute. In other words, the idea of setting God's power as absolute, in whatever form, may move to irreconcilable contradiction to human dignity because it could become just as dehumanizing as the pharaoh's or that of any despot. It too would then have a traumatizing effect. In other words: the archaic superego is both caused by trauma and newly traumatizing, and thus is the idea of God that is imbued with its characteristics, especially the absoluteness of condemnation and jealous passion (*Eifern*).

What about the Origins of the Archaic Superego?

Today we have gained a much better understanding of the nature and effect of traumata in early childhood than was the case in Freud's time and during the early years of psychoanalysis. Freud's important case histories (e.g., Little Hans and also Dora) leave out or underplay unequivocally severe traumata that we would consider today as child abuse, so that in order to understand and explain them he had to resort to allegedly phylogenetically inherited traumata and to the death instinct.

Instead of looking at putative phylogenetic traumata, we instead study the manifold disturbances and severe interpersonal traumata throughout childhood and youth—not only looking at physical violence and sexual abuse, but also at emotional mistreatment resulting from a severe lack of empathy ("soul blindness"), by "soul murder," by severe humiliation (Wurmser, 2000, 2007).

Another indispensable bridge toward understanding is provided by the transgenerationally "inherited" traumata and defenses, which are at least in part unconsciously transmitted and received, as they show up in the development of the superego. In this bridge building over centuries, even millennia, the "cultural memory" is decisive.

How can we understand the connection of the archaic superego with severe traumatization? This question we believe to be central for an understanding of the dynamics underlying much of NTR.

We can define trauma as an overwhelming, unsolvable external conflict between self and environment that leads to a conscious but unsolvable inner conflict. The affects battling each other overwhelm the capacity of the ego to master them, a failure that leads to an inner split: the act of making the connections unconscious. Dissociation and even hypnoid states remain important concepts for the understanding of the traumatic genesis of the severe neuroses.

Severe, repeated traumatization means that every emotional experience resonates as if it were a recurrence of the original trauma. It leads to the standstill, usually partial, of affective development: the differentiation, verbalization, and desomatization of the emotions are blocked. Thus in traumatization, by definition, the feelings, once roused, very rapidly become overwhelming, get out of control, are global ("dedifferentiated"), beyond symbolization ("deverbalized"), and are being experienced as if they were physical ("resomatized"). These three concepts of dedifferentiation, deverbalization or hyposymbolization, and of resomatization represent, according to Krystal (1988, 1998), affect regression. The standstill of time illuminated by several of the book's chapters is part of this affect regression and standstill of development.

But there is something else of great importance, especially in the recurrent traumatization in childhood: These affects tend to appear in sexualized form. Sexualization is an archaic defense set up to regulate affect. The affect flooding, combined with this very primordial defense by sexualization, leads, however, to an overwhelming sense of humiliation and embarrassment: Not to have any control over one's own emotional life is just as shaming as the loss of sphincter control, if not more so. Aggressive wishes are then being used to reestablish control, a form of further archaic defense to deal preventively with a spiraling out of control, an important way of turning passive into active.

The result of such severe disturbance of affect regulation is an archaic equation we typically encounter in the intensive, long term treatment of the severe neuroses. The following five states and contents are equated, and each of the five may be an entrance point into the equation:

Overstimulation by something on the outside which is being experienced as traumatic, as intolerable, and to which one feels helplessly, passively exposed;
Overwhelming, but usually contradictory feelings, the sense of bursting, "I cannot stand it anymore," the traumatic state (that inner state of passivity);
Something devouring, consuming (i.e., the imagery of orality), like rapacious animals or elements (fire, floods);
Sexual excitement;
Aggressive fantasies and of violence, even cruelty (see also Shengold, 1989).

Losing control over the affects, the collapse of affect regulation, and the conflict between global but opposing affects, is indeed a primary danger, evoking a most profound sense of helplessness, of "fragmentation" and "splitting," and thus deepening in circular form the basic anxiety and shame. It is not even necessary theoretically to resort to fears of abandonment, rejection, castration, or self-condemnation to explain this anxiety.

All these latter dreads simply give the necessary concrete and specific form, rooted in personal history, to those overwhelming, repetitive, traumatic experiences.

The archaic equation of traumatogenic affective storms, sexualization, and aggression is in turn again very deeply frightening and humiliating, calls for equally global defenses, and eventually to massive counteractions by the superego in pervasive and global forms of guilt and shame: "and conscience, turned tyrant, held passion by the throat" (Brontë, 1847). A very central part of such an overweening superego is the omnipotence of responsibility: "It is in my power to prevent all these disasters. If they recur, my guilt is total."

The archaic superego manifests itself by pervasive, internalized, global guilt feelings and shame. These may be conscious or unconscious, with a strong sadistic (i.e., sexualized) component.

We may presume that this is the kind of dynamics that is reflected not just in NTR, masochism, and depression, but also in the idea of the intolerant, jealous God of what Assmann called "exclusive monotheism" and the language of violence, witnessed in its currently most extreme form in jihadism, in centuries past in the Inquisition and the burning of the heretics—or books.

Jealousy: The Dilemma of Love and Power

With the exclusivity of the claim for adoration and submission we also enter into the domain of jealousy that occupies us psychoanalysts very often and centrally. It can best be expressed in these words: "I am the excluded third and want to be the excluding first."

Recurrently we read in the Bible of God's zeal and passion, His *qin'ah*, but also specifically as jealousy against revering other Gods, as in the scene of the Dance around the Golden Calf, as Jan Assmann has impressively elaborated. Similarly, the Zohar, the main work of Jewish mysticism (13th century), claims: "Whoever loves without being linked to jealousy—his love is not love. Once he becomes jealous, love is complete" (III, 498). Oh *really*?

Does not this postulate throw us right back to what we encountered in this volume as that "unholy trinity"? How does the psychoanalyst respond to this challenge?

Quite concisely: Jealousy is founded upon the feeling of entitlement to the exclusive possession of the other. A very important aspect to be considered in much love is the often quite unabashed wish for such exclusive possession. In its midst, there crouches devouring, even murderous jealousy. It seems that this wish for exclusivity can be observed already in very small children. Certainly this wish to take possession of the other person is an innate disposition. According to Freud, there is "normal" jealousy in love, besides the excessive, hence pathological, especially delusional jealousy.

However, if we reflect more about "normal" jealousy, the question is justified: Doesn't this concept of its "normality" rest on a concept of infatuation or even of love that is founded on ultimate possession and disregards the individuality of the other? There may be complex compromise formations between the claim for exclusivity and mutual respect. Still, the double question remains hanging in the air: On the one side, how is trust, the core of love, possible if the claim for possession is dominant? On the other side, how is trust possible if because of such possessiveness the attractions and ties to other people have to be hidden (i.e., if it has to come therefore to lies and secrecy)?

In short: The feeling of jealousy as such is ubiquitous and "normal" from the first few months of childhood and throughout life. As an attitude held and a claim obsessively pursued, jealousy is pathological, and no religion or law can justify it, try as they might (see Wurmser & Jarass, 2007).

One of the great insights seems to be that love is divisible and that it grows in the very sharing and does not get reduced. We are reminded of the beautiful parable of the Kabbalist Rabbi David ibn Abi Zimra (1479–1573):

> Just as a woman becomes pregnant and gives birth without lacking anything [of her own being], so too the souls of the righteous and the pious become pregnant and give birth and emanate sparks into this world, to protect the generation or for some other reasons, like one who lights one candle from another, where the first candle is not diminished. (Scholem, 1991, p. 223)[1]

This observation—that we have more by giving, and certainly not less—is true not only for love (and having children is the most beautiful example for it) and for goodness, but also for wisdom and justice. They all become more by being shared. The good German phrase, "Shared grief is half the grief; shared joy is double the joy," can be extended to love, as unusual as it may sound.

Another very important conclusion is this: Fidelity and exclusivity are not identical and have to be uncoupled from each other, as much as this may contradict conventional morality. There exists a deep and lasting fidelity to the other, beloved person without that this faithfulness and loyalty would have to entail exclusivity. Quite to the contrary! The more broadly, strongly, and deeply our love and need for being loved are being fulfilled, the better we are toward those next to us—more understanding and patient; and the more loving and giving we are toward others, the less we blame them and are intolerant toward them. It was, after all, one of the main insights of psychoanalysis that chronic or constantly repeated frustration of the desire for love (i.e., of libido) is centrally pathogenic.

Thus it appears that this one conflict is a kind of leitmotif for the tragic character inherent in the NTR (see especially chapters 1 and 5): It is the conflict between love and power. It is manifested, for example, in the tipping over of the yearning for the beloved into the compulsion to control this other person completely and thus to functionalize and dehumanize the beloved.

An image of God that has its core in jealousy cannot be reconciled with that of love. Jealousy is a betrayal of love, a perversion of love. A jealous God is not a loving God. The word *love* is misused for purposes of power. It is quite persuasive when Assmann derives much of this dangerous idea from the Assyrian despotism, an early form of totalitarianism and massive historical trauma suffered by ancient Israel and Judah. A jealous God is the God of all the holy wars, the crusades and jihads.

There is a wonderful Midrash in "Echa Rabba" which critically comments about it ("*Petichta*," i.e., "opening" to the Midrash Echa Rabba, "Echa" being the Biblical book of "Lamentations"). We could call it the "tolerance Midrash." It stands in connection with the lamentation about the fall of the Temple and the "shame and contempt" of Israel, the massacre of its children, and the chasing of the parents into exile and slavery. The angels, Abraham, Isaak, Jacob, and Moses step before God to decry and raise accusations about the suffering, devastation, and humiliation.

> At that moment, the matriarch Rachel broke forth into speech before the Holy One, blessed be He, and said: "Sovereign of the Universe, it is revealed before You that Your servant Jacob loved me exceedingly and toiled for my father on my behalf seven years. When those seven years were completed and the time arrived for my marriage with my husband, my father planned to substitute another for me to wed my husband for the sake of my sister. It was very hard for me, because the plot was known to me and I disclosed it to my husband; and I gave him a sign whereby he could distinguish between me and my sister, so that my father should not be able to make the substitution. After that I relented, suppressed my desire, and had pity upon my sister that she should not be exposed to shame. In the evening they substituted my sister for me with my husband, and I delivered over to my sister all the signs which I had arranged with my husband so that he should think that she was Rachel. More than that, I went beneath the bed upon which he lay with my sister; and when he spoke to her she remained silent and I made all the replies in order that he should not recognize my sister's voice. I did her a kindness,

> was not jealous of her and did not expose her to shame. And if I, a creature of flesh and blood, formed of dust and ashes, was not envious of my rival and did not expose her to shame and contempt, why should You, a King who lives eternally and is merciful, be jealous of idolatry in which there is no reality [lit.: "jealous about serving little pseudo-gods in whom there is no substance"], and exile my children and let them be slain by the sword, and their enemies have done with them as they wished." Forthwith the mercy of the Holy One, blessed be He, was stirred, and He said: "For your sake, Rachel, I will restore Israel to their place." (pp. 48–49)

Several friends who read this story vividly expressed their unease about the masochistic attitude in this "altruistic surrender" by Rachel in what we know as a leading defense against jealousy. Looked at psychologically in regard to Rachel this is entirely correct, just as we might question the wellsprings of a hero's suicidal audacity in his self-sacrifice for family, people, and religion (what is known, for example, in Jewish tradition as the "sanctification of God's name," the "Kiddush hashem" of the martyr, and similarly for the Christian martyrs).

Looked at ethically, however, Rachel's plea (or the hero's quest) is a symbol for something vastly different: It is a great manifesto from very ancient times against the idea of a God who is jealous and retributive. It is a protest against narcissism, calling for transcending it in spite of extreme traumatization, a metaphysical and existential turning away from jealousy and shame, from revenge and dehumanization—an appeal for an encompassing justice that even God is called upon to accept.

Or we could say, it is a sign of the deep transformation when the other person is intimately accepted, a deep sense of Buber's I-You relationship: no possession of the other, no power over the other, no "thingness" of what is human.

Thus it is a powerful voice against that "harrying" figure, within and without, that insists: "Nothing good is allowed to stand."

Note

1. The same metaphor had been used about 1,000 years earlier in the commentary of Midrash Rabba to the Torah (Shemot Rabbah, pp. 439–440).

References

Assmann, J. (2003). *Die mosaische Unterscheidung oder der Preis des Monotheismus* [The Mosaic distinction, or the price of monotheism] Munich, Germany: Carl Hanser Beck Verlag.

Assmann, J. (2006). *Monotheismus und die Sprache der Gewalt* [Monotheism and the language of power]. Vienna, Austria: Picus Verlag Wien

Brontë, C. (1994). Jane Eyre. In *The Brontës: Three great novels* (pp. 1–363). Oxford, England: Oxford University Press. (Original work published 1847)

Freud, S. (1937–1939). Moses and monotheism. In J. Strachey (Ed. & Trans.), *The standard edition of the complete psychological works of Sigmund Freud* (Vol. 23, pp. 3–137). London: Hogarth Press.

Holton, G. (1973). *Thematic origins of scientific thought.* Cambridge, MA: Harvard University Press.

Ibsen, H. (1991). *Brand: Et dramatisk dikt* [Brand: A dramatic poem]. Oslo, Norway: Gyldendal. (Original work published 1866)

Kant, I. (1983). Metaphysik der Sitten [Metaphysics of morals]. In *Werke* (vol. 7). Darmstadt: Wissenschaftliche Buchgesellschaft. (Original work published 1797–1798)

Krystal, H. (1988). *Integration and self-healing: Affect, trauma, alexithymia.* Hillsdale, NJ: Analytic Press.

Krystal, H. (1998). Desomatization and the consequences of infantile trauma. *Psychoanalytic Inquiry, 17*(2), 126–150.

Nietzsche, F. (1878–1880). *Menschliches, Allzu-Menschliches: Der Wanderer und sein Schatten* [Human, all too human: The wanderer and his shadow]. Stuttgart, Germany: Kröner, 1978.

Nietzsche, F. (1882). *Die Fröhliche Wissenschaft* [The gay science]. Stuttgart, Germany: Kröner.

Nietzsche, F. (1976). *Morgenröte* [Dawn]. Stuttgart: Kröner. (Original work published 1886)

Rashi (Rabbi Shmu'el ben Jitzchaq). (1946). *Pentateuch with Rashi's commentary* (A. M. Silbermann, Trans.). London: Shapiro, Vallentine.

Scholem, G. (1991). *On the mystical shape of the godhead: Basic concepts in the Kabbalah* (J. Neugroschel, Trans.). New York: Schocken.

Shengold, L. (1989). *Soul murder. The effects of childhood abuse and deprivation.* New Haven, CT: Yale University Press.

Shemot Rabbah. (1983). *Midrash Rabbah,* Vol. III. (H. Freedman, Trans.). London: Soncino.

Twain, M. (1918). *Huckleberry Finn.* New York: Greystone Press. (Original work published1884)

Twain, M. (1924). *Autobiography.* New York: Greystone Press.

Wurmser, L. (1999). *Magische Verwandlung und tragische Verwandlung: Die Behandlung der schweren Neurose* [Magic transformation and tragic transformation: The treatment of severe neurosis]. Göttingen, Germany: Vandenhoeck & Ruprecht.

Wurmser, L. (2000). *The power of the inner judge.* Northvale, NJ: Jason Aronson.

Wurmser, L. (2007). *"Torment me, but don't abandon me": Psychoanalysis of the severe neuroses in a new key.* Lanham, MD: Rowman & Littlefield.

Wurmser, L., & Jarass, H. (2007). *Jealousy and envy: New views about two powerful feelings.* New York: Routledge.

INDEX

Page locators in *italics* indicate figures.